MARENGO
and
HOHENLINDEN:

Napoleon's Rise to Power

MARENGO
and
HOHENLINDEN:

Napoleon's Rise to Power

James R. Arnold

Pen & Sword
MILITARY

To my parents,
Joyce B. and Robert C. Arnold

First published in the United States in 1999 by James R. Arnold.
Published in Great Britain in this format, in 2005 by
Pen & Sword Military
An imprint of
Pen & Sword Books Ltd
47 Church Street
Barnsley
South Yorkshire
S70 2AS

ISBN 1 84415 279 0

A CIP catalogue record for this book is
available from the British Library

Designed by Graham Beehag Book Design
Maps by Max Sewell and Jerry Malone

Printed and bound in UK
By CPI UK

Pen & Sword Books Ltd incorporates the Imprints of Pen & Sword
Aviation, Pen & Sword Maritime, Pen & Sword Military, Wharncliffe Local
history, Pen & Sword Select, Pen & Sword Military Classics and Leo
Cooper.

For a complete list of Pen & Sword titles please contact
PEN & SWORD BOOKS LIMITED
47 Church Street, Barnsley, South Yorkshire, S70 2AS, England
E-mail: enquiries@pen-and-sword.co.uk
Website: www.pen-and-sword.co.uk

Contents

List of Maps
(in the order they appear)

A Matter of Rank

To honor the leaders and to distinguish officers in the service of France or Austria, leaders are usually referred to with their French or Austrian rank. The following provides the hierarchy of rank and for the Austrians, the abbreviations used in the text, and the United States Army equivalent.

French   U.S.

French	U.S.
general of brigade	brigadier general, usually commanding a demi-brigade
general of division	major general, usually commanding a division
lieutenant general	lieutenant general commanding either a corps or army

Austrian   U.S.

Austrian	U.S.
Oberst	colonel
Inhaber	regimental proprietor, usually an honorific position
General-Feldwachmeister (GM)	major general
Feldmarschall-Leutnant (FML)	lieutenant general
General der Kavallerie (GdK)	full general, cavalry
Feldzeugmeister (FZM)	full general, infantry
Erzherzog	archduke
Kaiser	emperor

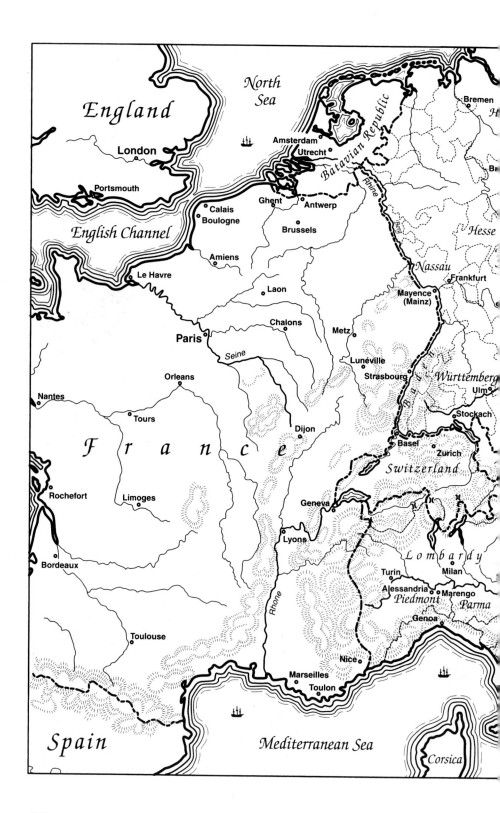

England

North
Sea

London

Portsmouth

English Channel

Calais
Boulogne

Ghent
Antwerp

Amsterdam
Utrecht

Batavian Republic

Bremen

Rhine

Hesse

Brussels

Amiens

Le Havre

Laon

Paris

Seine

Chalons

Metz

Lunéville

Strasbourg

Nassau
Frankfurt

Mayence
(Mainz)

Württemberg
Ulm

Orleans

Nantes

Tours

Dijon

Stockach

France

Basel
Zurich

Switzerland

Rochefort

Limoges

Geneva

Bordeaux

Lyons

Lombardy

Turin
Milan

Alessandria
Marengo

Piedmont
Parma

Genoa

Toulouse

Nice

Marseilles
Toulon

Mediterranean Sea

Corsica

Spain

European Theater: 1800

SCALE OF MILES
20 0 20 40 60 80 100 120 140

IX

Acknowledgments

I am deeply grateful to Robert and Joyce Arnold, who underwrote the first edition; Graham Beehag, for his outstanding design work; David Chandler, who kindly loaned me his photo of Fort Bard; Patrick Crusiau, who located maps and source material in Brussels; Paddy Griffith, who shared his insights on the wars of the Revolution (and the perils of self-publication!); Philip Haythornthwaite, for responding to obscure queries and providing research material; Grace McCrowell, who cheerfully processed inter-library loan requests; George Nafziger, who provided research assistance and encouragement; Robert Paulley, whose Portell Production provided essential publishing contacts; Ralph Reinertsen, who labored on my behalf through the Mras manuscript and altered his vacation plans in order to explore with critical eye the battlefield of Hohenlinden; John Slonaker for providing access to the wonderful collection at the U.S. Army Military History Institute; Bernhard Voykowitsch, who shared material from the Vienna Kriegsarchiv and cheerfully responded to queries about the background of various obscure Austrian general officers; Roberta Wiener, my indispensable chief of staff who accompanied me on a tour of Marengo and had the patience to edit and proof read this book; and the administrators and librarians at the University of Virginia, Washington and Lee University, and the Virginia Military Institute, who open their collections to the public.

The Napoleon Series is a valuable and interesting Internet site where participants "converse" about a wide array of Napoleonic topics. There I posted queries about the first names and backgrounds of various military leaders and received helpful responses from kind contributors including Ian Jackson, Bruno Nackaerts, and Digby Smith. Thank you gentlemen.

Via the Napoleon Series I also "met" two skilled cartographers, Jerry Malone and Max Sewell. These gentlemen undertook the enormous labor of translating my sketches into the fine maps contained in this book. They worked long and hard, motivated solely by a love for the period's history. Their combination of graphic talents and knowledge about the period proved invaluable. So a special thanks to Jerry and Max: well done!

Lastly, a word about the illustrations. All are from the author's collection except for GdK Melas, courtesy of Bernhard Voykowitsch and the Vienna War Archives; Fort Bard, courtesy of David Chandler; and the Hohenlinden terrain photos, courtesy of Ralph Reinertsen.

Prologue:

Afternoon on the Field of Marengo

The afternoon sun seemed to linger. Its position told Napoleon Bonaparte that there was no chance that darkness would come to save his army. Seventeen thousand Frenchmen were retreating before an ascendant Austrian army. Unless something dramatic occurred, this battle was lost.

The young leader's position as First Consul rested precariously upon a coalition of diverse interests. Win this battle and his support would solidify. Lose, and his many enemies in Paris might surface to rally around some other popular general whom they would anoint as titular leader of state. Protected by that general's sword – perhaps Bernadotte's, more likely Moreau's – they would methodically purge his supporters and eventually annihilate the Bonaparte clan.

That matters had reduced to such a state was his own fault. His overconfidence had blinded him to the possibility that the Austrians might attack. When they had stormed out of their bridgehead this morning, his army had been badly dispersed, its front line units surprised. Yet his lieutenants – old comrade Victor, gallant Lannes – had conducted a brilliant tactical battle until overwhelmed by numbers. Thirty minutes earlier Bonaparte had committed his own elite Consular Guard to help cover their retreat. The Guard performed prodigies, until it too fell back before superior numbers.

Everything depended upon Desaix, who commanded the army's only available reinforcements. Six hours earlier, Bonaparte had sent a message recalling him. It read, "Come, in the name of god, if you still can." At that time the Army of Reserve was still holding its position. Now the situation was far worse. Along the main road from Marengo came the battered remnants of Lannes' and Victor's corps. The knots of men who still marched beneath their smoke-blackened standards were those stalwarts whom the officers had managed to hold to their duty. Yet a glance to either side of the road revealed that many others had thrown away their weapons to flee as fast as possible.

A mud-splattered officer approached at the gallop. It was Desaix. "Well, what do you think of it?" Bonaparte asked.

1

Desaix pulled out his timepiece. "This battle is completely lost, but...there is time to win another."

Heartened by his comrade's response, Bonaparte rode among his troops to rally them for one more desperate effort. He called out, "Soldiers, you have retreated far enough; you know that it is my habit to bivouac on the field of battle."

"Chins up!" replied a sergeant of the Consular Guard.

Around such men, Bonaparte cobbled together a final defensive line and awaited reinforcements. When the first of Desaix's men appeared, the French soldiers cried out, "Here they are, here they are!"

Meanwhile, from the west came the steady beat of drums that heralded the appearance of the elite of the Habsburg army, the grenadiers. The Austrians had fought long and hard to gain this position. Now they marched east, a surging tide sweeping the debris of battle before it. The Habsburg army's chief of staff was with them to share this moment of glory. He believed that one more hard push would be sufficient. Victory lay on the far side of a small vineyard, 300 yards farther east, where Desaix's battle line formed behind a hedge. The pivotal encounter of the battle of Marengo was about to occur.

Chapter I
Coup d'etat

PART 1.
FRANCE IN PERIL

"The Directory trembled at my return. I was very cautious; that is one of the epochs of my life in which I have acted with the soundest judgment...Every one was taken in my toils; and, when I became the head of the State, there was not a party in France which did not build some special hope upon my success."[1]

BONAPARTE REFLECTING UPON BRUMAIRE FOUR YEARS AFTERWARDS

In 1792, Austria and Prussia formed the First Coalition, an alliance dedicated to crushing republican France. The execution of Louis XVI brought Great Britain into the coalition the next year, followed by Spain. Thereafter, Russia, Holland, Naples, and Tuscany participated, their roles like that of jackals, risking little but hoping to glean pieces of the kill. Amazingly, there was no kill to be had.

The French Revolution unleashed a type of energy perhaps never before seen in Europe. This energy, coupled with French martial skill, allowed France to resist her enemies. But France's survival also depended upon her enemy's blunders. They stemmed from the difficulties any coalition of diverse interests experiences when trying to pull in harness. One by one they left the coalition until the only important members left fighting were Austria and Great Britain. Then a French military genius appeared on the scene in 1796.

Twenty-six-year-old General Napoleon Bonaparte conducted a campaign in northern Italy of such brilliance that it remains to this day a benchmark. His conquests, along with limited French successes on the Rhine, prompted Austria to accept peace in the spring of 1797. When Austria and France signed the Peace of Campo Formio in October of that year, the First Coalition finally collapsed.

Europe breathed a sigh of relief. Campo Formio seemed to indicate that within France the crusading zeal of the Revolution had matured into old-fashioned power politics. This was something familiar, something that European diplomats could understand and deal with. For France itself, the peace was extremely favorable and could not have come at a more welcome time. A host of internal troubles required attention, not the least of which were an economy hopelessly ruined by corruption and restive pockets of Royalist sympathizers quite willing to continue the fight against the hated republicans. Had French leaders, the so-called Directors, pursued a rational policy, the peace might have endured while they made internal reforms. But such was not their way. They employed the time honored strategy of creating external incidents to distract the population's attention from internal woes.

In 1798 the Directory overstepped by ordering its armies to occupy Switzerland and the Papal States. This extended French military force "into areas where the French presence could be justified neither by historic right, racial or cultural identity, or even strategic necessity, and the rest of Europe did not like it."[2] Consequently, Great Britain assembled a Second Coalition to defeat France that eventually included Naples, Turkey, Russia, and Austria. Conflict initially centered upon Rome and Sardinia, until July when Bonaparte invaded Egypt.

As early as the summer of 1797, Bonaparte had broached the idea of an Egyptian expedition to the Directory.[3] A year later, when the expedition departed, the Directory's thinking focused on three considerations. Because of the seizure of the Bernese treasury the effort could be financed. More important was the desire to strike somehow at Great Britain on land since the Royal Navy prevented a direct cross-channel invasion. Of almost equal significance was the Directors' desire to see a popular general as far from Paris as possible. While Bonaparte campaigned in Egypt and Syria, fighting in Europe in 1799 spread to Naples, northern Italy, Switzerland, the Rhine, and Holland. By all rights the Second Coalition should have crushed France.

To win the war, the allies had to invade France and subdue the crusading spirit of the Revolution "in its citadel at Paris."[4] There were four potential invasion corridors. The southernmost required an advance through Lombardy and Piedmont across the Maritime Alps and into Provence. Here the initial advantages were that the flat plain of the Po River favored the Coalition's superiority in cavalry and artillery while negating the French infantry superiority on broken ground. It was a fertile region, which reduced supply problems. It also offered the possibility of cooperating with the Royal Navy upon reaching the coast. On the other hand, upon entering the highly

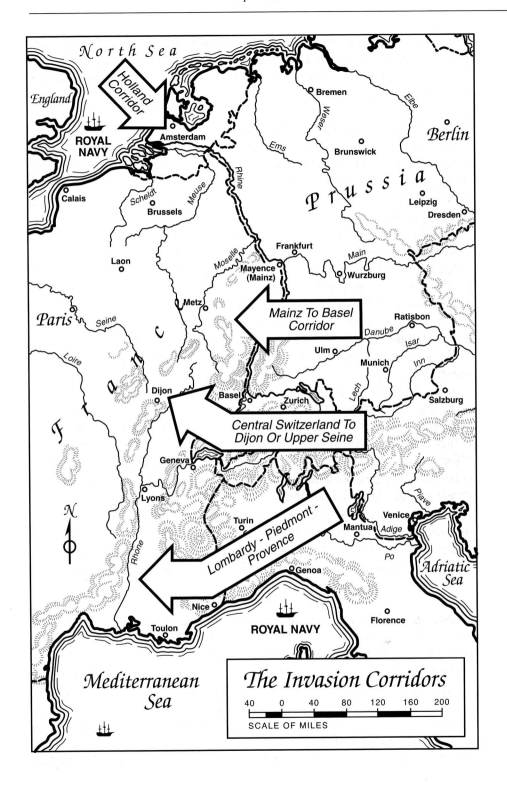

The Invasion Corridors

defensible Maritime Alps, all the advantages switched to the French. Moreover, the Italian corridor did not lead to a decisive objective. A successful allied advance would capture valuable territory but would not deliver a death blow.

Like the Italian corridor, an advance through Switzerland presented allied strategists with a mixed bag, some good, some bad. The mountainous terrain favored the defender. The French already possessed the country's limited road net. However, if the allies could overcome these obstacles and clear central Switzerland, they could then continue west across the Jura Mountains toward Dijon or head northwest through the Belfort gap and into the Upper Seine Valley. Although neither route immediately threatened Paris, both provided a means to deliver a significant body blow to the French Republic.

The easiest corridor by which central European powers could assault France was the 165-mile long space between Mainz and Basel. It provided the most direct route and enjoyed an excellent road net providing numerous alternative lines of advance. Although the Rhine River would have to be crossed, overall there were far fewer terrain difficulties than existed along the two more southerly corridors. In contrast to northern France, there were few fortresses blocking the way. Best of all, an advance over the Rhine led to Paris.

Since Prussia was neutral at this time, the region from Mainz to the Dutch frontier could not be crossed. What remained was a fourth invasion corridor through Holland. Like the Italian corridor, an advance through Holland offered the allies an opportunity to cooperate with the Royal Navy and any expeditionary force Great Britain might decide to deploy. Also like the Italian corridor, an advance would not lead to a decisive objective. Worse, it would have to contend with dike-constricted lines of march through waterlogged ground. For the campaign of 1799, the strategists of the Second Coalition resolved to utilize all four invasion routes.

From a French perspective, the beginning of the 1799 campaign was full of setback. The allies successfully cleared the Danube and Po Valleys. A succession of battles; Stockach, Magnano, Cassano, ended in French defeat. Italy, save Genoa, was lost. Switzerland was again in revolt with a certain Colonel Robert Craufurd – the future leader of Wellington's Light Division – poised to take command of a new Swiss army. Brittany and western France stood ready for armed insurrection. An Anglo-Russian Expeditionary force prepared to land in Holland. It appeared that France toppled on the edge of defeat.

PART 2.
DATELINE TO A COUP

Paris, Early Summer, 1799

The government of the Directory grows ever more unpopular. Weakness and corruption might be tolerable if the armies gain victories. But the Directory's short-sighted and erratic strategic meddling produces defeats. Thousands of troops badly needed in northern Italy are sent on a plundering expedition against Naples. In southern Germany, the Austrians cannot be effectively opposed because thousands of French veterans are instead fighting Royalists and other insurrectionists in the French interior. People wonder if the fault lies not with their army but rather with their government. Indicative of the lack of confidence in civilian rule is a growing tendency to look to generals as candidates to serve on the five-man Directory. When General François Lefebvre, the future marshal, receives votes to fill a place on the Directory, his wife reputedly comments, "They must be in a bad way when they want to make a dolt like you a King!"

Paris, June 18, 1799

Directors Paul Barras and Emmanuel Siéyès stage a coup, getting rid of three colleagues in exchange for three new ones. Siéyès intends this coup to be only a first step toward the dissolution of the Directory and its replacement by autocratic rule. Naturally, when the dust clears he plans for himself to be at the top of the heap. However, he requires the support of the military, since the army has replaced the terrorist mobs as the force to provide the necessary muscle to effect change. The plotters know that the army will ignore their orders but will march behind the sword of a popular leader. Siéyès selects the thirty-year-old Barthélemy Joubert to wield that sword.

Joubert's Lodgings, Paris, June 1799

Joubert enjoys popular renown, won while serving in Italy during Bonaparte's 1796-97 campaign. He is quite willing to employ his blade against the detested lawyers who seem to control the government. During this time of political intrigue, he grouses "they lose time in words. When they like, I will finish it all with twenty grenadiers."[5] Siéyès judges the situation too unsettled for immediate action. First

7

Joubert must win another victory to earn popular gratitude and then return for the necessary housecleaning. Before leaving Paris, Joubert tells both the Directory and his new bride that he will conquer or perish.

Bay of Aboukir, July 25, 1799

General Napoleon Bonaparte gazes at the Turkish army of Mustapha Pasha as it deploys northeast of Alexandria, Egypt. He has come full circle since landing near Alexandria a little more than one year ago. He had taken a select force to Egypt. Responding to criticism that his command included too many of France's best generals, he had replied, "I leave you Joubert." Early successes had prompted Bonaparte to dream of establishing himself as an eastern potentate. Perhaps he would march on British-controlled India and rival the accomplishments of Alexander the Great. But Nelson's destruction of the French fleet at the Battle of the Nile isolated him from most contact with home and forced him to modify his ambitions.

Nelson's victory proved a triumph of enormous strategic importance. As Bonaparte reported, "On this occasion as on so many others Destiny has shown that, if it gives us great preponderance on the continent, it has given the empire of the seas to our rivals."[6] Whereas in the spring of 1798 the French and Spanish fleets commanded the Mediterranean and the British had no port of call east of Gibraltar, by year's end it was the Royal Navy who controlled the sea. The threat to India was eliminated. Great Britain had re-established direct contact with the Mediterranean powers and with the Russian forces in that region. The surviving French naval units lay scattered or closely blockaded in Toulon.

Consequently, Bonaparte worked to establish Egypt as a self-supporting French base. News that Turkey had entered the lists against France forced him to consider the threat of a Turkish offensive. It would probably come in two prongs: an amphibious landing by the Army of Rhodes somewhere on the Egyptian coast; and an overland march by the Army of Damascus from Palestine. Rather than passively await the blows, Bonaparte led his army across the Sinai desert on an ill-fated invasion of Syria. The vigorous Turkish defense of Acre – a defense greatly aided by a French émigré engineer officer who had once been Bonaparte's classmate – and the ability of the Royal Navy to resupply Acre, thwarted the French. Bonaparte abandoned the siege and hastened back to Egypt to meet the amphibious prong of the Turkish offensive.

So today he orders his 7,700 men to advance and crush the 18,000-man Army of Rhodes. While French infantry led by General Jean Lannes charge over the Turkish redoubts, Colonel Joachim Murat conducts a brilliant cavalry charge that leads to the Turks' annihilation. The Turks suffer some 12,000 losses and 3,000 prisoners while the French lose about 150 killed and 750 wounded.

HMS Tigre, off the Egyptian coast, August 2, 1799

The Turks' defeat much vexes Captain William Sydney Smith, who has labored long to bring the Army of Rhodes to this coast. Outside of a devoted cult of worshipful followers, his fellow captains dislike him. Nor does he get along with Nelson. Smith is one of those dynamic naval officers who thrives on independent command. Sometimes his restless imagination can lead him astray.

One of his units has intercepted a French vessel carrying the latest news from Europe. Everywhere it seems that the forces of the Second Coalition are ascendent. Smith decides to leak information through the blockade in the belief that news of setback and defeat will demoralize Bonaparte's beleaguered army. In this instance, Smith proves too clever by half.

Cairo, August 11, 1799

Starved for news, Bonaparte eagerly digests the two-month old papers. It appears that most of the territory that Bonaparte had previously conquered in northern Italy is lost while the retreat over the Rhine places France again in direct peril of invasion. Bonaparte resolves to return to France, "well convinced that he alone could repair the harm that the Directory's bad government had inflicted upon the country."[7]

The Battlefield of Novi, August 15, 1799

Joubert leads the 35,000-man Army of Italy into battle. The army's former commander, Jean Moreau, has told him that he faces only 8,000 enemy soldiers. Moreau's assertion is wrong. Midway between Genoa and Alessandria, 65,000 Russians and Austrians commanded by the redoubtable Marshal Alexander Suvorov confront Joubert's army. The goad of winning a spectacular success spurs Joubert to risk battle. Early on Joubert senses his mistake. Having failed to conquer, he chooses a glorious death. He shouts to his aides, "Let us throw ourselves amongst the skirmishers!" and rides into the maelstrom of combat. Almost immediately a Russian musket shot drives through his left side and penetrates his heart.

A ferocious 16-hour battle ensues. The Austrian General Michael Melas personally leads his soldiers up to the cannons' mouths in a successful effort to turn the tide, and by day's end 11,000 French and 8,000 allies are casualties. In Suvorov's rustic words Joubert is "a young madcap, run away from school to get a thrashing."[8] When Joubert falls, the coup plotters in Paris must look anew for a sword.

The French Frigate *La Murion*, Midnight, August 22, 1799

In great secrecy Bonaparte gathers his core followers and orders two frigates readied to run Smith's blockade. Without even bothering to meet with his successor, he boards the *Murion*, his dream of rivaling Alexander the Great unfulfilled. He leaves behind a thoroughly disgruntled army. None are more displeased than the new senior commander, General Jean-Baptiste Kléber. Kléber formally complains that Bonaparte has left him a ragged, sickly, under strength army with a too extensive territory to defend. Informally he expresses his contempt at Bonaparte for deserting his post: "That little fellow has left us his breeches full of shit...we are going to return to Europe, and rub his face in it."[9] Some ten months later Kléber will be dead, stabbed to death by a Moslem assassin.

Zurich, September 26, 1799

General André Masséna learns that Suvorov, fresh from his victory at Novi, is marching into southern Switzerland to join forces with General Alexander Korsakov who commands the Russians near Zurich. Simultaneously, Erzherzog Karl has abandoned his ally and marched his Austrian army to southern Germany. This will not do. Masséna detaches a division to delay Suvorov and attacks Korsakov. Ably seconded by such notable divisional generals as Nicolas Soult, Michel Ney, Dominique Vandamme, Edouard Mortier, and Jean-Baptiste Drouet, Masséna routs the Russians. He then turns on Suvorov, destroying about half his army. It is Masséna's greatest achievement as a soldier.

The Battlefield of Castricum, October 6, 1799

The Anglo-Russian invasion of Holland bogs down amid the rain-soaked polders when confronted by General Guillaume Brune's well-conducted defense. The Duke of York resolves upon a final offensive to salvage the campaign. General Ralph Abercromby successfully drives back the French outpost line, but a Russian commander pursues too far. Brune skillfully organizes a counterattack with Jean Boudet's Division and a ten-hour long general action ensues. Defeated and discouraged, the Duke of York arranges a truce to allow the allied evacuation of Holland.

Richard Sheridan, the wit whose credits include *The School for Scandal*, provides his critique of Prime Minister William Pitt's strategy: it has been "an expedition of discovery", by which Great Britain has learned that "no reliance can be placed on Pitt's knowledge of human nature; that Holland is a country intersected with ditches, dykes and canals; and that the weather in October is not so good as in June.[10]

The Russian Tsar takes a darker view. The allied debacle in Holland coupled with Suvorov's defeat will convince Tsar Paul to leave the Second Coalition. In "a memorable fifteen days", Brune and Masséna have delivered France from immediate peril.[11]

The French Countryside, Early October, 1799

In spite of these successes, anger against the Directory's misrule intensifies. France is "groaning under the weight of her arbitrary government."[12] The Directory has created an unpopular conscription decree. Everyone knows that the conscripts will go unpaid and ill-clothed while the contractors make money. Once they arrive at the front they will be thrown away in some poorly conceived offensive whose real objective is plunder to prop up the government. The Directory also has decreed a forced loan that amounts to an extortion scheme. The rich employ every dodge including sham bankruptcy, shell companies, and emigration to avoid payment. Everyone else reduces expenses and participates more thoroughly in the underground economy. Consequently, businesses decline and unemployment soars. Bad as are these decrees, worse is the requirement that each commune with a potential for insurrection furnish a list of hostages who will be accountable for the misdeeds of their émigré or royalist relatives. The hostages will be either fined, imprisoned, or deported. It is so transparently open to corruption that it undoes most of the pacification work performed over the past many years. Georges Cadoudal and his men rise again in Brittany. The Vendée, Anjou, and even the heretofore quiet Midi become inflamed. The threat of royalist insurrection grows.

Consequently, the public's overweening desire is for change leading

"The news from Europe," dictated Napoleon Bonaparte in a proclamation to his Army of Egypt, "has determined me to depart for France."

to stability. One dedicated royalist who has managed to survive the terror speaks for most Frenchmen when he explains that he and his friends are prepared to support any government that possesses "A sincere desire to restore order in France."[13]

Paris, Early October, 1799

Prominent civilians and soldiers jointly denounce the government for its pervasive corruption and its stunning administrative incapacity. Legislators understand that reform without constitutional change is impossible. Few have any scruples about employing force to accomplish it.

However, power is divided among many factions. On the left stand the Jacobins, on the right the Royalists. In the middle are ardent republicans who sincerely believed that in spite of the hysteria and bloodshed of the Revolution, there are important ideals worth defending. To succeed, each faction needs a leader willing to risk all to execute a coup d'etat; a man who possesses enough reputation to attract sufficient followers. At this juncture, thirty-year-old Napoleon Bonaparte returns to France.

PART 3.
TO DARE ALL

The Bay of Saint-Raphaël, October 8, 1799

Bonaparte again sets foot in France. He appears:

> "very thin and very sallow, his complexion being copper-coloured, and his eyes deep-set and perfect in shape...His brow was very broad and open; he had little hair, especially about the temples; what there was very fine and thin. It was chestnut-coloured; and he had fine blue eyes that, in incredible fashion, depicted the divers emotions which stirred him, being sometimes extremely sweet and caressing, and anon wearing a severe, harsh expression."[14]

His physique conceals his ambition; a drive so powerful that Bonaparte considers it one and the same with his essential being. An acquaintance who had known Bonaparte in Italy encounters him again: "His manners were less abrupt, and he cultivated a more graceful method of speech, but his impatient nature still made itself felt throughout."[15] In a word, Bonaparte has matured.

Not for him are the quarantine regulations, although they are designed for the serious purpose of preventing Egyptian diseases from spreading to France. The legend will grow that when Bonaparte lands, he warns the crowd that they risk infection and people respond "We prefer the plague to the Austrians!"[16]

Avignon, October 11, 1799

Crowds line the road and receive Bonaparte with gratifying enthusiasm. In Avignon, an immense throng gathers to see the heroes of Italy and Egypt. Upon, "sighting the great man, excitement reached a fevered pitch, the air rang with acclamations".[17] In Paris, news of Bonaparte's landing causes the regimental bands belonging to the city's garrison to conduct spontaneous parades in which they are joined by soldiers and citizens alike. That evening illuminations light up the city. At the theaters people shout "Long live the Republic" and "Long live Bonaparte."[18]

In contrast to the general public, the Parisian political elite are not partial to the young general. His public dispatches from Egypt contained much braggadocio that prompted ridicule. Bonaparte's partial declaration of faith in Mohammedanism elicited distrust and contempt. Senior army officers are far from solidly pro-Bonaparte. Those who have not served with him dismiss his accomplishments by saying that he has gained his celebrity against second rate Austrian generals and Turks.

President of the Directory Louis-Jerome Gohier's Residence, Paris, October 16, 1799

Bonaparte appreciates that his unauthorized departure from Egypt hints of desertion while his presence in Paris at a time when the city buzzes with rumors of a coup d'etat looks suspicious. Bonaparte blurts out to Gohier his explanation: "The news that reached us in Egypt was so alarming that I didn't hesitate to leave my army, but set out at once to come and share your perils."

Referring to France's perils, Gohier replies with some sarcasm, "General, they were indeed great, but now we have gloriously overcome them. You have arrived in good time to help us celebrate the numerous triumphs of your comrades-in-arms." [19]

Luxembourg Palace, Offices of the Directory, Paris, October 17, 1799

Bonaparte lamely tries again to explicate his conduct before the Directory. He concludes by laying his hand on the hilt of his Turkish saber and pledging that he will never draw it except in defense of the Republic and its government. Gohier is dubious. At meeting's end the two exchange a fraternal embrace, which is "neither given nor received in a markedly brotherly fashion." [20] Later, when some of Bonaparte's entourage encourage him to strive for a posting in Italy, he responds, "When the house is crumbling, is it the time to busy oneself with the garden? A change here is indispensable." [21]

The Residence of Director Siéyès, Paris, October 23 (2 brumaire), 1799

For Siéyès, Bonaparte's return is a godsend. Here is a sword to replace the fallen Joubert. Reputedly, Moreau has told Siéyès that Bonaparte will carry out a coup far better than could Moreau himself. However, Bonaparte detests Siéyès. Today, he treats Siéyès so rudely that the Director remarks that his overbearing conduct is a bit much given that he has the authority to have Bonaparte executed for desertion.

Crime makes for strange bedfellows. After listening to some strong persuasion from his brothers, Minister of Foreign Affairs Charles

Talleyrand, and a handful of others, Bonaparte accepts that he has to cooperate with Siéyès. It is an uneasy alliance. In private, Bonaparte refers to Siéyès' recent diplomatic mission to Berlin and calls him a priest sold to Prussia, while Siéyès calls Bonaparte a rebellious soldier who ought to be shot.[22]

Paris, October 25 to November 5, 1799

The plot matures. The conspirators will rely upon the *Conseil des Anciens* (the upper house or Council of the Elders) to provide the coup's necessary veil of legality while dealing with the *Conseil des Cinq Cent* (the lower house or Council of the Five Hundred) summarily. The plot's essence involves three phases. On the first day the Anciens will use the pretext that a Jacobin conspiracy necessitates the transfer of the assemblies to Saint-Cloud to escape the Parisian mob. Second, to secure the execution of this decree, General Bonaparte will be given command of the Paris garrison. Having moved to Saint-Cloud where Bonaparte's soldiers can provide 'security', on the second day the *Anciens* and the *Cinq Cent* will complete the third phase by resolving to revise the Constitution. During the transition period, they will appoint three consuls to serve as a provisional government; namely, Bonaparte, Siéyès, and Roger-Ducos. For Bonaparte and Siéyès, there is "no chicane they were not prepared to use in order to maintain the pretense that the Government was actually willing to vote its own overthrow, and that the Constitution could be violated constitutionally."[23]

Bonaparte utilizes his talents as if directing a military campaign. Aware that he lacks a sufficient political base, he enlists allies and disarms potential foes by dint of insightful man management. "Remember," he tells Bourrienne, "you must always meet your enemies with a bold face, otherwise they think they are feared, and that gives them confidence."[24]

Paris, November 6 (15 brumaire), 1799

Not everyone proves susceptible to Bonaparte's manner. Jean-Baptiste Bernadotte is an ardent republican who carries the slogan "Death to Tyrants" tattooed on his arm. He is also a popular general. Because he has served under Bonaparte in Italy, is Joseph Bonaparte's brother-in-law, and is intensely ambitious, the conspirators believe he will join with them. However, when Bernadotte receives an invitation to a dinner to honor the hero of Egypt, he replies that the dinner should be postponed until Bonaparte accounts for his abandonment of his army. Then, alluding to his violation of the quarantine laws, Bernadotte observes that Bonaparte might be infectious and concludes, "I do not care to dine in the company of a plague-stricken man."[25] Bernadotte will bear careful watching. He is one of a handful of rivals who has the popular stature to thwart the coup.

Paris, November 7 to 8 (16-17 brumaire), 1799

Even for a city accustomed to political upheaval, the days leading up to the coup attempt feature unparalleled intrigue, suspicion, and betrayal. Josephine Bonaparte uses her friendship with Director Gohier and his wife to keep the conspirators informed of Gohier's position. Joseph Bonaparte uses his family connection with Bernadotte's wife to monitor Bernadotte. But no one outdoes policeman Joseph Fouché who has informers in every camp, not the least prized of whom is Josephine.

Unlike his potential rivals, Bonaparte has a group of devoted officers with him in Paris who are ready to obey any order. He deploys them with precision and purpose. Louis-Alexandre Berthier conspires with officers of the general staff. Lannes, Murat, and Auguste Marmont sound out officers of the infantry, cavalry, and artillery, respectively. Fellow Corsican Horace Sebastiani can be counted on to deliver the support of his cavalry regiment which is conveniently quartered in Paris. Brother Lucien Bonaparte, acting in his capacity as President of the Council, prepares the legal necessities. Bonaparte even enlists his wife into the plot. Josephine, who charms most men she meets, invites President Gohier to an 8 a.m. breakfast scheduled for the day of the coup. Bonaparte hopes to convince Gohier to accept his coup; if not, it will be simplicity itself to arrest him.

Bonaparte's Residence, 6 a.m., November 9 (18 brumaire), 1799

Bonaparte and his staff awake early. Events proceed with clock-like precision. General Lefebvre, who commands the Paris garrison and the Directoral Guard and is not in on the plot, receives a summons to Bonaparte's chambers at 6 a.m. He is uncertain what to do until Bonaparte announces to a select group of National Guard officers that the *Anciens* have transferred command of the garrison to him. The officers respond enthusiastically at which point Bonaparte asks the wavering Lefebvre whether he wants to allow his cherished Republic to collapse at the hands of the lawyers who control the Directory. He requests the now thoroughly excited Lefebvre to unite with him to save the Republic and hands him a saber exclaiming, "Here is the saber I wore at the Pyramids. I give it to you as a pledge of my esteem and confidence." Won over, Lefebvre replies, "Yes, let us throw the lawyers into the river."[26] Meanwhile, Berthier, Lannes, Murat, and Marmont each host a breakfast party for key officers while troops take up positions to repulse any countermoves.

Hall of the *Anciens*, 7 a.m., November 9 (18 brumaire), 1799

The *Anciens*, whose support or at least neutrality has already been assured, convene and dutifully authorize the move to Saint-Cloud and the transfer of command to Bonaparte. Then, Bonaparte appears before them to accept the appointment as "executor" of the plan to transfer the councils and receive command of the Paris garrison. By law, a quorum of three out of five Directors is necessary to order executive action and only such action can now delay the coup. To prevent a quorum, Siéyès and his collaborator Roger-Ducos are to resign. This leaves Barras holding the pivotal role.

Director Paul Barras' Residence, Paris, November 9 (18 brumaire), 1799

Since they first met during the siege of Toulon in 1793, Barras has been instrumental in Bonaparte's rise. Barras selected Bonaparte to defend the government against the mob in 1795. When Barras left the Army of the Interior to join the Directory, he chose Bonaparte to replace him. He appointed Bonaparte to the Army of Italy and gave him Josephine, albeit after Barras himself had tired of her. But he did not want to give Bonaparte absolute leadership of France by resigning. Exactly how Talleyrand persuades him to change his mind is unclear, because, "when two such men as Talleyrand and Barras do business together, the odds are that history will never know for certain whether bribery or blackmail clinches the matter."[27] By afternoon, Barras departs Paris with undamaged reputation – it could sink no lower – and a considerable sum of money. These actions isolate the remaining two Directors, Gohier and Moulin.

Bonaparte's Residence, late evening, November 9 (18 brumaire), 1799

Not everything has proceeded perfectly. When Joseph Bonaparte squired Bernadotte to an early morning meeting with Bonaparte, Bernadotte saw the plotters assembling and hastened away. The wily President Gohier sensed a trap and did not attend Josephine's breakfast. The soldiers of the 86th Demi-brigade refused to march until Bonaparte delivered a convincing harangue. But overall, when a weary Bonaparte and his conspirators retire for the night they are well satisfied. All that remains is a formal appearance the next day before the *Anciens* and the *Cinq Cents* to give the coup an acceptable cloak of legality.

But the plotters have made a cardinal error. The overthrow of a government should be done in one sudden stroke. By extending it over two days, they give opposition a chance to organize. Bonaparte may sense this when he bids goodnight to his secretary, "we shall see what will turn up to-morrow."[28]

The Jail of Moulin and Gohier, Paris, November 9 (18 brumaire), 1799

Bonaparte has dealt with the popular General Moreau by overwhelming him with affable civilities and giving him a diamond-studded Damascus blade brought from Egypt. Somewhat surprisingly given his cautious nature, Moreau actively participates in the coup by serving as the jailer for Moulin and Gohier, the two deposed Directors. By day's end, after listening to General Moulin denounce Bonaparte as an enemy of the Republic, Moreau's commitment to the coup weakens. He tells them "If I have committed a grave mistake, I will repair it."[29]

The Gardens of Saint-Cloud, November 10 (19 brumaire), 1799

The problem comes on the coup's second day, triggered by the most mundane, but thoroughly French cause. Laborers have not finished preparing the halls so the legislators can convene. The ensuing two-hour delay provides a chance for Bonaparte's opponents to confer. The Deputies circulate outside in the gardens to exchange views, to inquire what is the motive behind this extraordinary move to Saint-Cloud? Jacobin opposition quickly coalesces. The Jacobins have two champions in Generals Pierre Augereau and Jean-Baptiste Jourdan. The noted fence-squatter Bernadotte senses the tide shifting and prepares to support Bonaparte's rivals.

The Halls of Saint-Cloud, November 10 (19 brumaire), 1799

When the doors finally open, a full debate ensues. Speaker after speaker rises to denounce the coup plotters while in a nearby room Bonaparte waits impatiently. The general is politically still rather naive and completely unfamiliar with legislative niceties. Impulsively, he enters to deliver a rambling tirade to first the *Anciens* and then the *Cinq Cents*. Before the latter, the general learns "that he could not deal with the representatives of France in the same arbitrary fashion that had served to overwhelm the sheikhs of the Cairo Divan."[30]

He appears flanked by four grenadiers and followed by his military entourage. The presence of armed men upsets the politicians. Questions beget rude interrogation as the delegates egg one another on. When he begins to hear mutterings about his status as "outlaw" Bonaparte replies with bluster: "Remember that fortune and the god of war march beside me." The next day he will candidly confess, "I got heated and ended with a silly sentence. The French do not like bad taste; no sooner had I said the words than a murmur made me aware of it."[31]

In fact, the deputies raise far more than a murmur. They interrupt with shouts of "Long live the constitution! No dictatorship! Down with the dictator!"[32] The old revolutionary cry to suspend the law, the first step to nominating a dictator to put down the coup, arises.

In a proclamation delivered to the nation the next day, Bonaparte will melodramatically describe the scene: "I then appeared before the Council of Five Hundred, alone, unarmed, bareheaded...The daggers which threatened the deputies were immediately raised against their liberator: a score of assassins threw themselves upon me, seeking my breast."[33] In reality there are no assassins and probably no daggers. Instead, there is a hostile crowd of deputies who drive Bonaparte from the hall.

Temporarily dazed and off balance, Bonaparte staggers on the precipice of oblivion. At this juncture, the *Cinq Cents* can declare Bonaparte an outlaw and find enough support to make the decree stick. It is one of those rare occasions, a true turning point in history. Instead of acting, the *Cinq Cents* reverts to debate and threat making.

The Courtyard of Saint-Cloud, November 10 (19 brumaire), 1799

For one of the few times in his life, one of Bonaparte's siblings does something really useful. Lucien Bonaparte despairs of mastering the *Cinq Cents* and departs the hall with a dramatic flourish. Outside, he finds his brother trying to rally the soldiers by claiming that he has been attacked by assassins. The soldiers seem confused. Lucien mounts a horse so as better to be seen and heard. Gesturing toward the uproar within, he tells the soldiers that a handful of armed delegates are trying to take control of the Council. Hearing these words from the President of the Council himself, the soldiers waver. Cries of "Vive Bonaparte!" begin, but many still hesitate. Lucien continues with a stirring speech, explaining that those who oppose his brother are "not the representatives of the people, but rather the representatives of the dagger."[34] The President has told the soldiers exactly what they want to hear. His words dissolve their last doubts. Drummers sound the charge. Bonaparte and Murat order the soldiers to clear the hall. Grenadier Jean-Roch Coignet relates: "Suddenly we heard cries, and Bonaparte came out, drew his sword, and went up again with a platoon of grenadiers of the guard. Then the noise increased. Grenadiers were on the stairway and in the entrance. We saw stout gentlemen [the legislators] jumping out the windows."[35]

Discommoded by their 'togas' and holding their classical headgear in their hands, the Deputies ignominiously flee into the woods. It is said that as he evicted them, the commander of the grenadiers told the Deputies that they neither knew how to make peace nor war and thus there was no reason for them to remain.

That evening Joseph and Lucien Bonaparte manage to assemble a fraction of the Deputies who vote to adopt the measures suppressing the councils, abolishing the Directory, and creating three provisional consuls. Before his near fatal misstep in front of the *Cinq Cent*, their brother had hoped that this would come about by discourse and verbal persuasion. Instead, change has occurred at bayonet point.

The Residence of Foreign Minister Talleyrand, November 10 (19 brumaire), 1799

While waiting to see who will come out on top, Talleyrand characteristically enjoys the second day of the coup in pleasant company with friends. When word comes of Bonaparte's success, he responds, "We must go and dine." Years later, when Bonaparte asks him how he came to make his fortune so fast, Talleyrand refers to the dates straddling the coup's first day and replies, "Nothing could be more simple. I bought stock on the 17th Brumaire and sold it again on the 19th."[36]

The Residence of Chief of Police Fouché, November 10 (19 brumaire), 1799

Uniquely among all who lusted for power, Bonaparte has calculated the odds and accepted the gamble. The consequences of failure can be readily assessed. Among those straddling the fence during the coup has been Joseph Fouché. On the coup's second day, Fouché orders his police to close the roads to Paris and sends a spy to observe Bonaparte's reception at Saint-Cloud. Meanwhile, Fouché marshals his forces to arrest Bonaparte should he commit 'the crime of failure.' In all likelihood Bonaparte would have then faced the firing squad.[37]

Seeing Bonaparte, for the moment at least, safely in charge, the former ardent republican throws his support to the new regime.

By daring all, a mere thirty-three days after landing in France Napoleon Bonaparte has won more than anyone, himself included, ever anticipated.

NOTES

1. Claire Rémusat, *Memoirs of Madame de Rémusat* (New York, 1880) p. 100.
2. Alexander B. Rodger, *The War of the Second Coalition* (Oxford, 1964), p. 71.
3. See: "To the Executive Directory", Aug. 16, 1797 in John Howard, ed., *Letters and Documents of Napoleon*, I (New York, 1961), p. 199.
4. Secretary of State for Foreign Affairs Grenville's words cited in: Piers Mackesy, *The Strategy of Overthrow 1798-1799* (London, 1974), p. 69.
5. Ramsay W. Phipps, *The Armies of the First French Republic*, V (London, 1939), pp. 312-313.
6. "To the Executive Directory", August 19, 1798, Howard, *Letters and Documents of Napoleon*, I, p. 267.
7. Antoine-Marie Chamans, Compte de Lavalette, *Mémoires et Souvenirs* (Paris, 1994), p. 220.
8. Phipps, V, p. 318.
9. Rodger, p. 132.
10. Mackesy, *The Strategy of Overthrow*, p. 311.
11. Louis-Jerome Gohier, *Mémoires des Contemporains,* I (Paris, 1824), p. 165.
12. Etienne Macdonald, *Recollections of Marshal Macdonald*, I (New York, 1892), p. 279.
13. Etienne-Denis Pasquier, *Memoirs of Chancellor Pasquier*, I (New York, 1893), p. 48.
14. Wairy Constant, *Memoirs of Constant*, I, trans. Percy Pinkerton (London, 1896), p. 263.
15. André Miot, *Memoirs of Count Miot de Melito* (New York, 1881) p. 155.
16. Louis de Bourrienne, *Memoirs of Napoleon Bonaparte*, I (New York, 1906) p. 240.
17. Jean François Bon Boulart, *Mémoires Militaires du Général Bon Boulart* (Paris, 1892), pp. 67-68.
18. Paul Thiébault, *Memoirs of Baron Thiébault*, II (New York, 1896) p. 13.
19. Gohier, I, pp. 199-200.
20. Gohier, I, p. 202.
21. Auguste Marmont, *Mémoires du Maréchal Marmont Duc de Raguse,* II (Paris, 1857) p. 89.
22. Paul Barras, *Memoirs of Barras*, IV (New York, 1896), p. 45.
23. J.B. Morton, *Brumaire: The Rise of Napoleon* (London, 1948), p. 218.

24. Bourrienne, I, p. 257.

25. Barras, IV, p. 40.

26. Phipps, V, p. 458.

27. Morton, *Brumaire: The Rise of Napoleon*, p. 233.

28. Bourrienne, I, p. 269.

29. Gohier, I, p. 270.

30. David G. Chandler, *The Campaigns of Napoleon* (New York, 1966), p. 261.

31. "Speech to the Council of the Ancients," November 10, 1799 in Howard, *Letters and Documents of Napoleon*, I, p. 312. Also see FN on same page. Note that Bourrienne says that Bonaparte delivered no formal speech to the Ancients, but in his rambling he did make a threat. See: Bourrienne, I, p. 270.

32. Gohier, I, p. 273.

33. "Proclamation to the French Nation," November 10, 1799 in *Letters and Documents of Napoleon*, I, p. 313.

34. Lucien Bonaparte, *Révolution de Brumaire* (Paris, 1846), p. 123. Bourrienne has Lucien drawing his sword, pointing it at Napoleon, and exclaiming, "I swear that I will stab my own brother to the heart if he ever attempts anything against the liberty of Frenchmen." Lucien makes no such claim. See: Bourrienne, I, p. 279.

35. Lorédan Larchey, ed., *The Narrative of Captain Coignet* (New York, 1890), p. 54.

36. Rémusat, p. 85.

37. Antoine-Marie Chamans, p.233, relates that an old school colleague who worked with Fouché's police warned him, after the fact, that Fouché was prepared to arrest the conspirators.

Chapter 2

The Power of the First Consul

PART 1.
"THE REVOLUTION IS OVER"

"The First Consul has received many letters from young citizens expressing their desire to prove their devotion to the Republic...Glory awaits them at Dijon."[1]

PROCLAMATION OF MARCH, 20, 1800

When news of the coup's success spread, those who had waited to see who would emerge triumphant became committed Bonapartists, at least for the time being. A bystander observed how quickly favor-seekers and potential office-holders lined up in the streets to congratulate the latest 'great man'. Bonaparte returned a hard eye to their flattery, coolly identifying those whose talents he could use and those whose support he needed. Meanwhile, the day after the coup the Moniteur informed the nation of the change in government. It of course distorted the truth about how the changes had occurred. Yet, when a French diplomat returned to Paris after the coup, he found that the facts about what had transpired at Saint-Cloud were widely known. However, "success had justified the means."[2]

Bonaparte's position as Provisional Consul proved transitory. Soon his co-conspirators, Siéyès and Roger-Ducos, realized that the sword they had hoped to utilize for their own ascendancy was too strong. The night after the coup Siéyès had remarked, "We have a master who knows how to do everything, who can do everything, and who wishes to do everything."[3] By the time the consuls presented a new constitution to the French people on December 25, France's fourth in ten years, Bonaparte had emerged as First Consul while Siéyès and Roger-Ducos were pushed aside. The constitution came with Bonaparte's declaration that the violence and chaos of the

Revolutionary era had ended: "Citizens, the Revolution is confined to the principles which commenced it: it is finished."[4]

Indeed, while the French people desired stability above all, it was by no means clear that this latest change in government would produce that stability. Dispatched on a mission to Toulouse, a city which upon learning of the coup had pondered establishing its own Directory, Lannes informed Bonaparte that some areas were restless and confused. However, during his travels Lannes had heard neither "'Vive Moreau!' nor 'Vive Siéyès!' but rather 'Vive Bonaparte'"[5] Lannes concluded with an unwitting prophecy: if Bonaparte could give France peace, the people would idolize him.

The new constitution specified that there would be three consuls, each of whom would serve a ten-year term. All real power rested in the hands of the First Consul. He promulgated all laws, conducted foreign relations, and provided for national security. The other two consuls held a consultive voice only. The Third Consul was Charles Lebrun. During the Revolution, he had advanced because of his deep-held commitment to the ideal of equality. Lebrun's metier was finance, his personality that of an egotistical individualist. Bonaparte understood how to use such men. Within the Consulate, Lebrun played a useful role in reorganizing the government's financial and administrative activities.

The Second Consul was Jean-Jacques Cambacérès. He was a man of far greater talent than Lebrun. Amid the chaos of revolutionary France he had espoused moderate views and had been mainly concerned with codifying revolutionary legislation. Trained as a lawyer, he was a superb legislator, a role for which the First Consul had little skill or patience. Consequently, he complemented Bonaparte nicely. Unlike the Third Consul who shrugged his shoulders at titles and honorific distinction and was a thin ascetic, Cambacérès reveled in all manner of official display and was a fat gourmet. Bonaparte understood this sort of man as well. Cambacérès would remain a trusted advisor during his entire reign. Best of all, from the First Consul's viewpoint, neither of his fellow consuls aspired to supreme rule and thus neither was a threat to his own aspirations. First Consul Bonaparte's rule began on December 25, 1799. If recent French history was any guide, his reign would be temporary at best.

From his apartments in the Luxembourg Palace, the First Consul surveyed the strategic landscape. Unlike his predecessors, he recognized France's paramount need for peace. Because of the Royal Navy, France had lost her colonial trade which had accounted for a third of her imports and a fifth of her exports. She could not recover on the continent since many areas remained closed to French trade. To cite just one example, in spite of a growing population, cloth manufacture had declined by two-thirds since 1789. Accordingly, on December 26 Bonaparte offered peace to Austria and Great Britain. His sincerity is questionable; he probably merely sought a breathing space.

The allied perspective is well described by John Holland Rose: "In diplomacy men's words are interpreted by their past conduct and present circumstances."[6] Recent French conduct did not inspire confidence in Bonaparte's words. Moreover, Austria judged itself to hold an excellent strategic position and merely politely declined Bonaparte's olive branch. 'Present circumstances,' as assessed by British leaders, involved a more complex calculation. Prime Minister Pitt and his advisers could take comfort from the fact that the Second Coalition had endured in spite of hard knocks, but they had to ask how much more effort could its partners expend? Was now the time to take the long view, make peace, and prepare for the next round of hostilities, or should Great Britain continue the costly struggle to overthrow France's rulers?[7]

Britain's preferred ally remained Russia. However, the Russian army's defects had plainly emerged during its campaign in Holland. Bad officers, an inefficient staff, and a near useless commissariat reduced the army's potential to little more than that of a semi-barbaric horde. A British observer who saw them land at Great Yarmouth, where "they stole and drank the oil from the street-lamps", could hardly believe their shocking filth.[8] Their condition did not surprise British veterans of the Holland campaign who had seen neglected Russian soldiers butter their bread with axle grease scraped from the British artillery. Worse, they had seen the Russians repeatedly refuse to close with the enemy. Nonetheless, Secretary of State for Foreign Affairs William Wyndham, Lord Grenville, believed that such soldiers could form a substantial part of an amphibious landing on the French coast once the 1800 campaign season opened. He conceived that this would be one prong of a strategic offensive, a concentric series of blows delivered from the North Sea to Germany to Italy, designed to hammer Bonaparte into submission.

Pitt and Grenville knew that Austria had to provide most of the manpower for the German and Italian prongs. However, that country had proven itself an unreliable partner. Masséna's great victories in Switzerland had been possible only because the Austrian army had failed to cooperate with the Russians. Only slowly did British strategists come to realize that Erzherzog Karl had departed

Switzerland in order to capture territory the Habsburgs intended to use as bargaining chips once France fell. To overcome such selfish conduct, selfish that is from a British standpoint, Pitt and his ministers had to make a strategic determination whether substantial subsidies could keep Austria to the Coalition's business and ultimately defeat France. They concluded yes.

In the final analysis, British strategists regarded Bonaparte as a usurper, no different than his predecessors who had led France into revolution and war. As long as France remained in political turmoil, there could be no important negotiations since a new government might renounce prior agreements. A stable French government was a prerequisite. The restoration of the monarchy was the only path to permanent peace. In fact, Bonaparte's peace overture found Pitt's government deep in preparation for a combined British and French royalist amphibious strike against the French fleet in Brest. With this mindset, Pitt responded to Bonaparte's peace overture with an insulting set of demands that hinted strongly that there could be no meaningful discussions absent a Bourbon restoration.

Nothing could have been better calculated to elevate Bonaparte's popularity in France. Bonaparte, in turn, incisively noted the fallacy in the British logic. He replied that surely His Britannic Majesty recognized the right of a nation to choose its form of government since only by that right did King George III wear the British crown. Otherwise, the king was promoting a principle which would recall the Stuarts to Great Britain's throne!

Having demonstrated to his own people that he had tried to make peace, Bonaparte prepared for war. He resolved to spend the winter making a short, decisive campaign against the rebels in the west. Then, he would deal with the Austrians when active operations resumed in the spring. This gave Bonaparte a short amount of time first to win over the army – he well knew his ascent to First Consul was far from universally popular – and second to institute reforms to make the military a more effective fighting force.

He set about winning the army the day after the coup. He went to the Place du Carrousel to review the regiments which composed the Paris garrison. Traditionally the army's elite occupied the right flank of units drawn up in line of battle. This was the post of honor. On the *Place du Carrousel*, the two companies composing the Guard of the Directory formed the right of the line. Bonaparte halted before them to announce that henceforth it was to be the 'Guard of the Consuls.' The entire line exploded with cheers. No one present could know that one of the most fabled, elite units in military history, the Imperial

Guard, had been born. Later, when three veteran demi-brigades filed past him in salute, he observed that their banners were mere powder blackened shreds, the few intact threads riddled with balls. He doffed his chapeau and bowed in respect. The men cheered in response. To their minds, here was a leader who understood things; by honoring them he was honoring both France and himself, all in all a vast improvement over the lawyers who had formerly administered the government.

To forge bonds with the army, the First Consul extended the practice of handing out "arms of honor", the precursor to the Legion of Honor, to reward particularly gallant feats. Such feats included capturing an enemy flag or high ranking enemy officer or being the first to touch a captured cannon. For grenadiers and soldiers there were muskets with silver finishings and similar carbines or musketoons for the cavalry; for drummers and trumpeters, drumsticks or trumpets embossed with silver; gunners could receive a gold grenade insignia for their uniform. The highest reward was a saber of honor. When he rewarded a grenadier sergeant named Léon Aune with such a saber, Aune responded with a personal letter listing his exploits and asking to remain in the Consul's memory. Bonaparte, in turn, wrote back referring to the grenadier as "my brave comrade" and ordered him to come to Paris for a personal meeting.[9] He also had Aune promoted to second-lieutenant in the Consular Guard. Word spread quickly that the busy First Consul had time for a lowly sergeant whom he considered a comrade. It was an army-wide reassurance that the new government adhered to the old revolutionary, egalitarian ideal.

While symbolic gestures were well and good, most soldiers cared more about being fed and clothed and receiving their pay. For them, the events of Brumaire were just one more political upheaval in Paris. They would judge whether it had any significance on the basis of whether it led to an improvement in their lot. Under the Directory, pay had too often been late or not provided at all. Bonaparte understood that he could take a long stride toward gaining the army's obedience if he could contrive to pay it on a more regular basis. But, it required vast sums to maintain the 285,000 soldiers whom the official reports tabulated as serving in the armies on November 22, 1799.

As one of his first acts, Bonaparte had suppressed the unpopular forced loan legislation. He had appointed a very able Finance Minister to reform the tax laws. But reforms took time and the army needed money immediately. To finance the war, Bonaparte demanded huge payments from France's most wealthy merchants. Within two weeks of his coup he instructed his Finance Minister to summon "the twelve most powerful merchants" (of Paris) and demand the immediate payment of additional millions for the specific purpose of paying and supplying the French army. Marseilles, Bordeaux, Lyons all felt such demands. Simultaneously, Bonaparte refused to repay a 24 million franc loan he had used to finance his recent coup, thus proving that the rule of law he was returning to France could be rather elastic. The French 'allies' had large requisitions to meet as well. The First Consul ordered Augereau to "Imperiously insist on everything that government [the Dutch] owes us!"[10] The Swiss were to pay for the privilege of France's 'protection' of Helvetic territory. Even the Portuguese were expected to pay eight to nine million francs to help defray the cost of reconquering northern Italy. Extortion at bayonet point was a tool unlikely to foster enduring diplomatic relationships with other European nations. But in the short term it did garner the badly needed money to ready the army for the pending campaign.

Within France, Bonaparte's administrative capacity encouraged his partisans and won many converts. One of the secrets to his success was his ability to seek out men of talent and employ them in a suitable position. He cared not about their background, whether royalist or Jacobin, as long as they were henceforth loyal to his regime. General Lefebvre wrote to an officer who had not yet met the new First Consul: "times are much changed, my dear Ney. Places are no longer given through intrigue, every consideration yields to the public interest."[11] But republican ideals proved tenacious. Not everyone was ready to cede all power to an upstart general and a Corsican for all of that. Many officers and men who served with the field armies outside of Paris were either anxious about what had transpired or actively opposed the unconstitutional change. In Italy, when an officer in the 33rd Demi-brigade tried to convince his unit to accept the new Consular Constitution, angry officers replied, "they had not been fighting for eight years, they had not borne every possible wretchedness to serve as a footstool to a Cromwell."[12]

While Bonaparte's domestic administration is outside this book's scope, it must be noted that however admirable were many of his reforms, he simultaneously organized a dictatorship propped up by an efficient secret police. He discerned which aspects of the Revolution had captured France's heart and which could be fitted in with his despotism. He organized a government that observed certain republican forms while in reality he was responsible to no one. He could only be prosecuted by the Council of State, whose members he himself appointed. He alone possessed the right to initiate legislation. The legislature could merely vote 'yes' or 'no'. But if they voted 'no',

Bonaparte alone wielded decree power. By design it was rule without checks or balances. In January, a celebrated orator dared publicly to criticize Bonaparte during a legislative debate. Bonaparte could not tolerate criticism nor did he intend to learn. He fumed to an advisor, "My enemies deserve nothing from me but steel." [13]

He controlled all print outlets. In January he shut down 60 out of 73 Parisian journals. He made the Moniteur an official state organ. It printed whatever useful lies he desired. In April, in the midst of complex military planning, he found time to tell his Minister of Police "that the journals, *The Well-informed, Free Men,* and *Defenders of the Country*" should no longer appear; that news vendors "cry the names of no journals or pamphlets" without a police permit; that book stalls sell nothing contrary "to the principles of the government." He wrote to his brother Lucien, the Minister of the Interior, that "The First Consul would be glad to see suppressed the couplet referring to him" in a popular vaudeville play. [14] However, for perspective recall that in Great Britain Pitt asked for and received a new suspension of the Habeas Corpus Act in the spring of 1798, continued to suppress cruelly Ireland, and imposed a staggering income tax in order to procure money to subsidize Austria and other allies.

Lest anyone doubt who was in charge, on February 19, 1800, Bonaparte transferred the entire government from the Luxembourg Palace, the headquarters of the detested Directory, to the Tuileries, the place where kings had once reigned. Six white horses, who in 1797 had been a gift from the Austrian Kaiser to Bonaparte upon completion of the Peace of Campo Formio, pulled his carriage. To attract attention, he ordered some 3,000 soldiers to escort the vast procession, which included most of the government's functionaries as well as the State Council and cabinet minsters. In mid-parade Bonaparte, wearing the red consul's uniform, switched to a horse to inspect soldiers of the 30th, 40th, and 96th Demi-brigades. No one could know that in less than five months these soldiers would be fighting for their lives on the field of Marengo.

By occupying the Bourbon palace Bonaparte was symbolically announcing the nation's return to stability, and incidently, to one-man rule. By gesture, talk, and action he confirmed the fact that "The revolution is over." [15] In fact, before he took possession of the Tuileries, he had the palace thoroughly renovated and the caps of Liberty and other revolutionary symbols and inscriptions that 'decorated' the walls removed. At the beginning of the Consulate, the government's letterhead included a vignette representing the Republic in the form of a female figure holding a rudder in one hand and a crown in the other, with the inscription: "French Republic, Sovereignty of the People, Liberty, Equality, Bonaparte, First Consul." Bonaparte erased the reference to revolutionary principles and substituted the inscription, "In the name of the French people, the French government." As one dedicated republican observed, "The Sovereignty of the People, Liberty, and Equality soon disappeared from view."[16]

The First Consul recognized that he had come far but that his position was by no means assured. The day after occupying Louis' palace, he remarked, "To be at the Tuileries, Bourrienne, is not all. We must stay here."[17] Accordingly, Bonaparte labored hard in his private study at the Tuileries. Only his secretaries could enter to receive dictation. When he wished to confer with his fellow consuls or his ministers he moved to an adjacent room. This spatial division reflected his attitude toward work. Not for him were conferences and meetings. Rather, he preferred to receive written reports. He retained the office of the Secretariat of State but changed it into a mere central bureau for collecting dossiers submitted by the various governmental departments and transmitting Bonaparte's replies. Thus, with the notable exceptions of Talleyrand and Fouché, most ministers and their subordinates became mere clerks.

From Brumaire to the opening of the campaign season was a time of improvisation. It could hardly be anything else, given the low state to which the nation had sunk under the misrule of the Directory. As had been the case during the wars of the Revolution, improvisation – the lack of sound logistical preparation – meant the armies would suffer. It also meant that there could not be a protracted war. The first campaign had to be decisive because the war effort could not be long maintained "without demanding from the nation the kind of sacrifices which had made the Convention and the Directory so unpopular."[18]

PART 2.
THE STRATEGIC CHESSBOARD

The strategic situation First Consul Bonaparte confronted was daunting. A British expeditionary force of unknown size remained hovering along the channel coast. A large Russian contingent – Bonaparte judged it to number 25,000 men – camped in the Jersey Islands. Both seemed available to support the ongoing insurrection in western France. A second British expeditionary force was in the Mediterranean. There were two huge Austrian armies poised for invasion. In northern Italy General der Kavallerie (GdK or full general, cavalry) Michael Melas commanded a field army approaching 100,000 men of whom 14,000 were cavalry. Along the Rhine, Feldzeugmeister (FZM or full general, infantry) Paul Kray commanded a nearly equal sized force. Of the Republic's forces, Kleber's army in Egypt remained isolated while the Army of Italy was under strength and destitute. Thus Bonaparte focused on Moreau's Army of the Rhine, which numbered more than 120,000 men.

Jean Moreau was born at Morlaix in Brittany in 1763. His father was a lawyer who hoped that his son would follow in his footsteps. Showing a certain independence of spirit, the young man enlisted in the army only to have his father remove him and send him to the law school at Rennes. Moreau proved a natural leader among his fellow students. Upon the formation of the National Guard, he raised a volunteer company of gunners. His comrades elected him captain. The restless youth next applied to join the Gendarmerie and in his zeal was even willing to accept a low rank. Denied, his next chance came in 1791 when the government called for 169 new volunteer battalions to be raised by the departments. The popular young man became lieutenant-colonel of the first volunteer battalion raised in his department. On March 18, 1793, the battalion fought at the Battle of Neerwinden. Twice Moreau led it forward in the attack, twice he rallied it after it had failed. His commanding general praised his firm, brave conduct. By year's end, he had received a nomination for brigadier general. He rose rapidly within the Army of the North and became a favorite of General Jean Pichegru under whom he became a general of division in April 1794.

Back home, his father had been transmitting funds for several émigrés, a most unwise activity at a time when locally the Terror continued. In spite of the fact that he had four sons serving in the army, he was guillotined in July 1794. This event may mark the

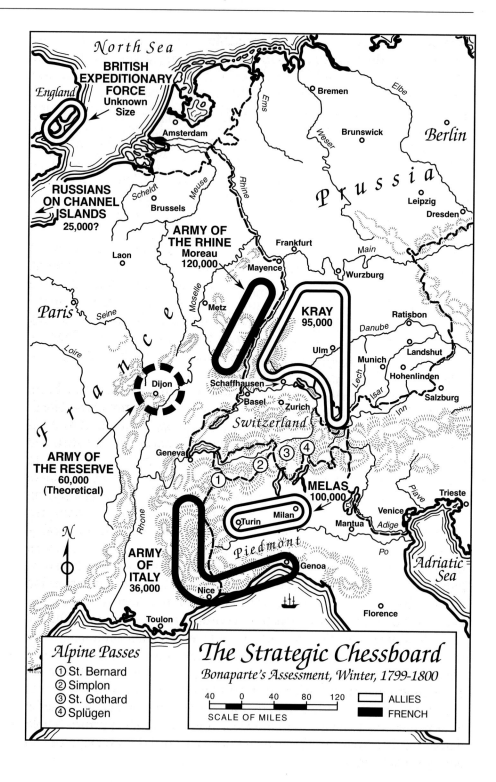

North Sea

BRITISH
EXPEDITIONARY
FORCE
Unknown
Size

England

Bremen

Elbe

Ems

Brunswick

Berlin

Amsterdam

Weser

Rhine

RUSSIANS
ON CHANNEL
ISLANDS
25,000?

Scheldt

Brussels

Meuse

P r u s s i a

Leipzig

Dresden

Laon

ARMY OF
THE RHINE
Moreau
120,000

Frankfurt

Mayence

Main

Wurzburg

Paris

Seine

Moselle

Metz

KRAY
95,000

Danube

Ratisbon

F r a n c e

Loire

Ulm

Munich

Landshut

Dijon

Schaffhausen

Basel

Zurich

Lech

Hohenlinden

Salzburg

Switzerland

Isar

ARMY OF
THE RESERVE
60,000
(Theoretical)

Geneva

③ ④

②

①

Inn

MELAS
100,000

Plave

Trieste

Rhone

Turin Milan

Mantua

Venice

Adige

N

ARMY
OF
ITALY
36,000

Piedmont

Genoa

Po

*Adriatic
Sea*

Nice

Florence

Toulon

Alpine Passes

① St. Bernard
② Simplon
③ St. Gothard
④ Splügen

The Strategic Chessboard
Bonaparte's Assessment, Winter, 1799-1800

| 40 | 0 | 40 | 80 | 120 |

SCALE OF MILES

ALLIES
FRENCH

beginning of Moreau's ambivalent feeling toward the Republic. An acquaintance describes him as henceforth merely giving lip service to republican ideals. Another describes him as talented, brave, but lazy. Lazy or not, he took good care of his men and continued to exhibit gallant conduct both on and off the battle field. Once he swam through roiling water to rescue a grenadier whose assault boat had swamped. In return, the army did well by him. Although he lacked a formal military training, by age 28 he had already become a general of division after just three years of military service. When Pichegru fell ill in the fall of 1794 Moreau took temporary command of the army. Upon Pichegru's recommendation, he assumed formal command on March 29, 1795.

Unbeknownst to Moreau, his friend Pichegru was now in treacherous communication with the enemy. An émigré general, whose correspondence was later captured, even wrote that the Royalists had hopes to subvert Moreau himself. In the coming years, Moreau would withhold documents proving Pichegru's treachery while he waited to ascertain who would come out on top. Then he publicly denounced his former friend and only barely managed to avoid being brought down with him.

None of these peregrinations speak well of Moreau's character. From a military standpoint, Moreau's successes with the Army of the North had more to do with the incompetence of his opponents that with his own tactical and strategic skills. Notably, "a General who has seen bad tactics and worse strategy win the day is less likely to find the way to success."[19] Yet he also had undeniable talents. Over the objections of his subordinates, including General Louis Desaix, he organized an army that heretofore had operated in divisions into an army composed of three corps and a reserve in which he placed all of the heavy cavalry. At this time, the corps was a rare organization. Having shown modern thinking, Moreau then employed his army in fits of energy followed by lethargy. Another characteristic that emerged at this time was a selfish nature. He was seldom willing to cooperate with fellow generals. The Directory had wanted Bonaparte to coordinate with Moreau in the fall of 1796. Bonaparte tried to oblige but Moreau responded that he dare not communicate his plan for fear it might fall into enemy hands! While commander in chief in Italy in 1799, Moreau contributed to Macdonald's defeat at the Trebbia; first by telling Macdonald, who was marching to unite with Moreau, that he would not find substantial forces blocking his route, and then allowing Suvorov to perform a bold flank march across the front of his army in order to dash south to engage Macdonald.

The first time Bonaparte and Moreau met, before the coup, conversation proved stilted and difficult until the topic became military strategy. Moreau observed that larger forces invariably defeated smaller ones. Bonaparte concurred. Moreau noted that during his Italian campaign Bonaparte had wielded inferior forces yet still triumphed. Bonaparte explained that it still was a case of superior force. He elaborated that when outnumbered he would utilize rapid marching to concentrate his entire force against one of the enemy wings. After defeating that wing, he would profit from the enemy's distress by another rapid movement to attack again with all his force a portion of his opponent's force. Thus he would inflict a defeat in detail. He concluded that Moreau was correct. Victory always resulted from the "triumph of a larger number over a smaller number."[20] Whether Moreau comprehended the nuances of Bonaparte's strategy was an open question as the two generals established a new relationship once Bonaparte became First Consul.

Bonaparte lacked the power to dictate orders and to know that they would be obeyed. In particular, he would have to handle the prideful Moreau very gingerly. One of Bonaparte's first decisions was sure to please Moreau while simultaneously improving operational efficiency. By decree of November 24, the armies of the Rhine and the Danube merged to become the Army of the Rhine under Moreau's command. The same decree named Masséna to command the Army of Italy. Later, Bonaparte gave Moreau a superb pair of pistols with the names of Moreau's battles engraved on the handles in gold letters. He delivered an amiable and graceful speech – an eyewitness observes that this alone was exceptional – and concluded by telling Moreau, "You must excuse their not being more richly ornamented, the names of your victories took up all the space."[21]

In spite of mutual flattery, a wide gulf remained between these two men. During the opening months of the new century, Bonaparte submitted a variety of plans to Moreau, and the latter found fault with them all. While recognizing Bonaparte's military talents, Moreau was deeply suspicious of his ambitions. At one point when Bonaparte proposed that he would come to the front to lead personally the Army of the Rhine, Moreau replied that he would resign rather than submit to such an indignity. One of Moreau's subordinates, the future marshal Nicolas Soult, relates an intriguing conversation in which Moreau acknowledged his suspicion and probed for Soult's support in the event of further political upheaval.[22]

But there was something beyond mere rivalry that accounted for Moreau's behavior. Whereas Bonaparte was developing an innovative strategic system based upon mobility and flexibility, Moreau remained wedded to the formal methods of the previous century. He could have been at home in the army of Frederick the Great or Louis XVI and in either he would have found distinction. Not for him were Bonaparte's madcap schemes that featured insufficient regard, in his mind at least, for an adequate line of communication and secure bases. Because of their political and professional rivalry and because they had very different ideas on the theory and practice of war, as winter drew to an end Moreau responded to Bonaparte's suggestions with a stream of endless objections. His complaints had a solid core of legitimacy: poor weather; lack of supplies; too many half-trained conscripts. But a thrusting general would have overcome them.

Even before Moreau demonstrated his repeated intransigence, the First Consul had concluded that if Moreau would not budge with the best army France could field, than he would fabricate an entirely new force and see what he could accomplish with it. Accordingly, on January 25, 1800, he ordered his Minister of War, his former chief of staff Alexander Berthier, to assemble a 60,000-man Army of Reserve around Dijon. The command of the army was to "be reserved for the First Consul." The selection of Dijon was brilliant since it provided a central position between the two main theaters of war, Italy and the Rhine. Yet it was so far distant from either front that the Austrians would hardly suspect that a 'reserve' army represented a serious peril. Moreover, labeling the army with the term 'reserve' suggested a training function rather than a field force. Bonaparte told Berthier, "You will keep extremely secret the formation of the aforesaid army, even among your own office force".[23] The First Consul knew that enemy spies would eventually detect its creation, so he arranged for the least threatening appearing units – raw conscripts, ragged veterans – to assemble in Dijon itself. He anticipated that the spies' reports about the Reserve Army's deficiencies would delude the Habsburg high command. Indeed, cartoons depicting the Army of Reserve became a regular feature in many European papers. A typical one showed a wounded veteran giving a hand to assist a toddler.

The true striking power of the Army of Reserve came from divisions that were dispersed throughout France. Two divisions had been engaged in western France. Another assembled in Paris. General Joseph Chabran's division comprised fourteen battalions formed from the depots of the Army of the Orient located in the southern Rhone Valley. Bonaparte also calculated that by carefully staging assembly marches through the Dijon area he would not alarm the Austrians. If they detected the movements they would think that they involved units moving to reinforce Moreau or Masséna. In sum, Bonaparte worked hard to ensure that the Austrians would not know until the last possible minute what he intended to do with the Army of Reserve. Bonaparte's stratagems succeeded. In Vienna, the Austrian high command judged that the army did not constitute a significant threat. For himself, even before he issued the order to form the Army of Reserve, he envisioned it as a mass of maneuver that could be hurled decisively against either Melas' army in Italy or Kray's army along the Rhine.

The First Consul wanted the various internal insurrections put down as quickly as possible in order to concentrate manpower for the Army of Reserve. He suppressed the counter-productive hostage law but this did not immediately have much impact. The Chouans, the name derived from the call of the regional owl, continued to fight. Unlike the case during their great rebellion of 1793, their activities more resembled hooliganism than purposeful guerrilla warfare. Royalist agents, operating from Jersey, kept them stirred up while the Royal Navy provided arms and supplies. From Paris, Bonaparte directed their suppression. After being squeezed between a government force north of the Loire and another operating in the Vendée, the Chouan chieftains agreed to an armistice on January 4, 1800. Bonaparte refused to negotiate with them. He offered amnesty to those who laid down their arms and treated those who complied generously. Among them was a certain Count Auguste Bourmont, the Judas of the Waterloo campaign. To deal with the balance, he suspended the constitution in the departments where the Chouans operated and sent Generals Brune and Lefebvre with orders to have their soldiers shoot anyone preaching rebellion or caught carrying arms.

After very little fighting, the Chouans began to surrender. In Brittany, the last holdout, Georges Cadoudal, submitted on February 14 and handed over thousands of British-manufactured muskets along with numerous cannon. The following autumn Cadoudal would appear in Paris to mastermind the attempt to assassinate Bonaparte. On February 16, the Norman rebel Frotté, who had come to negotiate under the promise of safe conduct, was arrested. While being taken to Paris he and six companions were executed. For the time being, that ended the Royalist threat in the west. Even if it had been driven beneath the surface, opposition to Bonaparte remained. If he suffered a substantial setback his enemies – royalists, liberals, and Jacobins – would reemerge. They shared the view of Madame de Staël who later wrote, "I wished for Bonaparte's defeat because it was the only means left to stop the advance of his tyranny."[24]

Bolstered by forces from the west, Bonaparte concentrated on the formation of the Army of Reserve. In reply to an anxious question regarding the capacity of the newly raised army, Bonaparte confidently said, "Four years ago did I not with a feeble army drive before me hordes of Sardinians and Austrians, and scour the face of Italy? We shall do so again. The sun which now shines on us is the same that shone at Arcola and Lodi."[25]

PART 3.
THE FRENCH WAR MACHINE

By 1798 French martial enthusiasm was nearly gone, having been killed off in battle or spoiled by the corrupt and cynical Directorate. The nation's paper strength was 250,000 men, hardly enough to defend a long defensive perimeter. Desertion, primarily from lack of pay, reduced further France's paper strength. The situation become so serious that the Directory accepted a proposal from General Jourdan and his committee that when the country was declared in danger, all Frenchmen between the ages 20 and 25 became liable for military service. They were to be called in five classes, beginning with the youngest, with no specified length of service. Director Gohier recalled that nothing was omitted in the new law to stimulate "the patriotism of young Frenchmen and their parents."[26]

The popular reaction was lukewarm at best. Even the police state efficiency of the Emperor Napoleon Bonaparte would experience difficulty enforcing conscription. In 1799 those conscripts who did report quickly found that patriotism carried a cost. They formed units based upon regional associations and received the privilege of inscribing their regional name on their banners. Then the Directory flung them into battle with the hope that this thin veneer of unit pride would substitute for professional training. That armies composed of such men managed to win important strategic victories in Holland and Switzerland is amazing.

The explanation for French success begins at the top. The Revolution's lowering of class barriers allowed officers of real merit to rise. Rapid promotion based on proven courage and skill meant that the typical French general was younger, smarter, and far more flexible in his methods than his rivals. Of the prominent leaders in the Army of Reserve, three were 45 years old; corps commander Moncey, divisional commanders Mainoni and Chambarlhac. All of the rest were under age 40 with divisional commander Boudet being a young 28.

The era's best staff system complimented the general's skills. The drubbing France had received during the Seven Years' War had stimulated a reform era which produced a regular staff corps. Bonaparte's faithful Alexandre Berthier, a greybeard at age 47, was merely one of many officers who provided invaluable service at drafting orders, siting camps, collecting intelligence about the enemy forces and the lay of the land, and coordinating operations with adjacent forces. French staff officers handled military correspondence and led storming columns with the same aplomb. Whereas many armies then and now preserve a distinction between staff and line, numerous French staff officers became renowned combat leaders including Nicolas Soult, Pierre Dupont, Nicolas Oudinot, and Jean Reynier. In the Consular armies a simplified chain of command, the precursor to the famed imperial corps d'armée, had evolved. This gave the Republic's armies a flexible maneuverability. The practice of attaching senior staff officers from general headquarters to the combat units so they could ensure that orders were carried out also augmented French combat strength. During both the Marengo and the Hohenlinden campaigns, French staff officers outperformed their Austrian counterparts.

The relationship between the French officer and his men was unlike that in any other European army. After a grenadier company made up largely of conscripts completed the dangerous task of hauling an artillery piece past Fort Bard, a captain gathered the men in a circle about him: "My grenadiers you have just accomplished a great work. It is a great credit to the company." The captain shook each man's hand and concluded, "I am much pleased with your first services. I shall remember you." [27] So it was on up the chain of command with officers noting deserving soldiers and rewarding them. On the battlefield of Montebello in June 1800, while the combat was still raging, Chief of Staff Berthier paused to interrogate conscript Jean-Roch Coignet about how he had performed in his first battle. Upon learning that Coignet had participated in a bayonet charge that had captured an Austrian cannon, Berthier carefully recorded his name, unit, and company officer in a memorandum book and told Coignet to tell his captain to bring him to see the First Consul that evening. So a valorous conscript met the commanding general and when word spread, conscripts throughout the army learned about a standard to try to emulate, and that they too had a chance for distinction. The bonds French officers forged with their men sustained soldiers in times of trial. During the darkest moments at Marengo, Coignet recalls, "the battalions were visibly reduced, and quite ready to give up but for the encouragement of their officers." [28]

The passage of the national draft in 1793, the famous '*levée en masse*', had allowed Revolutionary armies to substitute numbers for military skill. These citizen soldiers were highly motivated because, "Citizens had a personal stake in their government and were willing to fight to protect the regime". [29] Even after the abuses of the Directorate, recruits could still be inspired by republican ideals. Bonaparte reminded some conscripts of the importance of staying with their flag, their nation's sacred emblem. He had confidence in them, he said, but vowed that if they wavered he would ride into the midst of the canister fire to rally them. "March without fear; nothing can resist you; and don't forget that you are founders of liberty in the old world." [30]

In the French army, marksmanship ranked low among soldierly virtues. On the eve of campaigning, Berthier ordered "that in all demi-brigades the recruits shall fire a few rounds in order to learn how to sight, adjust, and load their muskets." [31] This was hardly adequate, but no continental army emphasized accurate shooting. But firepower was important and officers, including Bonaparte recognized this. One of the changes Bonaparte instituted in the Army of Italy during his 1796-97 campaign increased firepower by substituting muskets for the swords formerly carried by sergeants and lieutenants in the light infantry and the sergeants in the line infantry. However, what mattered more than marksmanship was the ability to stand firm and discharge one's musket while engaged in desperate combat and to maneuver as a unit while under fire. These attributes came from repetitive close order drill. Conscript Coignet entered the army in the summer of 1799. For more than two months his battalion was under arms all day long including two extended drill sessions. Then it was incorporated into the 96th Demi-brigade, a veteran unit whose experienced soldiers taught the conscripts how to use their weapons and whose officers drilled them incessantly. After three months of this, the conscripts performed before the First Consul, who commented that they drilled like veterans.

After the Seven Years' War, French military theorists worked on a new tactical approach that became codified in the Manual of 1791. It prescribed the three deep line for fire action and assault and the column for battlefield maneuver and assaults on towns and fortifications. The volunteers of 1792 could not master the complicated evolutions described by the manual. Their leaders herded them into position in column formations. A large number of men then advanced with no formation at all, each man operating on his own to take advantage of the terrain and shooting when a target presented itself. When their fire sufficiently shook the opposing forces, the remainder of the men rushed forward, supposedly in a column but really in something more akin to a mob. Alternatively, entire units broke out into open order and sought to overcome the enemy with skirmish fire alone. Such open order skirmish tactics had never been seen during Europe's horse and musket era. The combination of mass and mobility and the capacity to replace losses readily led to some surprising victories.

As the revolutionary armies gained experience and discipline, soldiers began to master tactical intricacies. During the campaigns of 1796-97, units had employed a flexible mixture of line and column supported by companies of specially designated skirmishers. The French infantryman evolved into an all-purpose soldier capable of fighting independently as a skirmisher, conducting a bayonet charge in column, or standing in a firing line. With such men, the virtues of the Manual of 1791 manifested themselves by providing officers with a choice of flexible, close order tactics. It imposed no tactical constraints but rather permitted field commanders to choose the combination of column and line best suited to the tactical situation. To cite one example, at the before-mentioned Battle of Montebello, the 43rd Demi-brigade charged with its center battalion in column and the two flanking battalions in open order. Experience had supplemented the Manual by teaching the value of large numbers of skirmishers who cooperated with the close order formations. Whereas the early revolutionary armies had employed mobs of skirmishers, the Consular armies employed them more judiciously. Their effect could be deadly. A British officer observed the French during 1796 and noted that they advanced "like a swarm of wasps."[32]

Once soldiers had been sent forward as skirmishers, it was difficult to recall them. As will be seen, at Marengo the inability to recall all of the skirmishers when the early afternoon retreat began caused a considerable diminution in the number of muskets available in the firing line when the climactic encounter occurred. On the other hand, if properly supported, skirmishers could contend against superior numbers because the Austrians lacked adequate light troops of their own. An émigré officer described a French counterattack outside of Genoa. The French: "Reassembled and formed in columns by battalions...they advanced with shouldered muskets. A handful of skirmishers scattered to lead the battalions' march: the battalions halted from time to time to gather breath, and then continued rapidly up the slope."[33] They climbed through plunging fire and took advantage of the dead ground to gain the heights.

Although local conditions heavily influenced tactical arrangements, in broad terms infantry on the defensive deployed in two lines of battalions. The battalions in the first line were in line with the third rank providing local reserves. Behind the first line stood a second line of battalions formed in column so they would be immediately available to counterattack. Infantry on the attack were preceded by a skirmish line. A line of infantry battalions followed, marching at the ordinary step of 76 paces per minute. The soldiers in the first rank carried their muskets at the charge, the others on their shoulders. They might be deployed in line or in column on a two-company front with intervals to permit deployment into line. A second line of battalions followed some 250 yards to the rear. The skirmishers aided the line troops by firing as they advanced and thereby creating a moving smoke screen. The skirmishers halted about 50 yards from the enemy line. Here they maintained their fire until the drums of the line troops sounded the charge. While the skirmishers fell back into the intervals, the line infantry conducted a bayonet charge at 120 paces per minute. If the enemy broke, the second line of battalions in column was ready to exploit the breach. If the attack failed, the front rank retired under cover of the skirmishers' fire. The second line advanced through the defeated troops, a difficult maneuver called 'the passage of the lines', to deliver a second charge. This tightly choreographed set of maneuvers explains why soldiers spent so much time practicing on the drill field.

The basic infantry formation was the demi-brigade with an authorized strength of 3,227 men. The term originated when General Lazare Carnot instituted the 'Amalgame' of January 21, 1793. The Amalgame fused one battalion of regulars with two of volunteers and substituted the term demi-brigade for the older designation of regiment. By 1796 there were 110 line demi-brigades and 30 light demi-brigades. A *chef de brigade* (colonel) commanded each demi-brigade. A *chef de battalion* (major) commanded each of the demi-brigade's three battalions, each of which, in turn, comprised nine companies. One of the companies comprised picked soldiers; grenadiers in the line and carabiniers in the light battalions. Two demi-brigades typically formed a brigade commanded by a brigadier general. A grouping of brigades combined with artillery and cavalry to form an all-arms division. Like the old Royal regiments, the demi-brigades retained a regional identity. In the Army of Reserve, some of General Louis Loison's division hailed from Gascony and were marked by an intolerance for discipline. The 9th Light was recruited in Paris and was known for that city's forward behavior.

Responding to concerns that too many soldiers were inexperienced, Bonaparte replied, "I have, it is true, many conscripts in my army, but they are Frenchmen."[34] The basis for his confidence is suggested by the records of two soldiers. They came from opposite ends of the social spectrum. Theophile Malo Corret descended from a bastard half-brother of Marshal Turenne and proudly bore the title "La Tour Auvergne." He served as a grenadier captain in the 46th Demi-brigade and was one of the best known junior officers in the French army. A scholarly man with at least two books to his credit, he had served in the Royal Army for 25 years. Rather than flee France as had so many bluebloods, he continued to serve in the Republican army where his magnetic leadership and surpassing bravery won him many admirers. He refused further promotion and voluntarily returned to the army in 1799 although he suffered from poor health. He served in Moreau's Army of the Rhine during the 1800 campaign. Following the battle of Neubourg, his unit bivouacked on the heights overlooking Oberhausen. Suddenly a party of Austrian uhlans charged the camp. The infantry ran in terror except for Captain La Tour Auvergne. When a French counterattack recovered the ground they found the dead captain lying in the road, a victim of three lance thrusts.[35] Minister of War Lazare Carnot proclaimed him "First Grenadier of France" on April 27, 1800. Thereafter, a grenadier sergeant of the 46th carried his embalmed heart in an urn attached to his crossbelts. First Consul Bonaparte decreed that the demi-brigade retain him on its roster. At muster, when his name was called, the sergeant replied, 'Dead on the field of honor.'

Léon Aune came from a much humbler background. A veteran of the Italian campaigns of 1796-97, in a letter to Bonaparte he described the highlights of his service to date:

> "at the Battle of Montenotte I saved the life of General Rampon and Colonel Masse, as they themselves informed you; at the battle of Dego I took a flag from the engineer commander of the enemy army; at the battle of Lodi I was the first in the assault and opened the gates to our brothers in arms; at the battle of

Borhetto I was the first to cross by pontoon, the bridge being blown, I fell upon the enemy and captured the commander of the position." [36]

Aune had already received five wounds and he begged Bonaparte for the opportunity to fight some more.

***

The Consular armies possessed a decided tactical superiority over all of its foes. Its organization and doctrine contributed to this advantage. The most scientific of the branches of the military, the engineers and artillery, retained throughout the upheaval of the Revolution a highly capable nucleus of professional soldiers. After Brumaire, the artillerists, sappers, miners, pontoniers, and workers constituted seven percent of the army's manpower. [37] However, Bonaparte's whole theory of war relied upon a speed of operations that avoided sieges, defensive fortifications, and set piece river assaults. Consequently, the engineers had few opportunities to display their talents in 1800. Of greater practical value for the soldiers who marched in the 1800 campaign were small pioneer detachments. During his first Italian campaign, Bonaparte had instituted the practice of assigning eight men – four to carry axes, two with spades, and two with picks – to each battalion. These soldiers cleared obstructions from the line of advance – during the passage of the Alps they were to perform prodigies – and converted hastily occupied buildings into miniature fortresses on the battlefield. In a characteristic exploit, at Hohenlinden the sappers cleared a fire-swept defile that was choked with wagons and carts in order to allow General Charles Decaen's men to continue their march.

Like the engineers, the artillery served in a decidedly secondary role during the 1800 campaign. Not until the wars of the empire would the artillery take center stage. When he had been a young artillery officer, Bonaparte had studied under Baron du Teil. Du Teil, in turn, was a forward thinking officer who urged reforms based upon experience during the Seven Years' War. One of Du Teil's central notions concerned artillery's proper battlefield function. He taught Bonaparte that guns needed to be concentrated and that in place of counter-battery fire, artillery should fire at opposing infantry and cavalry in order to prepare the way for an infantry charge. Bonaparte and his chief subordinates endorsed this tactical approach whole-heartedly.

The army's formal artillery organization had eight regiments of foot and eight of horse artillery. These were administrative entities. The field organization was the company with 111 men composing a foot artillery company and 76 a horse artillery company. The infantry's demi-brigade structure contained six, 4-pounder guns with the intent that each battalion would have the support of a two-gun section. Experience showed that battalion guns were an inefficient use of artillery. In theory, they advanced with the front line infantry, trundling forward in the intervals between battalions. In fact, they were 'neither fish nor fowl'; slowing the infantry down to the artillery's pace yet overlooked by the infantry officers in command once combat began. Thus, the battalion guns failed to contribute their full firepower.

The battery as a tactical unit was a far more efficient use of artillery. During his first Italian campaign, Bonaparte had instituted the practice of assigning a light and a horse battery to each division while assembling additional guns, particularly the heavy 12-pounders, into reserve batteries. In 1800, the passage over the Alps knocked the Army of Reserve's artillery arrangements into a cocked hat. In contrast, Moreau's Army of the Rhine received first call on all resources. Decaen's division, typical in all respects, had twelve pieces of 'light artillery' (presumably 8-pounders) as well as six 4-pounders.[38] Moreau's corps reserve included both horse artillery and 12-pounder batteries.

Batteries had six to eight tubes. Most of the field guns were either light 4-pounders or medium 8-pounders. Army-wide, one in four pieces was a howitzer. The horse artillery was already the elite arm: "They were renowned for their courage, and no less for their contentious spirit. They pushed esprit de corps far beyond the point of virtue and believed themselves infinitely superior to their comrades in foot artillery."[39] An anachronistic practice dating back to medieval times plagued the artillery. Horse teams and teamsters were civilians, hired by private contract. Too often in the past, civilian contract drivers had panicked under the stress of combat and prematurely driven their guns off the field or abandoned them to the enemy. Following Brumaire, when gunner Marmont became a Councillor of State in the War section, he corrected this flaw. Marmont arranged for the civilians who drove the artillery to be converted to soldiers. By the decree of January 3, 1800, henceforth they served as separate train battalions within the artillery. Moreover, whereas previously guns were unharnessed on the edge of the battlefield and dragged into action by the artillery men themselves – thus allowing the private contractors to preserve their valuable horses – from now on horse teams driven by soldiers hauled the guns into the heart of the battle.

This reform enabled Marmont to assemble rapidly a powerful battery during the crisis at Marengo.

The French cavalry during the last half of the eighteenth century had established a mediocre record. The Revolution had made matters worse by purging the mounted units of their numerous blue-blooded officers. By 1798 the cavalry was beginning to recover as a new set of young, aggressive, and talented officers emerged. The army comprised 84 regiments of cavalry: heavy shock troops of the cuirassier class; dragoons who carried carbines with bayonets and were supposed to be equally worthy of mounted or dismounted action; chasseurs who carried carbines without bayonets in order to practice their specialty of skirmish duty; and hussars whose specialty was outpost duty against enemy cavalry. All the cavalry nominally formed regiments of four squadrons each. Throughout the Napoleonic era the light cavalry was to commit notable omissions while on reconnaissance duty and such was the case during the Marengo campaign. However, during the War of the Second Coalition, the mounted arm as a whole was returning to an effective battle cavalry. A cavalry charge at Marengo clinched victory. Its superiority over the Habsburg horse at Hohenlinden surprised even Moreau.[40]

The infantry remained both the army's heart and its muscle. Among the junior officers, the egalitarian prospect of promotion stimulated a seemingly inexhaustible supply of raw valor. As for the common soldier, here are the words of the French military historian Henri Bonnal: "The French soldier was as he has always been: active, energetic and brave to the point of rashness when there was the prospect of combat, argumentative and poorly disciplined when there was nothing to excite his spirit."[41] The ethos of the day is revealed in a conversation between a young officer and his father. The son perceived he had been insulted, explained the incident, and asked his father what should be done. His father replied, "Challenge the aggressor."

"And if apologies are offered?"

"Refuse them." The son forced the duel, fired first and missed, and was shot dead. Presumably his father was proud of his conduct.

As would be the case under the Empire, the Directory's inability to pay for the bare minimum of food, weapons, and equipment needed to sustain their armies meant that the majority of the French armies had to be stationed in allied or occupied territories where they could live off the land. The Consular armies continued the habit of living off the

In 1800 the French cavalry performed well on the battlefield.

land that had been a hallmark of the Revolutionary armies. In addition, soldiers did not take tents or personal baggage into the field. Consequently, the French armies required far fewer wagons, carts, and draft animals compared to other continental armies and so enjoyed greater mobility.

In sum, the French armies had a hard core of seasoned veterans who enjoyed a superior system of organization and a superb set of officers. When everything was working harmoniously – as during the Battle of Stockach in May 1800, where Montrichard's division formed column and advanced at the assault pace (pas de charge) while retaining formation so perfectly that Nansouty's cavalry charged forward through the intervals – the French war machine possessed the type of well-drilled, irresistible fury reminiscent of the Roman legions.

***

The soldiers of the Army of Reserve had been waiting for more than two hours. On the other hand, as they reminded one another, they had been waiting months to receive their pay and recently had often waited days to receive their bread ration. So what difference did another few hours matter?

Finally the big shot from Paris appeared. General Chabran mounted his horse and escorted General Henri Clarke through the discontented ranks. A lieutenant shouted out, "We need bread."

The Parisians of the 9th Light possessed a turbulent reputation. Thus it was unsurprising when an old soldier stubbornly refused to present arms to the two generals. Resting his musket on the ground he said, "No reviews! Take us to the war with Bonaparte, it doesn't matter where. Without him, we will perish here, from misery."[43]

Bonaparte was in Paris. He knew that 140,000 conscripts had been ordered into the ranks. What he did not know was how many had answered the call and what was their condition. It was Clarke's duty to act as his eyes and inspect Chabran's conscripts in order to provide answers. So Clarke continued his tour of the ranks. All he heard was complaints about lack of food and pay. He saw that many soldiers did not have their weapons, their clothes were in tatters. It had taken a minor miracle even to get the soldiers to assemble for the inspection because lately they had refused all drill. Clarke knew that the First Consul would not be pleased. He candidly reported, "the 1st Division of the Army of Reserve exists only in name."[44] No one anticipated that three months later these disgruntled soldiers belonging to the 9th Light would occupy the critical sector at the climax of the Battle of Marengo.

What converted the men of the 9th Light, and thousands like them, from near mutinous rabble into reliable soldiers was the presence of a guiding administrative brain. Bonaparte demanded accurate information about his own forces. Toward this end he dispatched Clarke on his inspection tour and ordered Moreau's chief of staff to come to Paris and bring comprehensive facts and figures about the status of the Army of the Rhine. He pored over the numbers and took steps to improve the soldiers' lot. A lack of hard currency continued to plague his efforts. Still, he managed to scrape together coin. Then, to outwit corrupt army paymasters, he dispatched trusted aides to carry the money directly to the soldiers in the field. The arrival of trickles of money showed soldiers that things were improving.

While pressing ahead with his military and civic reforms, the First Consul simultaneously studied his maps to plan the spring campaign. Regardless of whether the Army of Reserve intervened on the Rhine or in Italy, any maneuver required Moreau's cooperation. To procure that cooperation, Bonaparte summoned Moreau's Chief of Staff, the nobleman General Jean Dessolles, to Paris. On March 13, 1800, Dessolles explained Moreau's plans for crossing the Rhine. They were at odds with Bonaparte's notions. Bonaparte and Dessolles wrangled heatedly until Dessolles played his trump card: he was authorized to inform the First Consul that Moreau would ask to be relieved of command if Bonaparte imposed his plan. Unbeknownst to Bonaparte, Moreau was already referring to him in less than flattering terms as 'a little Louis XIV.' This time Bonaparte backed down. Though against his inclinations, he authorized Moreau to proceed with his own plan. He told Dessolles, "The plan, which he does not comprehend, which he dares not venture to execute, I will execute myself...What he dares not do on the Rhine, I will do on the Alps."[45]

To Moreau himself, he was far less candid. In an effort to heal any breach, he employed outright flattery by writing to Moreau, "I would voluntarily give up my consular purple for the epaulet of a brigadier general under your orders." From Bonaparte's perspective, the minimum goal Moreau had to attain was to prevent the Austrians on the Rhine from interfering with the Army of Reserve or from sending reinforcements to Melas in Italy. His final orders to Moreau stated this clearly: "The object of your movement in Germany with your army corps must be to push the enemy into Bavaria, so as to intercept his direct communications with Milan".[46] He added that even if Moreau then had to retreat, as long as he thoroughly occupied Kray's attention for ten to twelve days that would be enough. By then, Bonaparte expected to have Melas trapped.

On the evening of March 17, the day after his 'offer' to serve as a brigadier under Moreau's command, he retired to his apartments where he spread out a map of northern Italy. Briefly he explained to his secretary, Louis Bourrienne, his plan and then gestured to show him where he anticipated the decisive battle would occur. His hand rested on the plain between the Scrivia and Bormida rivers, near a small village named Marengo.

NOTES

1. "To the Young French," March 20, 1800, *Correspondance de Napoléon Ier*, VI (Paris, 1860) pp. 193-194.

2. André Miot, *Memoirs of Count Miot de Melito* (New York, 1881), p. 154.

3. John Adye, *Napoleon of the Snows* (London, 1931), p. 21.

4. "To the French," December 15, 1799, *Correspondance de Napoléon Ier*, VI, p. 25.

5. Charles A. Thoumas, *Le Maréchal Lannes* (Paris, 1891), p. 65.

6. John Holland Rose, *The Life of Napoleon I*, I, (London, 1907), p. 241.

7. The evolution of Pitt's strategic thinking is comprehensively reviewed by Piers Mackesy in *The Strategy of Overthrow* and *War Without Victory*.

8. Piers Mackesy, *War Without Victory: The Downfall of Pitt, 1799-1802* (Oxford, 1984), p. 53.

9. "To Sergeant Léon Aune," January 15, 1800, John Howard, ed., *Letters and Documents of Napoleon*, I (New York, 1961), p. 341.

10. "To Citizen Gaudin," February 6, 1800, *Correspondance de Napoléon Ier*, VI, p. 117; "To General Augereau," April 27, 1800, ibid., p. 238.

11. Ramsay W. Phipps, *The Armies of the First French Republic* (London, 1926-1939), V, pp. 464-65.

12. François Roguet, *Mémoires Militaires du Lieutenant Général Comte Roguet*, II (Paris, 1862), p. 215.

13. Miot, p. 161.

14. "To Citizen Fouché" and "To Citizen Lucien Bonaparte," April 5, 1800, *Letters and Documents of Napoleon*, I , pp. 358-59.

15. "To Citizen d'Andigné," December 30, 1799, *Correspondance de Napoléon Ier*, VI, p. 61.

16. Antoine Claire Thibaudeau, *Bonaparte and the Consulate*, (New York, 1908), p. 5.

17. Louis de Bourrienne, *Memoirs of Napoleon Bonaparte*, I (New York, 1906), p. 379.

18. Georges Lefebvre, *Napoleon From 18 Brumaire to Tilsit* (New York, 1969), p. 94.
19. Phipps, I, p. 351.
20. Louis-Jerome Gohier, *Mémoires des Contemporains*, I (Paris, 1824), p. 204.
21. Claire Rémusat, *Memoirs of Madame de Rémusat* (New York, 1880), p. 41. Laure Junot has a slightly different version. See: Laure Junot, *Memoirs of Napoleon*, I (New York, 1880), p. 347.
22. See: Nicolas Jean Soult, *Mémoires du Maréchal-Général Soult,* II (Paris, 1854), p. 303.
23. "To General Berthier," January 25, 1800, *Correspondance de Napoléon Ier*, VI, pp. 107-108. Many historians say that by creating a new army Bonaparte skated around constitutional restrictions prohibiting a consul from assuming field command of an existing army. Napoleon at Saint Helena claimed this was so. In fact, there were no such restrictions.
24. Lefebvre, p. 94.
25. Bourrienne, II, p. 2.
26. Gohier, I, p. 74.
27. Lorédan Larchey, ed., *The Narrative of Captain Coignet* (New York, 1890), p. 64.
28. Larchey, p. 76.
29. Steven T. Ross, *From Flintlock to Rifle* (Rutherford, NJ, 1979), p. 61.
30. Édouard Gachot, *La Deuxième Campagne d'Italie*, (Paris, 1899), p. 51.
31. "Berthier to Dupont," May 12, 1800, *The Campaign of the Reserve Army in 1800 According to Documents Collected by Captain de Cugnac*, (Fort Leavenworth, KS, 1922), p. 115.
32. Thomas Graham, *The History of the Campaign of 1796 in Germany and Italy* (London, 1800), p. 397.
33. Jean Baptiste Crossard, *Mémoires Militaires et Historiques*, II (Paris, 1829), p. 226.
34. Bourrienne, II, p. 2.
35. For an account of this action see: Victor Dupuy, *Souvenirs Militaires* (Paris, 1892), p. 21.
36. Aune's letter is reproduced in Howard, *Letters and Documents of Napoleon*, I, p. 341.
37. 44,697 out of 653,923, based on Dubois-Crancé's report when he left the ministry. See: Edouard Detaille, *L'Armée Française* (New York, 1992), p. 234.
38. Charles Decaen, *Mémoires et Journaux du Général Decaen* (Paris, 1911), p. 131.
39. Baron Seruzier cited in John A. Lynn, *The Bayonets of the Republic: Motivation and Tactics in the Army of Revolutionary France*, 1791-95 (Chicago, 1984), p. 212.
40. "Moreau to Reynier," January 22, 1801, in Marquis de Carrion-Nisas, *Campagne des Français en Allemagne* (Paris, 1829), p. 423.
41. H. Bonnal, *La Vie Militaire du Maréchal Ney*, I (Paris, 1910), p. 290.
42. Gouvernet Henriette Lucie Dillon Marquise de la Tour du Pin, *Recollections of*

the Revolution and the Empire (London, 1933), p. 413.

43. Gachot, p. 4.

44. "Clarke to Bonaparte", 14 ventose, 1800, reproduced in Gachot, p. 316.

45. Adolphe Thiers, *History of the Consulate and the Empire*, I (London, 1845), p. 148. Thiers asserts that Dessolles related this conversation to him.

46. "To General Moreau," March 15, 1800 and March 22, 1800, *Correspondance de Napoléon Ier*, VI, pp. 190, 203-4.

Chapter 3
The Austrian Offensive in Italy

PART 1.
THE ARMY OF ITALY

"You are in a difficult position but what reassures me is that you are in Genoa; it is in cases such as yours that one man is worth 20,000."[1]

Bonaparte to Masséna, May 14, 1800

In 1796 an unknown officer named Bonaparte assumed command of the Army of Italy. He found it dispirited and destitute and led it to glory. Under Bonaparte's leadership, it became the most lethal of all the republican armies. When General Masséna assumed its command on November 24, 1799, it had reverted to its condition of 1796. The campaign season in northern Italy had ended unfavorably for the French. General Jean Championnet had succeeded in raising the siege of Coni but then was unable to resist *General der Cavalerie* (GdK or full cavalry general) Michael Melas' counterstroke. Defeated by Melas at the Battle of Genola on November 4, Championnet retreated to the high ground on the Alps and Apennines. Because of Moreau's advice dating from the time he had been involved with the Army of Italy, elements of the army continued to cling to the port city of Genoa. However, Genoa and the surrounding region had been stripped bare. The Royal Navy interdicted coasters bringing supplies from France. The Army of Italy starved and slowly fell apart.

Indeed, Masséna's journey from Paris had revealed how low all of France had sunk under the Directorate's misguided rule. Bandits prowled the countryside, compelling the army to have armed escorts for couriers and supply trains. Along the highway, the chateaux, villages, orchards, and woodlots showed signs of looting, burning, and

General André Masséna

destruction. Austrian and Royalist agents abounded, causing trouble when they could, but more importantly preparing the way for Melas' pending invasion. Civilians were hedging their bets by flying Royalist flags alongside the tricolor. In places the white flag stood alone.

In Provence the situation was worse. Something like 18,000 armed deserters thronged the countryside. If there was any civilian authority it deferred to the bandits belonging to the brotherhood of 'the Savior.' It was worse still along the mountains around Nice. Here the 'Barbets', so named because the men had cultivated beards while serving in the militia, had responded to harsh treatment from the French government by routinely ambushing convoys to seize food, weapons, and money. Offshore, corsairs plundered coastal shipping.

In person, Bonaparte could exert his considerable personal magnetism upon all he met. Distance weakened his pull. On Christmas day 1799, he wrote to the Army of Italy to remind them that "the first qualities of a soldier are steadfastness and discipline."[2] His words had little effect. When Masséna arrived in Nice on January 17, 1800, he measured his army's pulse and reported to Bonaparte that officers and men alike were far from happy about Brumaire. Bonaparte had hoped that Masséna might be able to conduct a surprise winter attack. Masséna bluntly reported that it was impossible: "The army is absolutely naked and barefoot...the pay is three months in arrears. We have not a scrap of forage or provisions of any kind, not a single means of transportation."[3] Masséna was not exaggerating. Even officers lacked boots. There were fewer than a million cartridges in the magazine, no lead to make bullets, the artillery immobile for lack of horses, the cavalry ruined. A crippling shortage of draft animals prevented the distribution of what rations were available. The malnourished soldiers fell victims to a variety of killing epidemics. More than 14,000 men were in the hospitals where they perished from lack of basic care.

There was an enormous number of deserters. The 29th Light had virtually disappeared, three-quarters of the 39th Demi-brigade deserted. Entire units returned to France in search of food while muttering we "will find Bonaparte in Paris and ask him for our bread."[4] General Louis Suchet found a 3,000-man demi-brigade that had retreated to Nice without authorization. In the past month they had received rations on only one day in five and thus taken it upon themselves to find food by moving to Nice. At least eight separate regiments and one entire brigade were in open revolt. It had been the inability of Masséna's predecessor to tolerate his army's wretched condition that had caused him to submit his resignation.

Authorized reinforcements failed to materialize. The 1st battalion of the Aude departed Carcassone with 1,600 men. All of the officers but only 68 rank and file arrived, the balance having deserted along the way. So it was with the other contingents: 22 arrived of 1,500 sent from the Lozère; 37 of 1,300 from the Ariège; 38 of 450 belonging to the 1st battalion of the Bouches-du-Rhône. According to official reports, of the 10,250 replacements sent to the army, only 313 actually reached their destination.[5] What particularly irked was that the deserters had received new uniforms and equipment while the men serving at the front wore rags.

The Army of Italy suffered from wretched logistical support.

Bonaparte had granted Masséna extraordinary powers. With great determination he set to wielding them. To restore discipline he ordered the chief organizers of a rebellion among the carabiniers and grenadiers of the 5th Light and 24th Demi-brigade executed; two grenadiers of the 2nd Demi-brigade shot for insubordination; a

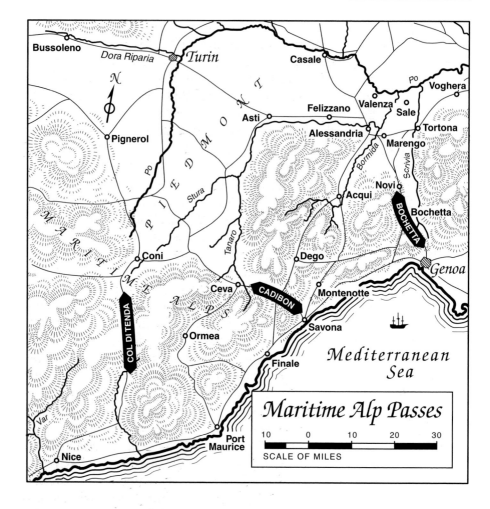

grenadier of the 106th Demi-brigade shot in front of his unit for having incited desertion. Among the officers he dismissed malcontents including two divisional generals who were unhappy about Bonaparte's rise to power. To regain some control over the coast, he commissioned twelve letters of marque to fight the corsairs. He personally inspected the hospitals and demanded improvements. By combination of force of personality and administrative reforms, Masséna was able to alleviate his army's sufferings. But the depth of the Marseilles commissary agents' venality was such that they managed to swindle the ex-smuggler Masséna. Their achievement prompted Soult to rage, "Is our army to be the plaything of this foul horde who enrich themselves at the soldiers' expense."[6] The army's impoverished status and sullen nature caused Masséna to recommend to Bonaparte on February 17 that the Army of Reserve not unite with the Army of Italy for fear that the latter would contaminate the former. Instead, he advised a descent through the alpine passes.

When the spring campaign began, Bonaparte's decision to dispatch most new men and material to strengthen Moreau's army and the Army of Reserve left Masséna with a force that had only 36,000 fit for active service to contest some 120,000 Austrians. Furthermore, much like the situation Robert E. Lee confronted in 1864 on the eve of Ulysses Grant's spring offensive, he knew an attack was pending but had to keep his army dispersed until the last minute in order to feed it. The army's position stretching east to Genoa was like a long, narrow finger. The Austrians threatened to lop it off by advancing from their base at Turin. There were three passes the Austrians could use: the Bochetta, leading to Genoa; the Cadibona, leading to Savona; and the Tenda, leading to Nice. After detailing General Louis Turreau and 4,000 men to defended the Mount Cenis Pass leading directly into France, a mere 32,000 remained to hold these three passes.

General Miollis occupied Genoa and its outworks with 8,000 men. Soult commanded 12,000 men defending the Bochetta Pass. Suchet, an ardent admirer of Bonaparte – when he had first learned that Bonaparte had returned from Egypt he had written a flattering letter and told the general that in Italy there remained "men anxious for your esteem and still proud to have marched under your orders" – commanded 12,000 men who held the left including the Col di Tenda, Nice, and the line of the Var River.[7]

Masséna's major advantage was the mountains of the Apennines and Maritime Alps. Combat experience had shown that such rugged terrain neutralized the Austrian superiority in artillery and cavalry while giving full play to flexible French infantry skirmish tactics. Bonaparte's experience in Italy had taught him how Austrian generals waged war. He shared his insight in a letter that explored how the Austrians would maneuver against Masséna: "The enemy, in the Austrian manner, will make three attacks" by using all three passes. Bonaparte explained how to deal with 'the Austrian manner': "decline meeting two of the attacks and take all of your force against the third."[8] Bonaparte further assured the commander of the Army of Italy that he confronted an opposing general who was "not a very clever man" and lacked Masséna's military talents and energy.[9]

The First Consul's optimism was about to be tested. Three weeks after he penned these words, Melas' army began its offensive.

PART 2.
THE AUSTRIAN WAR MACHINE

More than any other European army, the Habsburg military resembled a closely held family business. The head of the family was Kaiser Franz, who became the sovereign of the Habsburg Empire in 1792. Born in 1768, his military education and experience was limited. In 1789 he was the figurehead commander during the siege of Belgrade. At age 22 he received instruction in regimental, staff, and command duties. Two years later he observed military action on the Turkish front. Recalled to Vienna when his father died unexpectedly, Franz began his reign at age 24. He may not have appreciated the great difference between war against the Turks and against revolutionary France.

In any event, he was suspicious by nature, intensely conservative, and shared with his predecessors a distrust of outstanding soldiers. They represented a threat to family control. Franz's conservatism made him resist innovation. His distrust had two effects: he tolerated mediocre generals – students of the Napoleonic wars will note that many of the unsuccessful generals who participate in the 1800 campaign resurface for the 1805 and 1809 debacles – and he relied upon forceful civilian advisers. While history best remembers Clemens Metternich, who was Franz's dominant adviser from 1809 on, during the War of the Second Coalition, Chancellor Johann Thugut played the Metternich role. Still, after listening to whatever advice he chose, it was Kaiser Franz who made the final decisions regarding peace or war. When pondering such matters, his greatest goal was the preservation of the monarchy.

His title of Habsburg emperor referred to the Holy Roman Empire. By the time Franz ascended to the throne it was largely an honorific title. What remained was an empire from the Rhine to the Galician plains and from Bohemia to northern Italy. At its heart were the hereditary lands. These comprised Upper and Lower Austria as well as the Austrian territory touching the Adriatic, the Tyrol, Vorarlberg, Styria, Carinthia, Carniola, Bohemia, and Moravia. The Kaiser wished to protect these territories above all others, and in this resolve he had the support of his army's officer corps. Their correspondence reveals a patriotic attachment to the hereditary lands. Beyond the hereditary lands, the empire included the territory belonging to the Hungarian crown, Transylvania, that part of Galicia occupied after the First Polish Partition of 1772, a parcel of small territories in south Germany along the Rhine, and a good part of northern Italy. The Habsburg empire had also controlled the Austrian Netherlands, Belgium, and Luxembourg with its two million Flemings and Walloons, but lost these lands during the War of the First Coalition.

Like the empire itself, the army's officer corps was a multinational group of diverse social origins. Although some of the empire's great families – among them the families Liechtenstein, Lobkowitz, Colloredo, and Kinsky – regularly contributed their sons, generally the high nobility shunned military service. Consequently, Maria Theresa had opened her military academies to the sons of impoverished minor nobility and even commoners. However, the combined output of Austria's two military academies was only 60 graduates a year. Supplementing these academies was the artillery school in Vienna where artillery officers received formal instruction in their craft. Here they studied a comprehensive program ranging from mathematics and chemistry to military administration and tactics. Those who attended the seven-year course received commissions, those who chose the five-year course became enlisted gun captains.

Most Austrian officers entered the army by appointment as cadets. They learned their trade from experienced sergeants and then began a slow climb through the ranks. Promotion up to the rank of major was the prerogative of the *Inhabers* (regimental proprietors). The Kaiser personally appointed majors and above. Given the Kaiser's conservative attitudes, this system favored the capable bureaucratic administrator over the dashing combat leader. Officers exhibited little interest in military theory. Few among the staff officers displayed an ability to handle efficiently routine operational matters. To cite one example, at the Battle of Montebello a 300-man detachment occupied a position screening the right flank. When the army retired no one remembered to recall the detachment until the next day. Only the determined leadership of the French royalist officer in charge brought the unit to safety. The accumulation of such errors and oversights depleted the Austrian army as surely as enemy fire.

Because of indifferent staff work, Austrian route marches tended to leave the soldiers fatigued and hungry. When the Austrian commander in chief tried to concentrate men to oppose Bonaparte at Marengo, a British observer in Alessandria reported:

"I am sorry to say that General Elsnitz's corps, which was composed of the grenadiers of the finest regiments in the

army, arrived here in the most deplorable condition. His
men had already suffered much from want of provisions and
other hardships...and it will appear scarcely credible, when I
tell your Lordship, that the Austrians lost in this retreat from
fatigue only, near 5,000 men."[10]

Months later, to silence a complaining émigré officer, a superior
gave permission for him to arrange his division's march for one day.
The improvement was immediately noticed. This officer posted
guides at the intersections, arranged cross-country movement so as
to avoid traffic jams, and ended the march at a comfortable bivouac.
An infantry colonel commented, "This is the first time that we have
marched liked soldiers."[11] On the eve of Marengo, execrable staff
work compelled the entire army to sortie from its bridgehead through
one narrow gate and thereby lose much of the advantage of its
surprise attack.

For better or worse and unlike times past, Austrian staff officers
preferred bold strokes to caution. The British agent, William
Wickham, noted that they "seem disposed on every occasion to hazard
everything rather than remain on the defensive."[12] Their new-found
aggression influenced the campaign by helping convince Melas at
Marengo and Johann at Hohenlinden to attack the French. However,
Melas' Chief of Staff, *General-Feldwachtmeister* (GM or major general)
Anton Zach, was first and foremost a military theorist. He had served
ably at Novi and earned the nation's highest military order, the
coveted Order of Maria Theresa. Zach was a skilled mathematician
and had read widely on military topics, but was more comfortable with
the science of military engineering than with operational art or combat
leadership. Reflecting on Zach's role at the head of the troop during
Marengo's climactic encounter, an Austrian officer wrote that the
empire would have been better served had instead Zach been teaching
at one of the military academies.

The Habsburg officer corps was top-heavy with an astonishing
number of senior generals. At Marengo major generals commanded
infantry brigades with a mere two battalions while at Hohenlinden
they led units comprising only six squadrons. They were not young
men. The principle subordinates at Marengo were Kaim, age 70; Ott,
62; O'Reilly, 60; Zach, 54; Vogelsang, 52; and Haddick, 40. Among the
lesser subordinates, GM Karl Weidenfeld was typical. At the sprightly
age of 59, he commanded one of the army's grenadier brigades. In any
army, long years of service tend to erode mental flexibility and
diminish initiative. The Austrian army was over-officered with

antiquated senior generals. This made the army less responsive when the unexpected occurred. In addition, unlike their subordinates, most generals came from the minor aristocracy, the Austrian version of which was rife with rivalries and feuds.

There were a large number of French émigré officers in Habsburg service. Consider that in 1789 some 6,600 officers, two-thirds of the entire officer corps in the French Royal army, were noblemen. By the end of 1794, 5,500 were gone, the vast majority of whom had fled France for their lives. A number of these officers served in various royalist units or in the frei-corps (free corps). Many others found employment in the regular Austrian army. The French émigrés provided some of the army's most dashing soldiers. Typical was Oberst (Colonel) Konstantin d'Aspre, a former hussar officer in the Royal Army. During the combats around Genoa, his superior, GM Friedrich Gottesheim, noticed D'Aspre visibly chafing at the bit. Gottesheim asked him what could he possibly accomplish with horsemen across such difficult ground. "Beat them", replied d'Aspre.[13] There were also numerous soldiers of Irish or Scots-Irish blood, most notably *Feldmarschall-Leutnant* (FML or lieutenant general) Johann O'Reilly, who led one of the three columns at Marengo, but including GM O'Donel, who commanded a brigade at Hohenlinden.

Following defeat in 1797, an Austrian military commission gathered to analyze what had happened. The then up and coming Colonel Zach contrasted how France had witnessed the rise of numerous talented army leaders yet Austria had failed to produce "a single great man." Subordinate generals displayed no initiative, a fact he attributed to officers having to observe too many regulations. Regarding the ranks of captain to colonel, Zach noted that their interest in their craft never extended beyond mastering formal drill and their preferred topics for conversation were pay and privilege. There was, Zach observed, an enormous gulf between officers and men with the officers neither knowing nor valuing their men and the men returning neither love nor trust.[14] Among army commanders, only the Kaiser's brother, *Erzherzog* (Archduke) Karl, seemed able to inspire the soldiers.

Selective conscription supplemented by voluntary enlistment provided the army's rank and file. Authorities avoided using the lure of patriotism to attract volunteers. Very few men wanted to be soldiers except as a choice of last resort, and for good reason. In the absence of patriotic appeals no one thought army service particularly honorable. Worse, pay was low and discipline harsh. Corporal punishment was the norm, prompting one junior officer to wonder if "the defense of the fatherland can only be maintained with the whip and stick."[15] The conscripts' term of service was for life. Most of the rank and file came from the poor peasant and laboring classes. They, like most of their non-commissioned officers and a fair number of junior officers, were illiterate. Recruiting officers frequently turned to compulsion to meet their quotas. A startling number of recruits came from the smaller south German states where apparently the offer of a modest bounty proved more attractive than the certainty of an impoverished life as a peasant. For the British agents who dispensed the subsidies, they were a "cheap and easy" way to procure men.[16] Recruiters relied upon the time-honored mix of hard cash and alcohol to practice upon ignorant young men. A south German volunteer recalled that after a cursory medical examination he was "locked up in a large room with twenty young men in various stages of inebriation" until morning at which point an infantry platoon with fixed bayonets herded them to join fellow 'volunteers' and escort them to join their regiments.[17] A British diplomat estimated that half of the men serving in Austria's 39 German regiments were south Germans and an even higher proportion of non-commissioned officers. The cavalry attracted the better sort of recruits while the artillery accepted only literate, unmarried volunteers who were Austrian subjects.

The Austrian army featured ethnic diversity writ large. Multiple languages alone presented problems, but there were deeper issues. An Imperial officer wondered if an army of "Hungarians, Croats, Transylvanians, Italians, Bohemians, Moravians, Poles, Wallachs, Slavonians, Austrians, Styrians, Tyroleans, Carnioleans, and gypsies could march under one flag and fight for a cause it knows nothing about."[18] Likewise, Zach observed in 1798 that unlike the French soldier who possessed an intense national spirit, the Austrian fighting man had to rely on specific soldierly virtues: courage, fidelity, comradeship, and devotion to duty. This was asking a great deal. A British observer wrote, "The Austrian army is brave, very brave; well managed it would be the first in Europe. But nothing is done to excite and uphold the bravery and good will of the soldiers".[19]

Something that motivated all of the era's soldiers was the opportunity for plunder. Cavalry troopers who dispatched their foes and secured their mounts had captured valuable property. They could sell the horses to their own army. Thus, it was noteworthy when a cavalry unit did not pause after a combat to collect the enemy's riderless horses. If a soldier was captured, or wounded and abandoned by his comrades, he could expect to be stripped of his possessions. A French trooper at Marengo claimed that "Nothing is more shocking than the eagerness with which the Austrian strips off the spoils of his prisoner."[20]   Note however, that at the Battle of Montebello, Coignet describes rescuing a comrade from the clutches of three Austrian grenadiers. The first thing the rescued sergeant did after reclaiming his belt and watch was plunder all three Austrians!

For field service in 1800 the Austrian army had 62 line infantry regiments, 17 grenz regiments, and 42 cavalry regiments. In 1799 the army was at about 60 percent of its paper strength having a total of about 300,000 men including those assigned to garrisons and internal security. The infantry were either German – a designation that included Bohemian, Moravian, and Tyrolean – or Hungarian, which included Croatian and Transylvanian units. Each line regiment had an Inhaber who was the nominal colonel-in-chief and whose name was borne by the regiment. Regiments were numbered according to seniority and typically led into battle by a colonel who commanded in the absence of the Inhaber. Many Inhabers were merely wealthy or senior officers, although some officers received appointments to honor their battlefield conduct. The Inhaber system promoted nepotism to the detriment of martial efficiency. Yet in the hands of a good Inhaber, a regiment could shine. The Walloons of the Württemburg Infantry Regiment fought at Hohenlinden and endured the dispiriting retreat toward Vienna. While many regiments dissolved, their young Inhaber kept his regiment to its duty. Erzherzog Karl singled out both him and his regiment for its good conduct and high state of discipline.

Regiments had two or three field battalions with six fusilier companies in each. With everyone present, a field battalion numbered 1,432 men. Each regiment also had two grenadier companies. These were chosen men, dressed in showy bearskin hats to emphasize their special status. The grenadier companies merged to form 721-man grenadier battalions commanded by a lieutenant-colonel.

The grenzers served as the army's light infantry. They had been originally recruited from the hardy Slavic peoples who lived along the militarized eastern border of the Habsburg empire. Along this border every able-bodied man was a peasant-soldier, farming most of the time, taking up arms when the Turks attacked. At one time the grenzers had well performed scouting and skirmishing duties. But the receding Turkish threat had softened them while the decision to drill them as troops of the line spoiled their natural aptitude for skirmishing. They seemed unable to contest effectively against their French counterparts. In the 1800 campaign they appear with the army's vanguard but do not figure prominently once the battles begin. After learning about deteriorating conditions at home, in June 1800 several grenz units mutinied. This led many officers to doubt their reliability during the final campaigns of that year.

In response to French skirmish superiority during the 1796-97 campaign, the army formed fifteen battalions of light infantry from various frei-corps. To supplement them, when war began the Empire raised additional frei-corps. They attracted everyone from dedicated French émigrés to soldiers of fortune to outright bandits. Among the most useful was the Le Loup Frei-Corps; originally raised in Austria-controlled Netherlands by Major Johann Le Loup, which had six companies totaling about 1,000 men. At the other end of the spectrum were the so-called Red Mantles, a chasseur regiment that served in southern Germany. These men received a bounty for killing Frenchmen, a category they quickly extended to peasants, Austrian deserters, and anyone else they could safely execute. The Red Mantles preferred robbery and assassination to the risks and uncertain rewards of combat.

The terrain where the battles of 1800 occurred; the numerous ditches, vine-planted slopes, hedgerows and defiles of northern Italy or the forest covered terrain of Bavaria, required effective skirmishers. Whether grenzer, light infantry, or frei-corps, the Austrians never mastered skirmish tactics. Hefting an eighteen pound musket and carrying a poorly designed, heavily laden knapsack did not help. But in large part the problem was that senior officers continued to doubt the value of light troops. Melas' chief of staff offered this as tactical instruction in the spring of 1800: "In action, troops must remember not to lose time with firing. Only a few tirailleurs [skirmishers] are necessary to screen the front. If these are followed up by troops advancing courageously in closed formation, with bands playing, and keeping their formation, such an advance cannot be repulsed by an enemy fighting in open order.."[21] It is worth noting that Zach put his recommendation to practice at Marengo (including bands playing) where, in the absence of any skirmish screen to scout ahead, the French ambushed his advance guard, captured Zach himself, and turned the tide of battle.

To supplement the army in Italy, the Austrians hired a substantial Piedmontese force. Some of the soldiers were veterans of the Sardinian army that had opposed Bonaparte in 1796. Four national and ten provincial infantry battalions, each with an authorized strength of 876 men, composed the core of the Piedmontese contingent.[22] Along with the cavalry and artillery, there were 14,389 Piedmontese troops in Melas' army. Events would show them to be like most mercenaries; eager as long as the campaign progressed favorably, inclined to desert at the first reversal.

Regarding the relative quality of the Austrian infantry, it is impossible at this distance to distinguish them based upon ethnic origin. On both the Italian and Rhine fronts, the French seem to have considered the Le Loup Free Corps a particularly formidable lot. Hungarian units were renowned for their fierce fighting spirit yet something of their edge appears to have been lost. During the 1799-1800 campaigns they experienced an enervating desertion rate. After Count Palfi conducted a spirited nocturnal assault at Genoa, his commander, FML Peter Ott, embraced him and said, "You have attacked like a true Hungarian.".[23] When mentioning the grenadiers, French accounts invariably refer to the Hungarian units. Apparently they made quite an impression. Regarding them, Suchet had this to say: the "Hungarian grenadiers are the elite of the enemy's army; ordinarily they attack with impetuosity, but when their columns are a little unnerved after being defeated" they could be taken at a discount.[24] The Battle of Marengo would prove Suchet prophetic.

The mounted arm divided into heavy, dragoon, and light regiments. The Inhaber system also applied to the cavalry. A major reform in 1798 increased the heavy cuirassier arm to twelve regiments. They were the army's shock troops, big men wearing armored breastplates, riding big horses. The dragoons and chevauxlegers merged into fifteen light dragoon regiments. In the light cavalry, the hussars expanded to twelve regiments. A second uhlan regiment, armed like its sister regiment with 13-foot lances, was formed from Degelmann's Frei-Corps and a new corps of Mounted Jägers created from the mounted elements of various other Frei-Corps including a French émigré outfit.

Throughout Europe the Austrian cavalry enjoyed a high reputation. It was undeserved. In 1798, General Karl Mack noted that few regiments could gallop more than a short distance without falling into disorder. Undoubtedly this was due to a combination of poor equestrian skills and a lack of training in massed action. Moreover, although the mounted arm possessed many advantages – the light horse had been able to draft the finest animals from Germany, Poland, and Hungry – its tactical doctrine contained a crippling flaw. There were no precise instructions for coordinating charges by several regiments at once. The division, a unit of two squadrons, was the standard maneuver element. Consequently, the Habsburg cavalry never realized the potential of massed shock action. Occasionally, when led by a dashing officer with a good *coup d'oeil,* the cavalry could achieve notable results. An example occurred along the Mincio River in the fall of 1800 when an Austrian commander observed three French columns entering a valley. He ordered the Liechtenstein

Hussars to charge one of them. Obeying orders to ignore the enemy skirmish screen, the hussars advanced rapidly to strike the column before it could form square and dispersed it. More often the way Austrian generals utilized their mounted forces is reminiscent of how the allies employed their tanks against the German panzers during the early stages of World War Two. Both squandered numerical advantage by piecemeal commitment of small tactical units.

Austrian field artillery included 3, 6, and 12-pounder cannons and 7 and 10-pounder howitzers. Austria retained the practice of battalion guns. Each German and Hungarian battalion had three 6-pounders assigned to it while the grenzers included a detachment of three 3-pounders. Thus, the Austrian army labored under the inefficiency of the battalion gun system. About half of the artillery was assigned to 'position' batteries, each of which usually included four cannons and two howitzers. During the 1800 campaign the position batteries acted as a reserve artillery force. Theoretically this was a fine concept since they were subject to central control and could be massed, as occurred at Marengo, into an imposing gun line. But it depended upon the skills of the senior generals. Caught up in front line infantry combat, the generals might overlook the position batteries in which case, as occurred at Hohenlinden, they could be so thoroughly misused as to never enter combat.

The truism that military establishments prepare for the last war accurately describes the Austrian war machine. In the past, entire campaigns had been waged over the possession of one fortress city. As we will see, among Austria's army commanders the habits of siege warfare proved hard to overcome. If the rank and file lacked the patriotic zeal that fired the French, they still possessed qualities that made them formidable foes. Overall, British agent Wickham observed that the Austrian army presented a striking difference from the days of the First Coalition. In Switzerland in 1799 he detected "a manifest difference in the whole appearance and countenance of the officers, as well as of the men; instead of the discontented and dejected appearance which was but too visible among them during the campaign of 1796, they now appear cheerful and animated, and look as if they were conscious of their own strength, and of the glory and real superiority over the enemy which they have acquired."

The army's surpassing weakness was its officer corps. Wickham wrote that "the army is still miserably defective in generals."[25] Most Habsburg generals remained wedded to the habits of eighteenth-century warfare. As Karl observed, their spirit had fossilized and been replaced by the dead hand of regulations.

Part 3.
The Siege of Genoa

GdK Michael Melas

Given his three to one superiority, had the Austrian army commander, GdK Melas, shown any sense of economy of force, he would have overwhelmed Masséna in spite of the terrain. Born in Transylvania, Melas was 71 years old in 1800. He entered Habsburg service in 1746 and his formative experiences had occurred during the Seven Years' War. He received gradual promotion and fought against revolutionary France along the Rhine and in Italy. He assumed army command in Italy in 1799. A former cavalryman, he was undeniably brave but his capacity for high command was suspect. In 1799 he had participated in several victories, but he had benefitted greatly from Suvorov's presence and the blunders of his opponents. At the Battle of the Trebbia in June 1799, he had missed a fine chance while in command of a flanking column. He had been confronted with an unexpected appearance of a French force on his own flank. Cautiously he had committed only his cavalry to the main action while retaining his infantry to screen the enemy threat. By virtue of the fact that he received a wound at this battle he escaped most criticism. But it hinted that he was not up to the pace of contemporary battle. He seems to have learned little from Austrian failure in Italy during 1796 and 1797. He had served under Count Dagobert Würmser and attributed all poor results to the "foolish marches of Beaulieu, Alvinczy, and Würmser" rather than to Bonaparte's strategy and superior French tactics.[26]

Following a grand ball to celebrate the end of winter encampment, staff officers conducted a series of scouts all along the front. At Melas' headquarters, a lieutenant-colonel compiled their reports in order to identify avenues of advance and likely positions where the Austrians might meet opposition. On March 29, 1800, Melas issued a proclamation to inspire his troops for the forthcoming offensive. It was a rambling, turgid speech, notable only in that it borrowed Bonaparte's phrase from his Christmas proclamation to the Army of Italy regarding the importance of the soldierly qualities of "steadfastness and discipline." After scattering 20,000 men in garrisons throughout northern Italy and assigning another 31,000 under FML Conrad Kaim to watch the alpine passes leading to Switzerland, on April 4, Melas led his 62,000-man field army into the snow-covered Apennines to engage the French.[27]

While FML Ott and FML Friedrich Hohenzollern attacked toward Genoa, Melas and FML Anton Elsnitz advanced toward Savona and Finale to sever the coastal highway. To provide flank security, another column drove back Turreau's men at Mount Cenis. These maneuvers enjoyed initial success. The minor success at Mount Cenis caused both local French authorities and the commander of the Army of Reserve, Berthier, to worry that the homeland was about to be invaded. Best of all, Melas managed to penetrate the French defense and separate the Army of Italy into two groups, driving Suchet west toward the Var River and Soult toward the coast. With considerable assistance from local guerrillas who provided scouting and security services, after three days of tough mountain combat the Austrians occupied the heights overlooking Genoa.

Genoa lay beneath a spur of the Apennines. The spur divided into two ridges which extended down to the sea. The French had built fortifications atop these heights. Within the triangle formed by the two ridges and the sea lay the walled city. At the time of the siege some 70,000 people lived there and their presence contributed to Masséna's dilemma. Had there been sufficient provisions, he could have held the outer line along the heights in a prolonged delaying

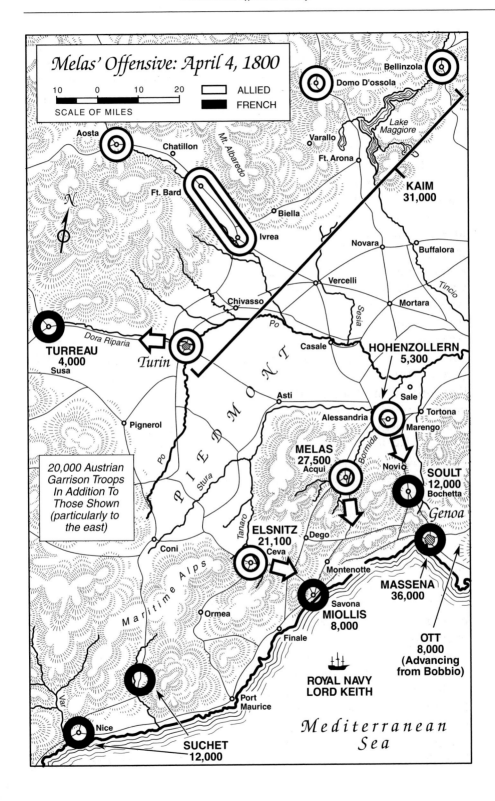

Melas' Offensive: April 4, 1800

SCALE OF MILES
10   0   10   20

ALLIED
FRENCH

Bellinzola

Domo D'ossola

Aosta
Chatillon
Mt. Albaredo
Varallo
Ft. Arona
Lake Maggiore

Ft. Bard
Biella
Ivrea

KAIM
31,000

Novara
Buffalora

N

Vercelli
Mortara

Tincio

Chivasso
Po
Sesia

Casale

HOHENZOLLERN
5,300

TURREAU
4,000
Susa
Dora Riparia
Turin

Sale

Asti
Tortona
Marengo

PIEDMONT

Alessandria

Pignerol

20,000 Austrian
Garrison Troops
In Addition To
Those Shown
(particularly to
the east)

MELAS
27,500
Acqui

Bormida

Novi

SOULT
12,000
Bochetta

Po
Stura

Genoa

Tanaro

ELSNITZ
21,100
Ceva

Dego

Coni

Montenotte

Maritime Alps

MASSENA
36,000

Ormea

Savona
MIOLLIS
8,000

Finale

OTT
8,000
(Advancing
from Bobbio)

ROYAL NAVY
LORD KEITH

Port
Maurice

Var
Nice

Mediterranean
Sea

SUCHET
12,000

action and then withdrawn behind the city's walls. But his army had barely been able to survive when they had been free to forage about the countryside. If confined within siege lines while sharing food with 70,000 hungry mouths, the army would quickly starve. Accordingly, Masséna resolved upon a bold assault to recapture the heights and cut his way free so he could retire to France.

On April 7 his army successfully stormed the heights after a series of desperate combats. Leaving an 8,000-man garrison in Genoa, Masséna and his chief subordinate, Soult, led the balance west. Meanwhile, Suchet marched east from Nice to unite with him. Over a ten day period Masséna conducted a series of ferocious attacks that inflicted considerable losses. On a smaller scale Suchet did the same, including a brilliant surprise attack out of the fog that enveloped a mountain top redoubt and captured 1,200 men. Struggle as they might, superior Austrian numbers told. Melas displayed good leadership and kept his balance amid a complex situation. By maintaining his central position between the converging French columns he blocked their union. When Masséna retired toward Genoa, Melas pressed him hard and managed to gain a position within cannon-shot of the city's walls. With the Austrians manning the mountain crests overlooking Genoa and the British dominating the sea, Masséna's soldiers were in a trap. Melas boasted, "In two days we will be in Genoa."[28]

The old veteran cavalier had done well so far. During the period April 6 to 19, his army had lost 276 officers and 8,037 men, while inflicting about 7,000 casualties on the French. On April 24, Melas demanded Genoa's surrender. He hardly expected a warrior like Masséna to comply. Indeed, Masséna responded characteristically, saying that he would rather be buried under the towers of Genoa than surrender. Recognizing that his two-day prediction had been a bit premature, Melas prepared for a siege. In an effort to capitalize on his success, he divided his army, sending Elsnitz with 30,000 men to pursue Suchet west along the coast while Ott retained a somewhat smaller force to capture the city. As he would do throughout the campaign, Melas tried to be present wherever command initiative might be needed. He judged that Ott could be entrusted with the siege, ordered him to pursue it vigorously, and departed to join Elsnitz.

On April 30 Ott's soldiers attempted a *coup de main* against Genoa. British gunboats provided close in fire support while the Habsburg infantry attacked in the pre-dawn hours all along the landward side. A nine-hour struggle ensued. For the French, the day featured emergencies rising hard on the heels of crisis. On the coast a French battalion dissolved in panic from the fire of a British gunboat. On the heights the intrepid Baron Palfi led his beloved Hungarians of the Alvinczy and Kray infantries in a bayonet charge against one of Genoa's key forts, the *Deux-Frères (Monte due Fratelli)* that sent the 24th Demi-brigade reeling. On another front, Oberst Johann Frimont skillfully infiltrated between the French outposts and captured a fort and 350 men of the 78th Demi-brigade. The Austrian officers expected that their successes would lead to the imminent collapse of the French position. Too many became complacent. They overlooked the fact that their men had become disorganized during the assaults and that they were clinging to perilous toeholds along the heights overlooking Genoa. Moreover, they forgot about the qualities of the general who opposed them.

Inside the siege lines Masséna seemed to be everywhere. At 3 a.m. he was at *La Lanterna* battery at the western entrance to the port to observe British and Neopolitan naval movements. At dawn he was directing the fire of two heavy 36-pounders against a British gunboat. During the morning he organized counterattacks. He sent a column of converged grenadiers to recapture the *Deux-Frères* while dispatching another force to attack the Austrians in flank. The combination of frontal and flank pressure triumphed and once again the republican colors flew atop the *Deux-Frères*. At 11 a.m. Masséna passed through the city's streets where he paused to rally troops and to receive reports while eating a hasty lunch of a few biscuits. In the afternoon he was at the front to supervise another series of counterattacks. At one point, after Masséna rallied the 3rd Demi-brigade and led a counterattack, he found that he had rescued the unit's twice wounded colonel. He embraced Colonel Georges Mouton who replied with a comment that applied to the entire garrison this day: "I didn't think I have any chance this time, I thought I had really bought it." [29]

Mouton, who would earn the title Count of Lobau for his conduct in the 1809 campaign, was one of many French officers who provided inspired front line leadership. We can catch glimpses of the confused and desperate combat and see General Paul Thiébault brandishing a fanion and leading his men to the attack or the entire staff of a beleaguered demi-brigade grabbing muskets from the fallen and charging like grenadiers. The garrison was so hard pressed that the only forces Masséna could send to reinforce Soult in his effort to hold the high ground were the Italian Legion – a unit of uncertain fighting value – the much diminished 1st Polish Legion, a militia company, and 50 hussars who still had their horses. Yet with Soult's superb tactical guidance they proved enough. Soult ordered his storming columns to advance with their muskets on their shoulders and "not fire a shot until they recaptured the trenches."[30]

In contrast to the French teamwork, Habsburg reactions were slow and muddled. When the impetuous French counterattack recaptured the *Deux-Frères*, a staff officer, Major Karl Stutterheim, sent a dispatch requesting reinforcements. He failed to specify how many men he needed. With pedantic formality, the general who received Stutterheim's request waited for his superior, FML Louis Vogelsang, to arrive before acting.[31] By the time Vogelsang had decided what to do it was too late.

The next morning Masséna continued his counterattacks. Overnight, the Austrians had hastily entrenched in an effort to consolidate their position. Initially, their earthworks proved no match for the French storming columns. As had been the case the previous day, individual Austrian units and leaders fought well. After a French column overran one Austrian post, a Hungarian second-lieutenant named Jugenitz organized a small band on the flank of the victorious column. Their enfilade fire followed by a sudden thrust caused the French to panic and break to the rear. However, what really put an end to the French effort was a lack of strength. By day's end, the French could do no more than regain the key posts on the heights. But their attacks imposed caution. After losing 3,147 men (the French lost 1,526) Ott concluded he would have to blockade the city and starve it into submission. Now began an epic siege.

Very few commanders possess the indomitable spirit that Masséna displayed over the ensuing days. For the two weeks preceding the formal investment, garrison soldiers and civilians had eaten a poor quality bread baked from a mixture of wheat and horse feed. Field soldiers had fared worse. Soult recalls eating nothing during a day of strenuous combat and then receiving a piece of old beef seasoned with gunpowder for supper. To his horror he learned that his own men were reduced to eating pieces of flesh hacked from dead enemy soldiers, and this before the blockade began.[32] By April 20 most horses had gone to the butchers. A week later, with the meat ration consumed, all that was left was a tasteless bread baked from whatever starches could be found. Soon the sick lists bloomed. About 18,000 soldiers were in the hospital. Among the 8,000 effectives were many who were too weak to bear the weight of the their muskets.

Nonetheless, by taking advantage of his interior lines Masséna aggressively disputed every effort the Austrians made to advance their siege lines. When Colonel Honoré Reille passed through the

British blockade in the pre-dawn hours of May 2 to deliver a letter from Minister of War Carnot, Masséna received his first solid intelligence of how matters stood strategically. It outlined Bonaparte's plan to cross the Alps, descend upon the Austrian rear, and relieve Genoa. Henceforth, Masséna clearly understood his mission: tie down as many Austrians as possible until Bonaparte arrived to rescue his garrison.

On May 5 a coaster ran the British blockade to deliver five days' worth of grain. Encouraged, Masséna conducted another vigorous sortie. Thereafter, Ott conceived a plan to take advantage of French impetuosity and trap the next French sortie. General Gottesheim was to give ground in order to lure the French onward and then Hohenzollern was to march in behind them and block their return to Genoa. When the French launched a sortie on May 11 in an effort to gather food, Ott's plan collapsed on contact. Gottesheim was a stubborn, tenacious fighter. Rather than retire, he contested every inch of ground. The French, under Soult's command, exhibited their tactical superiority and outfought Gottesheim's soldiers. Austrian casualties reflect the combat's intensity: 2 officers and 135 men killed; 13 officers and 315 men wounded, 41 officers and 1,321 men captured.[33] These losses again highlight the nature of Masséna's defense. Rather than passively accept the methodical advance of regular siege lines, he lashed out at every opportunity.

The sortie of May 11 proved to be the garrison's last success. On May 13 Masséna again ordered Soult to sortie. This time he suffered a costly repulse when Frimont, again displaying aggressive leadership, delivered a flank attack against Soult's columns that sent the French flying. French losses included Soult himself, who was captured after falling with a severe leg wound while leading an attack. Henceforth, the garrison lacked the physical strength to sortie beyond the city's walls. Inside, soldiers and civilians alike began dying from starvation. Typhus raged. Still Masséna resisted with an iron determination.

While Ott besieged Genoa, Melas pushed west along the coast. Suchet, who initially had only 7,000 men, could do little to oppose him. On May 3 the Austrians overran a French depot in Albenga. In their haste to escape, the French had spiked their cannons, burned the gun carriages, and flooded a powder magazine. Sensing he had his foe on the run, Melas accelerated the pursuit.

Early on May 6, GM Otto Hohenfeld's column stealthily captured a French outpost. Next, an Austrian colonel led a force under cover of a fog that surprised two more outposts before they could fire a shot. The French garrison of Tenda formed quickly on the heights only to be attacked in the flank and driven back into town. They fled to the next town which was already under Austrian assault. Here too the French abandoned their positions. From the Austrian viewpoint it had been a neat little operation. At a cost of 47 casualties, the Austrians captured 4 officers and 103 soldiers along with five cannons and a powder magazine.

Better still, the next day the Austrians attacked the French on the heights of Monto Carvo:

> "The battle continued quite heavily until [the Austrian flanking columns] got into the enemy's rear. Upon being attacked from all sides by the Austrians, the French fled Oneglia in great disorder. The divisional general Cravel, 60 officers and nearly 1500 prisoners including one color were in the hands of the satisfied victors by seven o'clock in the morning."[34]

Although the Royal Navy supplied the Austrians with food, forage, and ammunition, and also transported the heavy artillery, Melas could not march his army quickly along what were admittedly poor roads. It took Elsnitz's wing more than three weeks to close on Suchet's position on the Var River. Here Elsnitz found the French maintaining a fortified bridgehead on the river's east bank. Suchet's engineer officer, General Jacques Campredon, had designed the fortifications with such skill that the Austrians felt compelled to resort to formal siege approaches. The Royal Navy delivered the Habsburg heavy artillery on May 20 and disembarked some of their own to assist the methodical Austrian advance. Slowly, Elsnitz advanced the Habsburg lines. It seemed that he would have ample time to overcome the Var line and open the way to an invasion of Provence.

***

Meanwhile, well to Elsnitz's rear, the French position deteriorated. The garrison of Savona, some 30 miles southwest of Genoa, surrendered on May 16. Here the Austrians captured one general, 48 officers and 998 men along with 146 heavy cannons. In Genoa itself, Masséna's army wasted away. Although not completely isolated – general of division Nicolas Oudinot managed a round trip to confer with Suchet by running the British blockade in a bark commanded by a notable corsair named Bavastro – no provisions reached the garrison. By May 20 the troops had little to eat except a nearly indigestible bread baked from linseed, starch, and cacao. Men gathered herbs to make a thin soup. Many of the sentries were too weak to walk their rounds. Instead they maintained their vigil while sitting. Of course the privileged, generally officers serving in the rear or those with special connections to the quartermasters, could always find something better to eat. One officer who served as a courier slipping into and out of the siege lines, reported that a reasonable dinner could be purchased for five francs at a decent restaurant. On the other hand, the Austrian prisoners who were given one-quarter rations aboard their prison hulks, "had begun by eating the rigging and their shirts, and ended by eating one another."[36] On May 29 many Genoese rebelled against the twin dangers of bombardment and starvation. Masséna ordered the ringleaders arrested and had cannons strategically positioned to sweep the squares where the rioters assembled.

Masséna clung to the hope that relief had to be near. When a courier penetrated the lines to deliver a report that the Army of Reserve would proceed by forced marches and should arrive to raise the blockade on May 30, hopes soared. May 30, June 1, and June 2 passed with no relief in sight. Each morning the death wagons trundled through Genoa's streets to collect the emaciated bodies of those who had died the night before. Finally, with rations almost exhausted, Masséna opened negotiations for a surrender. Even then he proved tenacious. Masséna insisted that the garrison leave the city with the honors of war and be free to resume fighting once they cleared the Austrian lines. He demanded that his 4,000 wounded receive medical attention and be allowed to rejoin his army once they became well. Ott acceded to his demands.

His generosity resulted from the fact that unbeknownst to the beleaguered garrison, on June 2 he had received orders from Melas to abandon the siege and march to join the main army. Sensing Masséna's imminent surrender, Ott disobeyed orders and stayed put. His reward came on June 4 when Genoa capitulated. Two days later, about 7,000 French soldiers along with their arms, artillery, and baggage marched out of the city. Such was their state that 6,000 were unfit for further combat. Meanwhile, the Royal Navy transported the remainder of the garrison to Antibes along with its commander.

During the siege of Genoa, Masséna's officer corps had emulated their chief's sterling conduct. Masséna's second in command, Soult, had been wounded and captured. Of his three divisional generals, one died from disease and another received a serious wound; four of six brigadiers received wounds; among twelve adjutant-generals, one was killed, six wounded, and one captured. Eleven of seventeen colonels became casualties or were captured before the surrender. Among the staff, two officers were killed, fourteen wounded, and seven captured. Before departing, Masséna pledged to GM Francis Saint-Julien that within a fortnight he would be back in Genoa. Saint-Julien nobly replied, "You will find in this place, general, men whom you have taught how to defend it." [37]

From the Austrian viewpoint, six weeks of siege had netted very little. At a cost of perhaps 20,000 men, the Austrians had inflicted about 14,000 casualties and captured Genoa. To some extent logistical constraints had prevented Melas from accomplishing more. He had to subsist his army in the same barren territory where a smaller French army had starved. However, his deliberate pace of operations stemmed more from his experience of war in a different age, the time before Bonaparte.

It was a much more satisfactory entry on the French side of the ledger. Masséna and Suchet had accomplished Bonaparte's strategic aim. For two months they and the Army of Italy had thoroughly occupied Melas' attention. No man besides Masséna could have taken the abused, dispirited Army of Italy and managed such a defense. The soldiers had no particular attachment to Genoa and yet held it against overwhelming force and in the teeth of enervating privation. The Genoa garrison had been a sacrificial pawn within Bonaparte's master plan. By the time the survivors abandoned the city, the strategic impact of their sacrifice had already been felt.

NOTES

1. "To General Masséna," May 14, 1800, John Howard, ed., *Letters and Documents of Napoleon*, I (New York, 1961), p. 418.

2. "Proclamation á l'armée d'Italie," December 25, 1799, Jacques Campredon, *La Défense du Var et Le Passage Des Alpes 1800* (Paris, 1889) p. 16.

3. "Masséna to the First Consul," February 5, 1800, *The Campaign of the Reserve Army in 1800 According to Documents Collected by Captain de Cugnac* (Fort Leavenworth, KS, 1922), p. 71.

4. From the letter of Hector Legury, adjutant-general, to Bonaparte, Édouard Gachot, *Le Siège de Gênes* (Paris, 1908) p. 6.

5. See table in François Roguet, *Mémoires Militaires du Lieutenant Général Comte Roguet*, II (Paris, 1862) p. 594.

6. Sir Peter Hayman, *Soult: Napoleon's Maligned Marshal* (London, 1990), p. 34.

7. Bernard Bergerot, *Le Maréchal Suchet, duc d'Albufera* (Paris, 1986), p. 60.

8. "Le Premier Consul au général Masséna," March 5, 1800, Campredon, p. 96.

9. "To General Masséna," March 12, 1800, Howard, *Letters and Documents of Napoleon*, I (New York, 1961) p. 385.

10. William Bentinck's report cited in John Holland Rose, *The Life of Napoleon I*, I (London, 1907), p. 253, n. 1.

11. Jean Baptiste Crossard, *Mémoires Militaires et Historiques*, II (Paris, 1829) p. 370.

12. "Wickham to Grenville," October 31, 1799, William Wickham, *Correspondence of the Right Hon. William Wickham from the year 1794*, II (London, 1870) p. 320.

13. Crossard, II, p. 221.

14. Zach's writing are cited in Gunther Rothenberg, *Napoleon's Great Adversaries* (Bloomington, IN, 1982) p. 51.

15. A. Ellrich cited in Rothenberg, p. 54.

16. "Wickham to Minto," December 9, 1799, Wickham, II, p. 352.

17. Rothenberg, p. 24.

18. Ellrich, p. 251-2 cited in Rothenberg, p. 16.

19. Thomas Graham, *The History of the Campaign of 1796 in Germany and Italy* (London, 1800), p. 379. Zach's observation in "Zach to Alvinczy," April 18, 1798 cited in Rothenberg, p. 49.

20. Joseph Petit, *Marengo or the Campaign of Italy, by the Army of Reserve Under the Command of the Chief Consul Bonaparte* (Philadelphia, 1801), p. 35.

21. Rothenberg, p. 54.

22. Karl Mras, "Gefchichte Des Feldzuges 1800 in Italien," *Öestereichische Militärische Zeitschrift* (Vienna, 1822), p. 28.

23. Crossard, II, p. 257.

24. "Suchet au Premier Consul," May 30, 1800, Campredon, p. 347. Suchet uses the cant expression "vous en aurez bon marché."

25. "Wickham to Grenville," June 29, 1799 and October 31, 1799, Wickham, II, pp. 117-18, 320.

26. Cited in Gachot, *Le Siège de Gênes*, p. 50.

27. Ott: 8,000; Hohenzollern: 5,300; Melas: 27,500; Elsnitz: 21,100. See: Gachot, p 56. Melas' proclamation is in Roguet, pp. 594-95.

28. Gachot, *Le Siège de Gênes*, p. 108.

29. Édouard Gachot, *La Deuxième Campagne d'Italie* (Paris, 1899), p. 125.

30. Gachot, *Le Siège de Gênes*, p. 128.

31. Vogelsang was born in 1848 of Belgian extraction and so his first name is Louis instead of Ludwig. A courageous officer, as a major he received the cross of Maria Theresa during the Brabantine revolution.

32. Nicolas Jean Soult, *Mémoires du Maréchal-Général Soult*, III (Paris, 1854), p. 51.

33. Mras, p. 100.

34. Mras, p. 311.

35. Bavastro was a boyhood friend of Masséna's. He reappears, accompanying Masséna during his invasion of Portugal in 1810 where he hoped to outfit privateers in Lisbon once the French recaptured that city.

36. Marie Charlotte Oudinot, *Memoirs of Marshal Oudinot Duc de Reggio* (New York, 1897), p. 25.

37. Adolphe Thiers, *History of the Consulate and the Empire*, I (London, 1845), p. 225.

Chapter 4

Over the Alps

PART 1.
THE SAINT BERNARD PASS

"I note with pleasure that Paris is quiet. All the same, I repeat my advice to you: hit hard the first of them...who fails to come into line with us."[1]

BONAPARTE TO HIS FELLOW CONSULS, MAY 9, 1800

Throughout the early spring, units assembled to form the Army of Reserve. Having suppressed the rebellions in the west, divisions commanded by Jacques-Antoine Chambarlhac and Gaspard-Amédée Gardanne marched through Paris and continued toward Dijon. Logistical support remained poor. Soldiers lived off the land as if they were in enemy territory. Chambarlhac's men earned the title 'brigands' for their rapacious conduct.[2] Considering the number of conscripts who were in the ranks, the desertion rate was surprisingly low. About 3.7 percent of Chambarlhac's 'brigands' deserted en route to Dijon. The division made good time, averaging 16.5 miles per day. On April 11 the last major element of the army, the Consular Guard, departed Paris.

For the remainder of the month the First Consul perfected his plans. He knew that the army would use the Lake Geneva region as a staging area. He was as yet undecided which alpine pass it would then utilize to descend into Italy. Bonaparte anticipated that the alpine crossing would be difficult and consequently he applied his enormous appetite for work toward the challenge. He had dispatched officers to scout the various passes leading to Italy and to interview Swiss citizens who possessed local knowledge about climate, routes of travel, and methods and means appropriate for traversing the passes. Among those he contacted were the monks who lived in the hospice at the Great Saint Bernard Pass. This pass had the advantage that it was closer to Lake Geneva than alternative passes. But the road on the far side of the pass was little known to planners in Paris. The Simplon Pass, on the other hand, was better known and led to finer country that could better support the army. The Saint Gothard offered the attractive possibility of descending deeper in the Austrian rear. Most dazzling of all was the most eastern pass, the Splügen. If the army debouched here, it could sever all communications between the Austrian army in Italy and its homeland.

Much depended upon the supporting operations conducted by Moreau and Masséna. At all events, the army could be set in motion for Geneva before the choice was made. In the meantime, Bonaparte ordered Berthier, who had moved from the War Ministry to assume temporary command of the army, to travel to Basel to confer with Moreau. It was essential to Bonaparte's strategy that Moreau both prevent the Austrians from hindering the Army of Reserve's march through Switzerland and that he send an entire corps to reinforce Bonaparte once Moreau had driven Kray back from the Rhine. Accordingly, Berthier and Moreau signed an agreement on April 16 stipulating precisely how Moreau was to cooperate with the Army of Reserve. Based on this agreement, Bonaparte anticipated receiving 28,000 men from Moreau. In the event Moreau would send only 11,500. After concluding business with Moreau, Berthier hurried back to army headquarters. Among the dispatches he received was the order from the First Consul to "make certain of the nature of the roads" on the far side of the Saint Bernard pass.[3]

For the first time since the Revolution, a controlling genius was coordinating the maneuvers of all French armies. However, at this juncture his three principal subordinates were letting him down. Berthier was overwhelmed by his work. He showed little initiative and became despondent. Moreau added the military sin of moving slowly to that of obstinately disputing Bonaparte's strategy. The most surprising behavior was that of the most trusted of them all. In Italy, Masséna had seemingly maneuvered rashly and gotten himself in big trouble. When the first sketchy reports from the Army of Italy arrived in Paris, all seemed in order. Over the ensuing days, tension regarding Masséna's position increased. Bonaparte realized that if Masséna had retired into Genoa and if he failed to hold out long enough, Melas would have time to countermarch to engage the Army of Reserve as it debouched from the alpine passes. Specifically, Bonaparte calculated that an Austrian march from Genoa to Aosta would take only eight days. If Melas arrived in Aosta in force, he would be perfectly positioned to block the Army of Reserve, in much the manner of a cat waiting outside a mouse's bolt hole. Bonaparte knew that the Army of

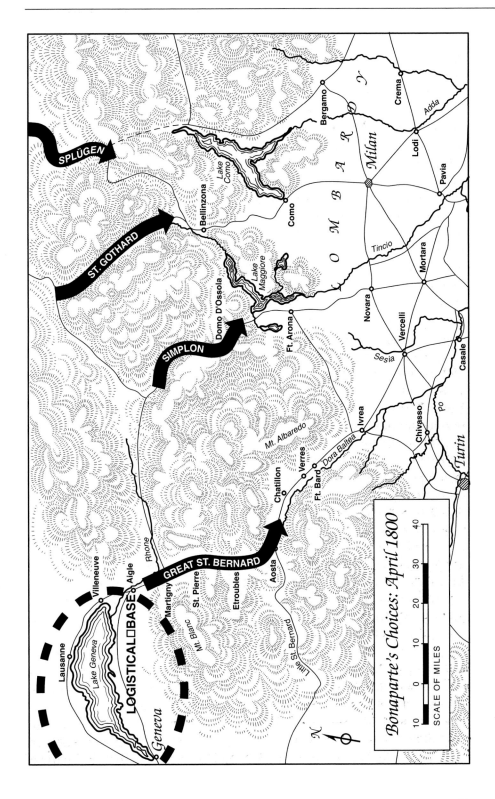

SPLÜGEN

ST. GOTHARD

SIMPLON

GREAT ST. BERNARD

LOGISTICAL BASE

Bergamo

Crema

Adda

Lake Como

Milan

Lodi

Pavia

Bellinzona

Como

L O M B A R D Y

Lake Maggiore

Domo D'Ossola

Tincio

Mortara

Ft. Arona

Novara

Vercelli

Sesia

Casale

Mt. Albaredo

Verres

Ivrea

Dora Baltea

Chivasso

Po

Ft. Bard

Turin

Chatillon

Aosta

Rhone

Villeneuve

Aigle

Martigny

St. Pierre

Etroubles

Mt. Blanc

L. St. Bernard

Lausanne

Lake Geneva

Geneva

Bonaparte's Choices: April 1800

SCALE OF MILES

10 0 10 20 30 40

N

Reserve could not long subsist in Switzerland. Even against little opposition, the effort to cross the Alps was based on a logistical shoestring. Everything depended upon Masséna, but there was little reliable information about how that general was faring.

In the absence of solid intelligence and even before he received reports from the reconnaissances of the alpine passes, on April 27 Bonaparte resolved to cross via the Great Saint Bernard. He rejected the passes farther east because Moreau had failed to win a great victory that would have permitted bolder strokes. Moreover, he had begun to worry seriously about Masséna: "it is possible that it is not to Milan that we must go, but that we may be obliged to move in haste to Tortone to disengage Masséna, who, if he has been beaten, will have shut himself up in Genoa, where he has provisions for thirty days."[4] The army could move most quickly to Masséna's relief by marching through the Great Saint Bernard. Simultaneously, there would be feints at other passes to distract the Austrians from the main blow.

On Sunday, May 5, one of Masséna's aides reached Paris. He informed Bonaparte that Masséna was besieged in Genoa and had only enough provisions to endure until May 20. Bonaparte sent a courier galloping to Berthier to relay this bad news. He concluded with the order "Force the march."[5] Masséna's plight also convinced Bonaparte to accelerate his own departure. He would leave Paris to join the Army of Reserve. The papers would claim that he had left on an inspection tour. On Monday, he met for one last time with his fellow consuls. The telegraph had just transmitted the welcome news that Moreau had gained a victory at Stockach. He dictated a short reply that included the compliment, "Glory, threefold glory!"[6] That evening, to maintain the appearance that everything was normal, he attended the opera. At two in the morning, dressed in a long grey cape, he descended the flight of stairs leading from his apartment in the Tuileries and boarded his gleaming black, new berlin. It flew through the Parisian night at a gallop. The First Consul dozed briefly. By the time the coach had departed the suburbs he was reviewing reports with his secretary Bourrienne.

For the First Consul to leave the capital before his government was solidly established was a risk. Recent history had witnessed three political upheavals preceding his own coup of Brumaire. He knew that in his absence his opponents might cause trouble. Indeed, a bureaucrat noted that Bonaparte's departure "produced a general sensation in Paris...His enemies – their number increased every day – hoped he might meet with reverses, and flattered themselves that defeat would wrest his power from him."[7] Bonaparte calculated that Fouché's police could control his foes in the short term. But he did not want to be away from Paris for long. This anxiety would explain several oversights that almost compromised the entire campaign.

To speed his journey, his chief aide, Geraud Duroc, had arranged fresh relays of the finest horses. Pausing only to change teams, Bonaparte's berlin traveled 143 miles in 15 hours. Additional news from Masséna confirmed the need for haste. When Bonaparte had devised his strategy, he envisioned Masséna's role as one of maneuver. While the Army of Reserve entered Italy Masséna was "to attract to yourself the attention of the enemy" in order to "oblige him to divide his forces."[8] When an aide de camp to General Soult named Franceschi encountered Bonaparte at midnight on May 6, he brought a much different tale. Eight days earlier, in the black of night, Franceschi had taken a boat from Genoa. An English corvette sighted the boat at dawn and gave chase. On the point of being captured, Franceschi had put his saber between his teeth, leaped overboard, and swam for shore. He survived to report to Bonaparte that the situation in Genoa was truly desperate.

Bonaparte rose at dawn to continue the journey to Dijon. Here he encountered the soldiers of the Army of Reserve and it was not a reassuring sight. Too many men were poorly dressed. Some lacked shoes. While inspecting the ranks of Chambarlhac's division, Bonaparte saw a veteran corporal among the conscripts. In a familiar tone he inquired if the corporal had served in Italy with him. Yes, replied the corporal. He had been at the bridge at Arcole. "It was hot work, general; without you, one might say, we would have been flambéed like chickens."

> Bonaparte turned to Chambarlhac, "Promote this brave man to sergeant."

> The new sergeant shouted out, "Vive Bonaparte!"[9]

After becoming emperor he would perform such scenes on a grander scale, nominating the chosen ones for the Legion of Honor, elevating some into the nobility. If just now he lacked the impressive baubles of later years, he already possessed the leadership skills to bond his army to him. He also knew when to show the back side of his hand.

The next day while inspecting Boudet's division he observed that the 9th Light was poorly clad. He summoned the commissary officer and laid into him. Forty days ago, he thundered, you were made commissioner for clothing. Now you give me troops dressed in rags. How can I ask such men to clamber over the alpine glaciers?

The unfortunate officer began to make excuses about the state of the magazines. Bonaparte interrupted him. "The magazines are full. You have in Lyon 8,000 uniforms and carts to haul them. Don't interrupt me, citizen...after such negligence, you should be shot. Leave this instant; if by the twentieth Boudet's division is not better clothed, never show your face before me again."[10]

Switzerland was thinly populated without a bountiful agricultural base. The normal French recourse to requisition simply did not work. In one Swiss district Bonaparte tried to requisition 1,000 mules to assist in the alpine crossing. His commissary could only locate 217 animals. Because of Switzerland's relative poverty, the army would have to rely upon an extensive network of magazines and wagon trains. Because he had ordered it done, Bonaparte expected to find a large magazine already established at Villeneuve on the eastern end of Lake Geneva. Instead he found a scene of grand disorder; a jumble of baggage wagons, caissons, powder carts, and cannons, precious supplies exposed to the rain. He sternly rebuked the commissary officer in charge who offered lame excuses about the difficult weather. Bonaparte replied, "While you and your mates sleep we march through the rain day and night." He explained that the government had paid a great deal of money to procure supplies. An "army on campaign without food and munitions, because of your omissions, is half way to defeat. It is impossible to tolerate your feebleness any longer."[11] In no uncertain terms the First Consul told the officer to get to work and that he could begin by immediately bringing his lists showing exactly what and how much was in the magazine. One can imagine the chill of apprehension the commissary officer experienced. Until now the commissary had been a plum posting that promised little work and great personal profit. The snarling Bonaparte promised that things had changed.

And again the promises to the rank and file:

> "Like those who followed me at Lodi...you are poorly clothed, poorly fed...In fifteen days all of that will change. Soldiers, I am going to ask a great effort of you before you meet the Austrians. Follow me with confidence and you will cover yourselves with glory."[12]

***

The crossing of the Alps was far from an improvised scramble up and down the mountains. Even a stripped-down French army had a significant logistical tail. The army's grand park alone counted 80 ammunition wagons for the heavy cannons pulled by 312 horses; 200 horses hauled 54 wagons loaded with ammunition for the 4-pounders along with two million paper artillery cartridges; 300 horses pulled 106 baggage carts laden with 25 million iron musket balls. There were 8 wagons carrying musket cartridges, 20 ambulances, and even a wagon loaded with semaphore equipment. The soldiers sensed that they were embarked upon something grand:

> "We kept constantly passing troops on the march, with officers and soldiers hastening to rejoin their several regiments. Their enthusiasm was indescribable. Those who had seen service in Italy were delighted at the prospect of returning to so beautiful a country, while those who had not had such experience were eager to see the fields of battle immortalised by French valour and by the heroic genius who marched at their head. All went forward as to a festival, singing and shouting as they scaled the Valais mountains."[13]

In spite of all preparations, not everything proceeded smoothly. Staff officers found that the convoys heading for Saint-Pierre, the staging area for the ascent, were very late. Most of the drivers were drunk. They roundly abused the officers who tried to straighten matters out. Many of the inhabitants of Saint-Pierre had fled when the army came to their village. Naturally the first wave of soldiers took everything of value leaving subsequent waves without food or fodder and the inhabitants, when they returned, destitute.

In the tenth century, Bernard de Menthon decided that something had to be done to alleviate the perils associated with crossing the nearby mountain pass leading to Switzerland. At 8,120 feet, the pass was one of the highest on the alpine frontier. Generally it could only be traversed five months a year. Adjacent to some Roman ruins near the summit, Bernard ordered a hospice built. Over time, it provided both a sanctuary for suffering travelers and, using its specially bred, giant tracking dogs, a rescue service for the frostbit or avalanche buried.

In 1798 a small French garrison occupied the hospice. The following year, in response to Suvorov's advance through northern Italy, 180 men of the 28th Demi-brigade and 30 artillerists defended the pass. Lower down on the Italian side of the pass, an Austrian force occupied Saint-Remy. General Melas had wanted to control the pass, but winter snows prevented active operations until April 12, 1800. Then FML Karl Haddick sent a column toward the hospice. The two French guns sited near the Roman ruins fired furiously while the well-positioned infantry of the 28th added their musket fire. The volume of fire convinced the cautious Austrians that they confronted several battalions supported by a 12-pounder battery! The game was not worth the candle and the Austrians withdrew to Saint-Remy. Because of this successful skirmish, the Great Saint Bernard Pass was available to Bonaparte in April 1800.

***

The steepness alone made the pass daunting. Even before entering the pass itself the track climbed so abruptly that the animal teams hauling the wagons were doubled. When that proved insufficient the soldiers supplemented animal power. At particularly steep places up to 300 men hauled the ropes attached to a single baggage wagon. The soldiers learned that the artillery sledges purpose-built for the crossing were useless. The local Swiss showed them how to hollow out a pine trunk and put an artillery barrel on top of it. A trooper in the Consular Guard describes the effort:

> "The exertion of a whole battalion was requisite for the conveyance of one field-piece with its necessary ammunition: one half of a regiment could only draw [haul] the load, while the other half was obliged to carry the knap-sacks, firelocks [muskets] cartridge-boxes, canteens, kettles, and more especially, five days provisions in bread, meat, salt, and biscuit."[14]

So acute was the avalanche danger that the first soldiers to try the pass, the men of Lannes' advance guard, waited until darkness on the evening of May 15, when the cold evening air could stabilize the snow, before attempting the pass itself. Some 6,000 men, each one hefting a load of between 60 and 70 pounds, 200 horses, and 215 laden mules formed a column three miles long. The head of the column departed at midnight. If all went well, a five-hour climb to the hospice was before them. Officers led the way, leading their horses by their bridles. Fifty men carried lanterns to illuminate the passage. The path was so narrow that the soldiers trudged two abreast. Pontonnier detachments marched between each battalion carrying tools to tackle any unexpected obstacles. Everyone maintained a strict silence so as to avoid triggering a snow slide.

The shoeless soldiers of the 6th Light had wrapped canvas around their feet. It provided poor traction on the icy rocks and little protection from the cold. Overheard loomed dark, forbidding summits. Suddenly, shouts from some ill-disciplined grenadiers loosened a mass of snow. An avalanche thundered down toward the column. Shouts of sauve qui peut echoed off the walls of the gorge. The wall of snow missed most of the soldiers but did bury three gunners and an 8-pounder. Only with the greatest difficulty could a lieutenant rally his men to dig out the buried gunners. Meanwhile, news of the avalanche swept through the line of march. Ahead, in a narrow gorge, teamsters conducting a mule train carrying biscuit and gunpowder refused to continue. So great was the perceived peril that the 6th Light refused to budge until daylight. To make matters worse, a snow squall enveloped the column. Shrouded by the snowfall some pontonniers who were leading the column left the ranks to seek shelter. Hard on their heels came the teamsters. The entire operation was on the point of dissolution when, near dawn, Lannes appeared. He harangued the men of the 6th Light and, avalanche be damned, ordered the drummers to sound the assembly. More effective than the music was a stiff breeze that dispersed the clouds. The sight of a blue sky overhead calmed the troops. Order restored, Lannes mounted a mule and led the column to the welcome sanctuary of the hospice.

Using funds provided by Bonaparte, the monks had purchased cheese, bread, and wine. They laid tables in front of the hospice. As the soldiers passed they took a cup of wine to wash down the bread and cheese. During the day, the monks served 1,295 bottles of wine and 83 pounds of cheese, which surely says something about the nutritional requirements of the French army. Meanwhile, using their keen-nosed dogs, the monks searched the trail and rescued several lost and half-dead soldiers. After a short rest, Lannes' soldiers descended into Italy.

The cavalry who were supposed to lead the advance guard were still back in Switzerland. Jean Rivaud's brigade of light cavalry, comprising the 12th Hussars and 21st Chasseurs à cheval, had never been known for its upstanding discipline. Two days without rations and a torrential rain did not improve their outlook. A disgruntled trooper shouted out to his commanding officer, "When are you going to give us a village to pillage?"[15] Nearing the village of Saint Pierre, troopers began threatening the handful of inhabitants who had remained with cries of "Bread or death!" Bonaparte had told the army that the fields of Italy were like a well-stocked granary and that the countryside would supply all of their wants. When they learned that yet again the supply wagons were late, Rivaud's men decided not to wait for Italian promises. Some men found a supply of alcohol. Soon the brigade began to professionally pillage Saint Pierre.

Rivaud vainly tried to stop them, reminding them they were looting their own allies. The French called it living off the land. For the hapless inhabitants of Saint-Pierre, it was ruin. Bonaparte, in turn, well knew that news of such incidents would spread quickly through the countryside. He was furious. He could not afford to have an insurrection break out along his line of communication in Switzerland. For the present, all he could do was order the brigade over the pass and promise Rivaud that he would put them in position to take the hardest blows at the next battle.

On the day Lannes' advance guard began its ascent, Bonaparte was back in Lausanne. He received a letter from Suchet informing him that Suchet had abandoned Nice and retired behind the Var River. Suchet promised to take up the offensive as soon as the Austrians to his front weakened themselves by sending detachments to confront Bonaparte. This was contrary to Bonaparte's plan since the Army of Italy was supposed to occupy Austrian attention until the Army of Reserve crossed the mountains. After digesting all available intelligence, Bonaparte concluded that the Army of Reserve would have to accelerate. He instructed Berthier, "you must immediately give orders to General Lannes to advance, even if the rest of the army has not passed the Saint-Bernard. It is necessary to be at Ivrea [where the Aosta valley opened onto the Po plain] as soon as possible, even if with only half the army."[16] This order, by which Lannes learned that he was to clear the Aosta valley, sped along the chain of command.

Meanwhile, Jean Rivaud received orders to cross the pass to support Lannes and arrive before noon the following day at Aosta. Because of the disgraceful pillage of Saint Pierre, he knew that Bonaparte would tolerate no excuses. At midnight the brigade began the crossing. Troopers led their horses by their bridles up the pass. They struggled through snow squalls, high winds, and cold. By 2 a.m, a layer of ice covered man and beast alike. A series of snow slides cascaded around them. Horses and troopers shivered from cold and from fear. About a mile and one-half from the hospice, the column stumbled to a halt. Rivaud and his senior officers unfurled the unit's standards and began to sing the *Marseillaise*! Amazingly, the singing stimulated the column to continue to the hospice. Here the monks provided food and wine for the men and hay for the shivering horses. The treacherous, ice covered path leading to Italy presented further frightful obstacles with banks of hanging snow hovering above and a roaring river torrent below. Yet the brigade met its deadline and in the end the cost was far less than the annihilation that had seemed certain during the black night: one hussar trampled, three horses injured.

The crossing had been hard for the advance guard. It was far more difficult for the artillery. To expedite matters, Bonaparte balanced the army's needs: supply wagons and ambulances versus cannons and howitzers. He ruthlessly reduced the army's trains to a bare minimum to obtain another 800 horses and 150 mules to help Marmont get the artillery over the pass. It still took the heroic labors of young Marmont, ably assisted by another gunner who was to make a big name for himself, Alexandre Senarmont, to manage the crossing. In his *Mémoires* Marmont recalled these days and described himself: "Young, active, and already convinced that the word impossible, in three-quarters of the circumstances, was an excuse for feebleness."[17] Marmont prevailed upon the unruly Gascons of Loison's division to cooperate by instructing half the men to carry two muskets and two haversacks and thus free the hands of the remaining half so they could carry disassembled cannons and ammunition. After one day of such labor, the civilian teamsters – the artillery had not yet been completely militarized – deserted. Marmont drafted additional men from the ranks and pressed on, launching the final ascent at 1 a.m. to avoid avalanches.

Still, conditions were frightening. A company of grenadiers abandoned their loads. In a narrow defile a platoon mutinied and refused to budge until General Louis Loison appeared, ordered his staff to seize some muskets, and threatened to open fire. Another delay came when a half-battalion of the 60th crouched in the snow and said they would rather die in the cold than continue to labor like animals. Lieutenant General Philibert Duhesme intervened, ordered three loyal companies to load their muskets, and threatened to decimate the 60th. Finally, at 11 in the morning the column reached the hospice. After a brief rest, Loison left 18 footsore men with the monks and began the march downslope to Italy.

So, in stages, the army traversed the pass: "Horses, cannon, waggons, huge quantities of ammunition, everything was dragged or carried pell-mell over glaciers that seemed inaccessible, or along paths that even one man could hardly pass." For a time, a heavy snowfall prevented the reserve echelons from crossing. On May 19 the Consular Guard climbed the pass with little difficulty. The next evening Marmont sent over the artillery park and the trains, including the treasury with 850,000 francs sewn into leather saddle bags.

Intermixed was a sizeable bevy of Parisian women of easy virtue who claimed they wanted to assist in the army's victories and inquired about the men of their beloved 9th Light Infantry. Ice covered the route of march. A thick fog descended. So awful were the conditions that Marmont offered bonuses for the men who successfully dragged cannons across the pass: 500 francs for a 4-pounder; 700 for the howitzers. It took two hours to progress three-quarters of a mile. The snow fell in large flakes. At 2:30 a.m. a tremendous wind swept the route of march. Yet the column persevered. Indicative of their spirit is the fact that the men of the rear guard declined Marmont's bonus. To have safely reached Italy was enough.

Earlier, General Berthier had ascended the pass on a mule until the balky animal bucked him into the snow. The 47-year old veteran had seen much of war and he was not going to let this bother him. He mounted another mule only to find the going so poor that he and his staff had to dismount and walk the final mile and one half to the hospice. The army's ability to conquer the Alps impressed Berthier. He remarked to an aide that the French army had done some very fine things since 1792, but nothing surpassed its audacious trek over the Saint Bernard.

The crossing of the Alps succeeded because of meticulous planning, a great deal of hard work by senior officers – among many, Chief of Staff Pierre Dupont went virtually sleepless for three days while attending to his duties – and above all, the soldiers' constancy. A total of 50,011 men, 10,377 horses, 750 mules, 76 guns and their caissons, and 103 wagons crossed the Great Saint Bernard. The cost was remarkable: three artillerymen and one hussar buried in an avalanche; one fusilier dead from congestion; 34 horses dead or maimed; one 8-pounder and five spare wheels lost in the gorge; three wagons and five gun carriages abandoned and burned.

On May 20 Bonaparte himself began a 2 a.m. ascent to the hospice. Although David's heroic painting shows him crossing the Alps on a magnificent horse, in fact he rode a humble, but more sure-footed mule. The chief monk greeted the First Consul at 5 p.m. and served him a meal that would, had they known about it, have made his soldiers' mouths water: dried beef and porridge, ragout of mutton, dried vegetables, chèvre and gruyère cheeses, an Italian white wine. Outside, troopers of the Consular Guard received only a very chilled glass of wine. But throughout his life, meals, whether hearty or gourmet, held little interest for Bonaparte. He ate in twenty minutes, inspected the hospice, and prepared to depart. Then came most unwelcome news when a courier from Berthier arrived at the hospice to report that "The fort of Bard is a greater obstacle than we had foreseen."[19]

This was an understatement. The fort blocked the army's exit onto the Lombard plain. It penned the Army of Reserve in the Aosta Valley with a precarious supply line straddling the Saint Bernard Pass. What should be attempted? Irritated, Bonaparte raged to his secretary that 'those imbeciles have allowed 200 Croats' to immobilize the army. Having spent only 90 minutes at the hospice, Bonaparte began walking toward Italy. At one place the slope was so steep that he ordered his younger aides to go first and slide through the snow. Satisfied that this was a viable mountaineering technique, Bonaparte likewise sat and slid down the slope. If it was undignified, it was effective. By 9 p.m. he was in Etroubles where another courier from Berthier delivered the news that scouts had located a path to bypass Fort Bard.

This was better. Bonaparte responded immediately by ordering Berthier to pass the fort and then occupy a position to cover the siege of Fort Bard. He should select a position to negate Austrian cavalry and artillery superiority and to begin work improving the bypass. It had been a long day. By midnight Bonaparte was asleep atop a mattress placed on a pile of straw.

PART 2.
BOTTLENECK AT FORT BARD

Austrian intelligence had begun receiving reports about the French build-up in Switzerland. However, Bonaparte's diversionary efforts succeeded famously. At his headquarters in Turin, FML Conrad Kaim, the general whom Melas has charged with defending Lombardy and Piedmont, understood that Bonaparte was marching for the Simplon and Saint-Gothard passes. His objective was apparently Milan. To block a French descent from the Simplon, Kaim ordered the 5th Hussar Regiment and the Bussischen Jägers to reinforce Fort Arona. He relayed his concerns to Melas and awaited the next French move.

Consequently, until contacted by hostile forces, the Austrian garrison of Saint-Remy had remained oblivious to what was taking place on the other side of the Great Saint Bernard. Whereas Bonaparte had dispatched spies and intelligence officers to northern Italy who were able to provide him with good information about his enemy, most Austrian agents had seemed unwilling or unable to penetrate the alpine passes. One who did was an Italian named François Toli. Disguised as a priest, Toli attempted the Great Saint Bernard only to be turned back by French guards. He traveled to a secondary pass where he spent 60 hours toiling through the ice and snow until finally reaching Switzerland. He began spying on the marching French columns only to fall into the hands of the French cavalry. At this juncture he asked to be taken to General Bonaparte.

Toli had spied for the French four years ago. Bonaparte recognized him immediately. Addressing him in Italian, the First Consul asked what was he doing in Switzerland? Toli replied that Moreau would not hire him and Masséna was besieged in Genoa. Desperate for work to feed his family, he had sold his services to the Austrian General Philipp Vukassovich. Bonaparte asked Toli how much money had the Vukassovich given him. Coyly, Toli hung his head and declined to answer.

> "Speak" Bonaparte demanded, "and I will recompense you. But if you remain mute, the French will shoot you in ten minutes."
>
> Toli stoically kept silent. Bonaparte summoned an aide. "Here is a spy. Take him away!"
>
> Toli cried out, "General Bonaparte, I have seven children; I will speak." [20]

Bonaparte listened, showed leniency, and recruited another agent.

In the absence of useful intelligence and because the garrison at Saint-Remy disregarded routine security measures – after all, what possible danger could approach over the 8,000-foot-high, snow choked pass? – the Austrians were taken by surprise on the morning of May 15. Lannes' advance guard swept through the village at bayonet point at the cost of only two killed. Having cleared a potential choke point, Lannes pressed on in hopes of clearing the entire Aosta Valley. To assist his offensive, Lannes' gunners reassembled two 4-pounders to provide fire support. The next objective was the village of Etroubles. Although mules dragged the cannons into combat position, they were not needed. The Austrians mined the bridge over the Buttier River and withdrew. In their haste someone blundered. The mine failed.

General of division François Watrin sent some voltigeurs to scour the nearby woods while establishing an artillery workshop to remount six more 4-pounders along with two 8-pounders and some howitzers. The next day Watrin marched on Aosta. Would the Sardinians resist?

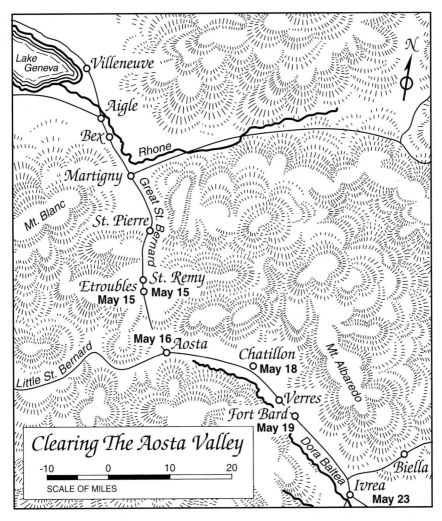

Clearing The Aosta Valley

No. The 6th Light led the way into Aosta thus completing a remarkable 27-mile march in 14 hours during which time they had deployed for battle at least five times. Observing standard intelligence practice, officers examined letters found in Aosta's post office. Lannes relayed the bad news to Berthier: "Genoa is being vigorously bombarded and cannot hold out long." [21]

By May 17, 12,300 infantry, 1,400 cavalry, and 14 cannons had crossed the pass and were operating in the Aosta Valley. Lannes was very much in his element as commander of the advance guard. With characteristic verve he continued his offensive. The first serious resistance came at Chatillon on May 18 where Oberst Rakithevich commanded six infantry companies and three cannons. Rakithevich stationed his men in the village, put a grenadier company in the old chateau, and waited for the onslaught. General Watrin, ignoring the hail of Austrian canister fire, studied the position up close and proposed to Lannes that he launch three columns against the village. One would attack frontally while the other two enveloped the Austrian flanks. Lannes gave the word and the 22nd Demi-brigade stormed the village. A forty minute street fight ensued, but the 22nd prevailed while capturing Rakithevich and two 4-pounders. GM De Briey arrived with some cavalry to cover the Austrian retreat. Colonel Fournier countercharged with one squadron of the 12th Hussars to fix the Austrian cavalry. He committed the remaining three against the Austrian flank. Fournier's tactics proved sound. His hussars routed the Austrians. The French cavalry harried the Austrian infantry, capturing some 350 prisoners. Overall, the French lost 90 while inflicting 550 casualties. More important, Rivaud's cavalry had begun to retrieve their sullied reputation. Then on May 19 the advance ground to a halt before the imposing edifice of Fort Bard.

Somehow the strategic implications of Fort Bard had escaped Bonaparte's gaze. One month ago, he had ordered Berthier to learn about the road past Aosta and had recommended that he consult with the army's Italians who would surely know the terrain. In response, an Italian general, who should have known better, had written to Berthier on May 6 that two columns advancing through the Great and Lesser Saint Bernard Passes "may attack the little fort of Bard in concert and capture it, in order to get rid without delay of this obstacle". Accordingly, while still in Switzerland Berthier had issued orders to Dupont telling him how to dispose of the fort.[22] From a distance it had seemed simple. The first French officers who saw the fort immediately appreciated otherwise.

Fort Bard sat on an isolated rock overlooking the narrow valley where ran the main road. The only alternative routes were mere mountain goat paths, inaccessible to wheeled transport. A battery in barbette occupied the highest point. Half way up the rock was an earthwork with seven large caliber guns which were sited to control the valley. At the foot of the rock was another seven-gun battery, but this one had a restricted field of fire. Beneath the rock and outside of the walls was a three-gun battery. The defenses of the town itself included guardhouses, a drawbridge, and a continuous entrenched perimeter. A loopholed wall ran parallel the main road. The fort's garrison composed 100 men from the Kinski Infantry Regiment, 50 Piedmontese invalides, and some 200 assorted gunners, local militia, and service personnel. There were hardly enough men to crew the 16 heavy caliber artillery pieces, 26 8-pounders, handful of 3-pounders,

Fort Bard from the bridge over the Doire River

and a variety of small-bore rampart guns. But the garrison commander, a Captain Stockard di Bernkopf, was a resourceful and determined officer.

When Berthier examined Fort Bard, he could see no alternative but to summon siege guns from Aosta. For two days, 1,500 infantry and sappers belonging to Boudet's division toiled to mount cannons to bombard the fort. The officers had little doubt that it would surrender. On May 21, General Dupont sent the usual summons: concede now and prevent useless bloodshed. Bernkopf replied, "I will never surrender Bard." After French infantry cleared the village of Bard, at 2 a.m. the next day, three 12-pounders, sited a mere 100 yards from the fort, opened fire. Their shot glanced off with no effect. After a five-hour bombardment, Dupont sent a second summons. This was an ugly ultimatum threatening to put the garrison to the sword unless they surrendered. Again Bernkopf refused.

***

At first, Bonaparte had not been overly concerned about the fort. How could a third-rate fortification stop an army that had conquered the mighty Alps themselves? After resting from his passage over the Saint Bernard, he awoke on May 21 in Etroubles. He inspected

Marmont's workshop where gunners and artificers were busily reassembling the artillery and rode on to Aosta. He received numerous reports: Murat had remounted the cannon for his cavalry; Victor had restored discipline among the infantry; the last troops had crossed the pass. He spent the next three days in Aosta. Slowly his complacency disappeared. Now he had ears for only the most recent news from "this devilish Fort Bard." [24]

On May 25 the First Consul departed Aosta. Twenty-seven miles ahead lay Fort Bard. Bonaparte and Duroc rode some 300 yards ahead of their escort, 25 troopers of the 2nd Chasseurs à cheval. It nearly proved a disastrous folly. Suddenly a pistol-wielding Austrian cavalry patrol approached at the trot along a side road. A Habsburg lieutenant shouted out "Surrender." With no hope of escape Bonaparte reined in his horse. He stalled for time: "Monsieur, who are you to speak to us like that?"

The lieutenant, who was a Belgian and spoke French, replied, "We belong to Vukassovich's corps of scouts."

Bonaparte pled that he must first consult with his fellow officer. In the meantime would the lieutenant please ask his troopers to stop menacing the two Frenchmen with their pistols? The obliging Belgian ordered his men to holster their weapons at which point the chasseurs of Bonaparte's escort appeared. With considerable satisfaction, Bonaparte spoke, "Now, lieutenant, you are the prisoner of the First Consul." [25]

Farther along he rendezvoused with Berthier who explained the problem at hand. Although Lannes had laboriously managed to bypass the fort, two attempts to sneak cannons past it had failed. It seemed impossible to prosecute a regular siege. Bonaparte ascended a height overlooking Fort Bard and studied the situation. Even his expert eye could detect no flaws in the Austrian defenses. He resolved to attempt a *coup de force*. He ordered three storming columns to assemble. Each was to number 200 grenadiers or carabiniers and was to include only the most experienced men. One column would attack the three-gun outwork. A second would march straight against the main gate. A third would cross the 50-yard wide Doire River aboard a raft and try to catch the garrison unawares. For two and one-quarter hours, until darkness had descended upon the narrow valley, the French artillery bombarded the fort. There was little return fire. Fortified by a double distribution of gut wrenching army brandy, at 9:15 p.m. the grenadiers and carabiniers stormed toward the fort.

The first column overran the outwork. The second column began tearing apart the wooden palisades that guarded the main gate while the third embarked upon their raft. Not until the French soldiers reached the walls of the fort itself did the defenders open fire. When they did, the result was devastating. Rockets illuminated the valley and revealed French soldiers laboriously dragging scaling ladders across the rocks. Captain Bernkopf, who throughout the siege provided inspirational leadership, directed his artillery against the hapless storming columns. A mortar bomb demolished the raft. A hail of canister and musket shot, thickened by grenades, bricks, and stones hurled from the parapet, fell upon the French. Beneath Fort Bard's walls, a boulder crushed Colonel Dufour of the 58th Demi-brigade. This renowned swordsman later died from his injuries. Leaderless, the milling French fell to flanking fire from concealed positions. General Loison tried to reanimate the assault and went down with a wound. A third of the storming column fell before the attackers gave up and retreated.

Bonaparte retired to a nearby monastery and gave Marmont orders to move somehow artillery past the fort to reinforce Lannes. Until he received artillery support, Lannes dared not risk open battle since he could do nothing to prevent the Austrians from battering his men at long range. Marmont, in turn, recognized that force had failed. The young gunner resolved to try stealth. The guns had to traverse a long section of road that was exposed to Austrian enfilade fire, pass within pistol shot of the fort's exterior wall, and then exit the town while again under artillery fire until reaching a bend in the road. Consequently, any attempt had to occur at night. In preparation, gunners carefully greased all wheels and chains. Piedmontese volunteers spread straw and manure on the road to dampen noise. Fifty men gathered at each gun to provide motive power.

On the night of May 26, the French waited for a nocturnal storm to gather power to provide concealment. Around midnight the storm's thunder intensified. Its rain quickly swelled the flow of the Doire River alongside of which ran the road. The briskly flowing current supplemented the noise from the sky. As the artillery started to run the gauntlet, fifty musicians began a loud drum and horn fanfare to cover further the noise of wheels on pavement. The first two 4-pounders passed safely before an Austrian sentry detected movement. The garrison tossed fire pots over the walls to illuminate the road and opened fire with the rampart guns. Their fire caught the men assigned to haul three howitzers at the back of the column. At least thirty were hit. The garrison began flinging grenades at which point the French realized that they could do no more. They abandoned one artillery piece in the street and retired.

In total, the French managed to drag six artillery pieces past the fort.[26] Furthermore, on May 24 additional infantry and some 3,000 troopers had skirted the fort by using a mountain track high above Fort Bard. This route was less practicable than the Saint Bernard Pass. In spite of improvements made by sappers and local peasants, it remained a difficult hand scramble, ten minutes of which was under artillery fire from the fort. Each foot soldier carried a cannon ball or artillery cartridge. Trooper Joseph Petit of the Consular Guard recalls, "The cavalry were still more fatigued than the infantry, for the horses were obliged, like the native goats, to leap from stone to stone."[27] The establishment of this precarious supply line, if an improved goat path may be so dignified, permitted the advance guard to resume its advance.

On May 26, Bonaparte passed the fort to join Lannes. He left behind Marmont along with 7,000 men to prosecute the siege against Bernkopf's gallant three hundred. The Austrians resisted until French gunners built a siege battery at a blind spot in the streets below the fort. When the battery opened fire the Austrians had no answer. As soon as the guns created a practicable breech, Bernkopf sued for terms. In spite of French threats, these proved surprisingly lenient; honors of war, officers keep their swords, men retain their private possessions. On June 2 Bernkopf marched out the gate and the French entered Fort Bard. The resistance that he and his men had mounted over a fourteen day span had purchased priceless time for Melas to regain his balance. Whether that septuagenarian warrior possessed the strategic skills to recover was an open question.

NOTES

1. "To the Consuls of the Republic," May 9, 1800, *Correspondance de Napoléon Ier*, VI (Paris, 1860) p. 259.

2. Lorédan Larchey, ed., *The Narrative of Captain Coignet* (New York, 1890), p. 57.

3. "Bonaparte to Berthier," April 24, 1800, *Correspondance de Napoléon Ier*, VI, 230-31.

4. "To General Berthier," April 27, 1800, ibid., p. 240.

5. "To General Berthier," May 5, 1800, ibid., p. 257.

6. "To General Moreau," May 5, 1800, John Howard, ed., *Letters and Documents of Napoleon*, I (New York, 1961), p. 408.

7. André Miot, *Memoirs of Count Miot de Melito* (New York, 1881), p. 168.

8. "To General Masséna," April 9, 1800, *Correspondance de Napoléon Ier*, VI, p. 215.

9. Édouard Gachot, *La Deuxième Campagne d'Italie* (Paris, 1899), p. 32.

10. Gachot, p. 53.

11. Gachot, p. 53.

12. Gachot, pp. 34-35.

13. Wairy Constant, *Memoirs of Constant*, I, trans. Percy Pinkerton (London, 1896), p. 50.

14. Joseph Petit, *Marengo or the Campaign of Italy, by the Army of Reserve Under the Command of the Chief Consul Bonaparte* (Philadelphia, 1801), p. 2.

15. Gachot, p. 109.

16. "Bonaparte to Berthier," May 16, 1800, *Correspondance de Napoléon Ier*, VI, p. 290.

17. Auguste Marmont, *Mémoires du Maréchal Marmont Duc de Raguse*, II (Paris, 1857), p. 115.

18. Constant, I, p. 53.

19. "Berthier to the First Consul," May 20, 1800, *The Campaign of the Reserve Army in 1800 According to Documents Collected by Captain de Cugnac* (Fort Leavenworth, KS, 1922), p. 125. Hereafter cited as *Captain de Cugnac*.

20. Gachot, p. 153 citing L'art de l'espionnage, pp 17-20.

21. "Lannes to Berthier," May 16, 1800, *Captain de Cugnac*, p. 122.

22. "Mainoni to Berthier," May 6, 1800, *Captain de Cugnac*, p. 40. Also see: "Berthier to Dupont," May 13, 1800; p. 116.

23. Gachot, p. 205.

24. Gachot, p. 165.

25. Gachot, pp. 200-01.

26. According to Berthier's orders there were two 4-pounders, two 8-pounders, and two howitzers that reached Lannes. See: "Berthier to Dupont," May 26, 1800, *Captain de Cugnac*, p. 137. Marmont's description of these events is not reliable. See: Marmont, V, pp. 119-120.

27. Petit, p. 9.

Chapter 5

Blitzkrieg
Through Italy

PART 1.
THE TRIALS OF GENERAL MELAS

"Keep Paris quiet. That will enable me to stay away a few more days,
which, I hope, will not be without interest to M. de Melas."[1]

BONAPARTE TO MORTIER, MAY 14, 1800

When GdK Melas began his offensive, he knew about the existence of the Army of Reserve. Initially, it did not overly concern him since he believed that it was en route to Provence. Then came rumors about a French buildup in Switzerland. On May 8, with Suchet retreating toward the Var River, Melas received reports at his headquarters in Nice that seemed to confirm the presence of the French in Switzerland. The next day, additional intelligence persuaded him to begin to gather a part of his force from Elsnitz and Ott and send them toward Turin. Here they would occupy a central position that could address a variety of threats. In addition, Melas forwarded two infantry regiments, the Nauendorf Hussars, all available cavalry batteries, and a field artillery reserve to reinforce FML Kaim. He even ordered the Thurn Infantry Regiment to assemble in Livorno so that it could be transported by sea to reinforce Kaim.

Melas remained in Nice through May 13. Austrian patrols delivered to him a letter addressed to the First Consul in which Masséna stated that he could hold out in Genoa through May 24 and that he hoped for prompt relief from the Army of Reserve. Melas resolved to leave Elsnitz on the Var River and Ott to complete the capture of Genoa. He would accompany three brigades, numbering about 9,000 men, on a march to Turin to join Kaim. From his perspective, the great objective of Genoa was about to fall and the French force in Switzerland did not present a dire threat. The idea that he might have to interrupt his successful offensive and counter-march some 100 miles to defend his own rear was too incredible to entertain. Indicative of his attitude was a letter he sent to a female friend living in Pavia on May 19. Alluding to the 'rumors' of a French presence in Lombardy, he advised her to have no fears on that score and remain in the city.[2]

During the time leading up to French contact with Fort Bard, all Melas knew for certain was that there were multiple enemy columns crossing the Alps. In fact, he confronted from west to east: Turreau's division advancing by Mount Cenis to Susa; the Army of Reserve in the Aosta Valley; Bethencourt's 1,000-man detachment crossing the Simplon Pass; and Moncey's corps from the Army of the Rhine marching through the Saint Gothard Pass. Melas did not know which column actually represented the major French offensive. As the days passed, he concluded that Turreau's division was the advance guard for the Army of Reserve. It was quite proper, therefore, for Melas to switch his headquarters to Turin. While en route he received a report on May 24 describing how the French were bypassing Fort Bard. He still did not know whether this was the major enemy effort, but the news was alarming enough. It was time to concentrate further his forces. He ordered Elsnitz to abandon his position on the Var River and fall back toward Genoa.

Meanwhile, well to the southeast of Fort Bard, General Lannes had been enormously frustrated by his enforced inactivity. Without artillery, Bonaparte forbade him to risk battle. Lannes' foes numbered some 7,000 to 10,000 men, many of them Piedmontese of indifferent fighting ability, commanded by FML Haddick. Haddick had the mission of covering Turin. Finally, on the night of May 22-23, the First Consul authorized Lannes to resume his advance. Lannes' conduct would be enormously important. He had to strike fast and far before Melas truly realized what was up. Otherwise, Melas could block the Army of Reserve from achieving the fertile Po Valley and thus force a return to Switzerland for lack of supplies.

Once unleashed, Lannes moved with characteristic verve. At 4 a.m. on May 23 he had the 22nd Demi-brigade up and marching on Port Saint-Martin. The 22nd found that this village had been abandoned by Haddick's men. The 22nd brushed aside a patrol in the next village, crossed the Doire River, and deployed in column of companies to assault Ivrea. Some 2,000 Austrians and 15 cannons defended Ivrea.

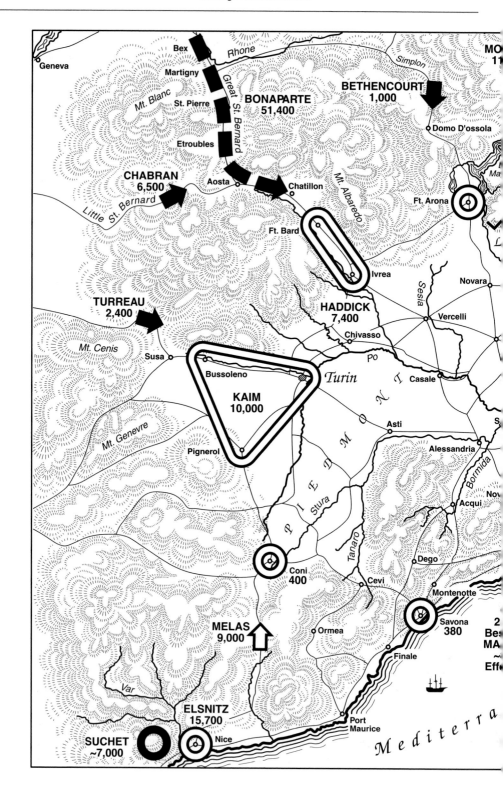

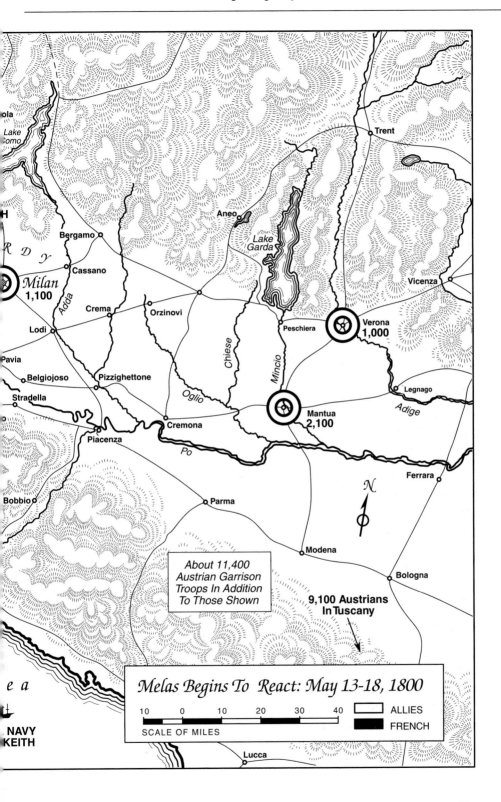

Trent

Lake
Como

ola

Aneo

H

Lake
Garda

Bergamo

RDY

Vicenza

Milan
1,100

Cassano

Crema

Orzinovi

Peschiera

Verona
1,000

Lodi

Pavia

Belgiojoso

Pizzighettone

Legnago

Adige

Stradella

Cremona

Mantua
2,100

Piacenza

Po

Ferrara

Bobbio

Parma

N

About 11,400
Austrian Garrison
Troops In Addition
To Those Shown

Modena

Bologna

9,100 Austrians
In Tuscany

e a

NAVY
KEITH

Melas Begins To React: May 13-18, 1800

| 10 | 0 | 10 | 20 | 30 | 40 | | ALLIES |
| SCALE OF MILES | | | | | | | FRENCH |

Lucca

One of their first shots killed a French battalion commander. Enraged, the 22nd made a bayonet charge that overran the Austrian artillery. Protracted, but relatively bloodless, house to house combat ensued. It ended abruptly around noon when a Captain Cochet forced the gate of the citadel and compelled the garrison to surrender. At the cost of seven killed and 25 wounded, Lannes was master of Ivrea and 500 prisoners along with 15 Austrian artillery pieces. Not content with this triumph, he drove his men along the road toward Turin until nightfall.

That evening the six artillery pieces that had passed beneath Fort Bard joined the advance guard. In addition, Olivier Rivaud's entire brigade arrived. At dawn Lannes resumed his march toward Haddick's entrenched line along the Chiusella River. The Chiusella defile was like a cork in a bottle, blocking egress from the Aosta valley. It was a formidable position made more so by the fact that Haddick had received reinforcements. Five thousand men, including the guards of the King of Sardinia and 20 cannons, manned the trenches overlooking the fast-flowing Chiusella River. Another 4,000 occupied the adjacent high ground to block flanking attempts. Haddick believed that he faced only one French division. He had no idea that the entire Army of Reserve was now in the Aosta Valley. Because of this misconception, he did not order the wooden bridge over the Chiusella destroyed.

Having spent a day reconnoitering carefully, Lannes ordered Watrin's division to storm the defile. At 5 a.m. on May 26, the 6th Light stealthily advanced through a wheat field toward the bridge. The vigilant defenders spotted them. From behind a log barricade, four cannons shot apart the unit's 2nd battalion. Under a hail of canister fire, officers reformed the demi-brigade. Arms on their shoulders, the infantry stormed across the bridge. The defenders retired and by so doing unmasked ten more Habsburg cannons. Again blasts of canister flailed the French column. Capitalizing on their disorder, a Major Weiss led a battalion of the Kinski Infantry Regiment, supported by the Banat Grenz, in a counterattack. They drove the French into the river. Seeing this debacle, Watrin ordered the 22nd Demi-brigade to counterattack. The 22nd assaulted the bridge in close column while the 40th Demi-brigade advanced in its wake. Simultaneously, the 6th Light returned to the combat. Moving through neck deep water, the 6th Light scrambled up the bank, endured point blank canister fire, and charged the Habsburg battery.

When the French assault began, Haddick had summoned his cavalry. They arrived at this juncture. Thick underbrush made the ground poorly suited for cavalry action. Nonetheless, General Palfy led four squadrons in a charge against the dispersed French light infantry. The 6th's buglers immediately sounded the rally. The men ran behind a nearby farm where they formed squares. The Austrian cavalry could make no impression against these human bastions. Palfy fell with a mortal wound. Enraged, his cavalry tried a charge against the adjacent squares formed by the 40th and 22nd. Again they failed in the face of disciplined musket volleys. Lannes sent Jean Rivaud's light cavalry brigade to reinforce his infantry. At about the same time the last Austrian reserve unit, the La Tour Dragoons, charged to cover the retreat of their fellow troopers. The dragoons overran a company of the 6th Light and advanced toward the 40th's squares.

Looming in the smoke behind the squares was a mounted party of French officers. Although the La Tour Dragoons did not immediately recognize them, they included army commander Berthier, corps commander Duhesme, and divisional commander Boudet. And there as well was First Consul Bonaparte. So perilous did the situation appear to the French that they all drew their swords. Before these officers had to engage, infantry fire struck the La Tour Dragoons and the Austrian charge dissolved. Although the dragoons rallied to conduct two more charges, the combat was lost. The 12th Hussars spearheaded a vigorous pursuit that chased the Austrians southward toward Turin.

Typically imprecise French accounting mentions 250 to 300 French casualties, a total Bonaparte reduced to 200 in the official report. On the Austrian side, in addition to gallant General Palfy, six Austrian officers and 115 men fell dead. The French captured 224 wounded along with 60 sound men. More importantly, Lannes had forced the Chiusella defile. If the Austrians could not hold this barrier, it was unlikely they could hold any other blocking position since the terrain now opened onto the great Lombardy plain. That evening, with the scales removed from his eyes, Haddick wrote Melas that he had battled against 20,000 Frenchmen. Unless Melas hurried to his succor, Haddick feared all of Piedmont and Lombardy would be overrun.

***

Bonaparte returned to Ivrea after the combat ended. He ordered Lannes to remain in observation at Chivasso on the Po River. Then he went to the city's Royal College where he conducted a long conference with Berthier, Murat, and his staff. Ivrea was at the intersection of the two major roads. One ran southwest toward Chivasso and on to Turin. Lannes wanted the army to march in this direction since it offered the quickest way to relieve Masséna. But the First Consul was playing for higher stakes. His aim was nothing less than the destruction of Melas' army. Accordingly, he turned away from this conventional solution and instead resolved to maneuver against Melas' line of communication. At 11 p.m. a flood of new orders issued from the Royal College; the objective, Milan. While Lannes diverted Austrian attention by continuing to menace Turin, Duhesme would march his two-division corps toward Vercelli, a city half-way between Turin and Milan and squarely on one of the major east-west highways that served as Melas' supply line. Murat with 4,000 troopers, supported by another infantry division, would take a different route to unite with Duhesme at Vercelli. The audacity of Bonaparte's strategy comes into clear view when one remembers that with this set of orders Bonaparte was committing his army to an offensive at a time when his entire available artillery comprised six guns along with a handful of captured pieces. Something like this would not recur until Erwin Rommel emerged on his western desert stage during the Second World War.

Bonaparte remained in Ivrea the next day. At 3 a.m. on May 28 he took horse to inspect Lannes' men. With practiced ease he traversed the ranks, singling out particularly brave soldiers with a hearty compliment and a tweak of the ear. "Here is the brave 22nd who was the first over the Chiusella. Good work. Lannes is proud of you." He addressed the 40th: "One can neither form square nor shoot better than you have done...You are all worthy of your comrades who served at Arcola." While inspecting the 12th Hussars: "Why here are my hussars of Chatillon; I greet you comrades; you are going to cover yourselves with glory in Italy." The First Consul spent the most time with the 28th Demi-brigade, an unfortunate unit that had spent the past two years in the mountains, including those companies which had garrisoned the Saint Bernard. Bonaparte commiserated with them; theirs had been a hard service. He complimented them for never complaining and concluded with the promise that at the first battle the 28th would serve in the advance guard as proof of his esteem.[3] Content that all was well along this line, Bonaparte returned to Ivrea.

On June 1 he was in Novare where he received a report from his spy Toli. Toli said that Melas had ignored reports from Fort Bard in order to prepare for his invasion of Provence. Not until a dragoon officer of the La Tour regiment told Melas in person that he had seen Bonaparte near Romano did Melas become alarmed. Then the Austrian general received Haddick's report of the combat at Chiusella. At last Melas recognized his peril. Toli claimed that Melas was bitterly angry at his subordinate's failure to detect earlier the presence of the Army of Reserve. The Austrian general reckoned that now Bonaparte would march on Turin. To protect that city he had ordered forces concentrated at Turin. Since Toli's report jibed with dispatches Bonaparte had received from Suchet, the First Consul felt confident that he understood Austrian intentions. When another spy provided detailed intelligence regarding Austrian dispositions in Lombardy, Bonaparte was well content. He informed Minister of War Carnot: "All goes here well enough. The enemy appears completely put off the track."[4]

Bonaparte's assessment was correct. By May 27, Melas had massed about 18,000 men around Turin. FML Haddick had rebuffed Turreau's advance from Mount Cenis and Melas no longer believed that this was the major French effort. He realized that Bonaparte was concentrating his forces at Ivrea. He remained wedded to the notion that the Army of Reserve's mission was the direct relief of Genoa. He decided to thwart his foe by defending the line of the Po River against a thrust from Ivrea. When Lannes failed to press an attack against the Po line, Melas concluded that his dispositions were sound and that victory remained within grasp. He did not understand that Lannes' efforts were actually a diversion to cover Bonaparte's march on Milan.

PART 2.
MILAN INTERLUDE

Two major rivers stood between the Army of Reserve and Milan. Under different circumstances, they would have presented serious obstacles. Because of the dashing leadership of Bonaparte's subordinates, they were easily overcome. A cavalry officer conducted the 2nd and 15th Chasseurs à cheval on a 36 mile march in order to surprise an Austrian cavalry brigade along the banks of the Sésia. To open the ford, the carabiniers of the 9th Light waded into water. The swollen water swept the first four downstream where they drowned. Undaunted, the officers and men who knew how to swim organized themselves to assist the nonswimmers across the ford. They formed a bridgehead on the far side to secure the ford. During the night of May 27-28, Murat and Duhesme personally scouted the river. At dawn, while the cavalry crossed the ford, grenadiers boarded two fishing boats to conduct an assault crossing. The defenders were a hard bitten émigré unit named the Legion of Bussy. But the Legion could not withstand the dynamic, two-prong attack.

Then it becomes a race to Milan between Duhesme and Murat. Murat, in hopes of deceiving his rival, failed to report his position and intentions. But Berthier informed Duhesme of the Gascon's plans. So as not to lose a minute, Duhesme was again at the front on May 30 searching for a ford over the Tessin River. From the heights across the river, Habsburg gunners opened fire. Ignoring the canister rounds flailing the ground around him, Duhesme calmly completed his reconnaissance and then ordered his adjutant to assemble the boats. Unbeknownst to one another, Duhesme and Murat conducted nearly simultaneous assault crossings over the last barrier before Milan. That timeless goad for good officers, the opportunity to earn distinction and honor, had inspired sterling conduct.

At 4 p.m. on June 2, Murat led six cavalry regiments through the Vercelli gate into Milan. Behind him marched the infantry to blockade two Austrian regiments which had holed up inside the central citadel. The First Consul planned a triumphal, Roman-like entrance for himself. He wanted to dazzle and awe the Milanese. His staff found a grand, gilt-leafed coach that had belonged to an Italian nobleman. They selected six white horses to pull it. Bonaparte dressed in a general's uniform and climbed aboard. Three gleaming postillions took their position. The highly polished troopers of the Consular Guard trotted alongside. While Bonaparte could command much, he could not control the weather. As the coach approached Milan, a terrific thunderstorm broke. Bonaparte took shelter in a nearby farmhouse where he had to content himself with preening before a handful of astonished peasants. Finally the storm let up and the bedraggled group entered Milan.

A large crowd had assembled along the streets. Most greeted the First Consul with silence. The Milanese had not liked its first encounter with Bonaparte's army back in 1796 – they had revolted and been brutally crushed – and they liked it no better a second time around. Bonaparte arrived at Milan's central square in a foul mood, angry at the rain, angry at his indifferent reception. His first administrative acts were designed to bring the proud Milanese to their knees in humble tribute to Bonaparte and to France. He worked until two in the morning and the labor put him in a better mood. He dictated the official bulletin that said in part that Milan greeted the First Consul with "great outbursts of joy."[5] French people had not yet coined the phrase 'to lie like a bulletin.' They would soon learn.

If the mood of the city was not what he wanted, the strategic situation remained promising. Bonaparte had switched his line of communication from the Saint Bernard to the more secure Simplon and Saint Gothard. Milan had provided sufficient food and material to nourish a continuing offensive. Murat brought captured Austrian correspondence. Careful study revealed nothing too threatening. With the capture of Milan, Bonaparte occupied all of northern Italy between the Alps and the Po. Within this territory he had captured several garrisons and the major cities, seized immense quantities of provisions and munitions including pontoons, and secured his own communications back through Switzerland. He now possessed a secure line of retreat in the event of a reverse. It was a great accomplishment, but now Bonaparte understood that his army needed a rest halt. Everything from shoes to wagon wheels had taken a hard pounding during the alpine crossing. A short break would also permit General Bon Moncey's 11,500-man corps to join the Army of Reserve.

But having achieved a central position, Bonaparte did not intend that his army remain totally idle. He ordered Duhesme to drive the Austrians commanded by FML Vukassovich east toward Mantua. This would ensure that no Austrians from the east could disrupt his plans. Meanwhile, the balance of his army refitted around Milan. Unlike Melas, who allowed the siege of Genoa to occupy a large number of men and most of his attention, Bonaparte had no intention of laying siege to any of the Lombard citadels. Instead he masked them with the smallest detachments possible in order to concentrate his army for field operations.

Duhesme's march east followed the path of Bonaparte's 1796 campaign. Now as then the situation demanded a succession of river crossings. In an assault much like Bonaparte's combat at Lodi, generals and officers placed themselves at the head of the 9th Light and led that unit across the Lambro River bridge into the face of Austrian cannon fire. An intrepid grenadier slew six enemy artillerymen and thus cleared the way for his unit to follow. The 11th Hussars pursued the fleeing enemy until encountering the Legion of Bussy. The Legion attempted a rear guard action but could not resist the hussars' impetuosity. Among the prisoners were five unfortunate émigré officers. These were not insignificant combats. On June 3 alone Duhesme's corps suffered 60 killed and 200 wounded.

After storming the bridge at Lodi on June 4, Duhesme received orders to cease his pursuit. He was to clear both banks of the Po River between Cremona and Plaisance with Loison's reinforced division and three cavalry regiments. The balance of his command was needed back west. Although disappointed, Duhesme obeyed orders with his customary energy. The 5th Dragoons spearheaded the drive on Cremona. They encountered 400 chasseurs commanded by an Irish major. Again it was a case of a gallant Habsburg officer fighting tenaciously but without support. When enveloped by the French cavalry the chasseurs had to surrender. The Austrian officers were furious about their plight and chose to break their swords rather than hand them to the victors.

Shortly thereafter, a Habsburg deserter told Duhesme that the Austrians had begun to fire Cremona's magazines. Because of Fort Bard's resistance, the Army of Reserve's logistical situation remained perilous. Therefore, Duhesme's orders had stressed the importance of capturing supplies. French sappers opened a breach in the city's walls. In an unusual maneuver, cuirassiers charged through the opening and scattered the defenders. At a stiff price, 5 French officers were killed, 11 wounded, and at least 300 rank and file knocked out of action, Duhesme was master of the city. Service personnel immediately organized the captured materiel, sending 200 wagons to Boudet and Murat and 50,000 pairs of shoes to Lannes.

In the coming days, all that remained was to drive the Austrians east toward Mantua. On June 14 came a last, fierce combat, pitting 800 Tuscan hussars and the remnants of the Legion of Bussy against the French cavalry. The Legion was determined to die game. Its foot contingent formed square and, exhibiting rare bravery, advanced toward the French cavalry. Brave but foolish; Duhesme ordered up two horse guns which began to pulverize the square with canister fire. A platoon of dragoons charged a side of the square that had collapsed from this fire. They hewed left and right and the square dissolved. The Tuscan hussars charged to relieve the Legion infantry. Duhesme, in turn, committed his own staff alongside the French chasseurs à cheval and dragoons in a countercharge. A memorable melee ensued during which the Tuscan hussars mounted at least four separate charges before conceding the field. As the French cried victory, the Legion's second in command, an émigré named Curtius, and General Barko each seized a standard, placed themselves at the head of the remaining infantry and charged! A French captain engaged Curtius in a furious sword fight. The captain delivered three saber cuts to Curtius' head and back, forcing him to relinquish his reins. As he fell from the saddle, Curtius cried out "Long live the King!"[6] General Barko also received a sword wound but managed to escape thanks to the devotion of ten of his Tuscan troopers who conducted a determined rearguard action as they escorted him from the fray. By the time the combat ended, 300 of the Tuscan hussars had fallen.

Events to the west overshadowed Duhesme's brilliant little campaign. Yet he had accomplished much. His successes allowed Bonaparte to turn his back on the Austrians operating east of Milan and concentrate on dealing with Melas. Napoleon Bonaparte would recognize Duhesme's service with a series of minor promotions. However, as Emperor he would find him lacking until Duhesme again distinguished himself during the 1814 campaign. The valorous Duhesme rallied to Napoleon in 1815. While leading the Young Guard in the defense of Plancenoit at the Battle of Waterloo, Duhesme received a mortal wound.

Duhesme had his counterparts among the Frenchmen who had served in the Legion of Bussy. Many who escaped from the fighting in Italy joined a British-sponsored regiment, the Chasseurs Brittanique, and continued the fight to overthrow the Corsican usurper for the next fourteen years.

***

At the spy's hour of 11 p.m. on June 5, Toli returned to Milan. Bonaparte greeted him, "You haven't been shot yet?"[7]

Indeed, Toli was playing a dangerous game, shuttling back and forth across the lines and reporting to both Bonaparte and Melas. The First Consul was uncertain if Toli could be trusted but concluded that while Toli was certainly receiving pay from both sides, on balance he was still Bonaparte's man. Toli's latest intelligence described Melas as in the process of concentrating his forces between Alessandria and Tortona. He related to Bonaparte Melas' desire to have Toli locate the French army and learn its strength. Accordingly, Bonaparte dictated the report that Toli would take to Melas. To be convincing it could not be too wild. Still, Bonaparte could deceive Melas by either undercounting or exaggerating his strength. He chose the latter, hoping to gain time to perfect his dispositions by imposing caution upon his foe. So Toli departed in the darkness to convey to Melas the intelligence that about 80,000 French were in northern Italy when in fact there were closer to 50,000.

Part of that 50,000 had just arrived. General Moncey's 11,500-man corps had endured a long trek from the Rhine front and through the Saint Gothard pass. With Moncey present Bonaparte had his entire strength mustered. When planning his campaign back in Paris, the First Consul had anticipated having 70,000 or even 80,000 men. But

Moreau had sent fewer than half the 25,000 men he had promised. Bonaparte had also counted upon the Army of Italy, but Masséna's soldiers lay besieged in Genoa. Undaunted, Bonaparte resolved to bring Melas to battle. He sought nothing less than a battle of annihilation. To begin, he intended to seize the main Austrian route to safety, the highway running from Alessandria through the Stradella defile to Piacenza. In addition, he had to cover Melas' possible secondary lines of retreat to the north and south of the Po River and guard his own new line of operations by the Saint Gothard Pass. These secondary operations required about 20,000 men and left him with only 30,000 to engage Melas. Consequently, if the Austrian commander concentrated his forces, Bonaparte was unlikely to have sufficient manpower to win a decisive tactical success.

The First Consul also worried about prolonging his absence from Paris. He believed that his insecure position demanded an overwhelming victory and that it had better come soon. Yet he did not exhibit any sense of immediate urgency. Instead, he spent seven nights in Milan, and it may well be that the presence of the enchanting opera diva, Giuseppina Grassini, partially explains the hiatus in his campaign. Bonaparte also spent a fair amount of time attending to the establishment of the Cis-alpine Republic. While the creation of this vassal state would benefit France in the long run, it was hardly the stuff of great moment. Likewise, on June 6 Bonaparte reconnoitered the Austrian-held citadel in Milan and dictated instructions for its reduction. This too was not a vital objective. The schedule the next day also involved less than urgent business when the First Consul held a very satisfactory troop review that featured his Consular Guard.

Bonaparte's secretary had standing orders never to awaken him to report good news, but to inform him immediately upon the receipt of bad news. So it was that Bourrienne entered his chambers at 11 p.m. on June 7 to find Bonaparte in bed with Madame Grassini. Bourrienne reported that Murat had intercepted one of Melas' couriers who was carrying a report to Vienna. It announced the fall of Genoa. Initially Bonaparte refused to credit it: "Bah!" he snapped at Bourrienne, "you do not understand German."[8]

Closer scrutiny revealed that Bourrienne was right. This intelligence changed everything. Suddenly 20,000 of Austria's finest soldiers, men whom Bonaparte had dismissed from his plans, entered the calculus of battle. Thoroughly aroused, Bonaparte issued a flurry of orders. He postponed his proclamation regarding the Cis-alpine Republic, took steps to ensure that nothing and no one – particularly a disgruntled local populace – interrupted his line of communication, and sent Berthier to the front to explain to Lannes the new situation. In sum, he discarded his bedroom clothes and statesman's robes to put back on his soldier's uniform.

NOTES

1. "To Major-General Mortier," May 14, 1800, John Howard, ed., *Letters and Documents of Napoleon*, I (New York, 1961), p. 415.
2. The French intercepted this letter. It is mentioned in "Bonaparte to Carnot," June 4, 1800, *Correspondance de Napoléon Ier*, VI (Paris, 1860), p. 333.
3. "Bulletin of the Army of Reserve," May 29, 1800, ibid., pp. 223-24.
4. "To Citizen Carnot," May 29, 1800, ibid. p. 321.
5. "Bulletin of the Army of Reserve," June 3, 1800, ibid. p. 328.
6. Édouard Gachot, *La Deuxième Campagne d'Italie* (Paris, 1899), p. 341.
7. Gachot, p. 247.
8. Louis de Bourrienne, *Memoirs of Napoleon Bonaparte*, II (New York, 1906), p. 9. Bourrienne describes this incident as occurring at 4 a.m. on June 8 but he mis-remembers. It is another illustration of the need to use Bourrienne with extreme caution. Melas' report is probably the one reproduced in Jacques Campredon, *La Défense du Var et Le Passage Des Alpes 1800* (Paris, 1889), beginning on p. 381.

Chapter 6

To the Plain of the Scrivia

PART 1.
THE VISE TIGHTENS

"The result of all our efforts will be cloudless glory and secure peace."
Army of Reserve Order of the Day, June 6, 1800[1]

The time Bonaparte spent in Milan provided Melas with another opportunity to recover his balance. He had planned to concentrate a formidable force around Turin to repel the anticipated French attack. The inept performance of FML Anton Elsnitz subtracted a significant fraction of that force. Back on the night of May 26 Elsnitz, who commanded on the Var front after Melas marched to Turin, began his retreat from the Var River. Initially Elsnitz's goal was to cover the siege of Genoa. From the beginning it was a disorderly withdrawal. When the French entered Nice the next day they found that the Austrians had abandoned 800 sick and numerous cannons. Although he outnumbered Suchet's command, Elsnitz offered only feeble resistance along a succession of fine defensive positions between Nice and Genoa. Austrian morale plummeted as Elsnitz marched east. Elsnitz's Piedmontese soldiers in particular began to desert. Evidence of this decline encouraged Suchet to try to move around the Austrian flank and block Elsnitz's retreat through the Col di Tenda.

On June 1 the French overtook the Austrian rear guard and captured 400 men. A vigorous pursuit compelled Elsnitz to abandon 10 artillery pieces. After a two hour rest, the French advanced to attack a new Habsburg rear guard that had taken position behind earthworks atop a mountain pass. Exhibiting great elan, Suchet's men overran the works and secured another 500 prisoners. Prevented from using the main road through the Col di Tenda, Elsnitz struggled to extricate his force via secondary routes through the coastal mountains. On June 3 the French pursuit again contacted the Austrians. Elsnitz abandoned his baggage, and more artillery, and barely escaped.

Elsnitz had managed to prevent Suchet from interfering with the siege of Genoa, but at great cost. Suchet reported that his pursuit from the Var to the Col di Tenda netted 7,000 prisoners, 30 artillery pieces, and six flags. Well might an Austrian officer whine in a letter to his family, "affairs here have taken a turn for the worse."[2] Indicative of the decline in Austrian morale, the officer concluded with instructions about how to dispose of his possessions in the event of his death. Melas had counted on Elsnitz bringing him about 17,000 men. Instead, Elsnitz brought only 7,876 demoralized soldiers.

Unaware of Elsnitz's looming debacle, Melas continued to assess intelligence and make reasonable adjustments. When the French failed to do the expected and advance on Turin, he revised his plans. On May 31 he ordered a general concentration at Alessandria. His Chief of Staff, GM Anton Zach, vigorously endorsed this notion. While waiting to achieve the desired concentration, Melas took comfort in the fact that although the fall of Milan had severed his main line of communication, he retained a secondary connection with the fortresses of eastern Italy and with Vienna itself. That secondary route was the Alessandria to Mantua highway. One strategic point along that highway was Piacenza. Melas well recognized Piacenza's importance since it was a major road hub and it contained a valuable supply depot. Because Piacenza was on the south side of the Po River, it seemed secure from any French thrust. The Po also presented a major obstacle to a direct westward French advance from Milan.

Sheltered by the Po River, Melas conceived a strategy whereby he would first unite his forces at Alessandria and then attack Bonaparte. At this time his preference was to strike the French flank by marching north from Piacenza. Zach concurred. Accordingly, Austrian headquarters issued a flurry of additional orders on May 31. To Ott: send a brigade from Genoa to help defend Piacenza. To FML Andreas O'Reilly: march with a 3,000-man force through the Stradella defile to that city. To the reserve artillery: accompany O'Reilly and move into Piacenza's fortified bridgehead on the north side of the Po River. There it would be well-positioned to support an offensive. To units in the Parma area: march north to join in the defense of Piacenza. On the map, a three prong convergence on Piacenza seemed feasible. Although the sudden loss of Milan was a shock, in his June 5 report to the Aulic Council Melas optimistically wrote that the campaign was progressing favorably.[3] What he failed to account for was the speed of the French advance.

Ever since he had bypassed Fort Bard, Lannes had had to balance carefully the need to avoid bringing on a major battle with the glittering opportunities available if he maneuvered boldly. Although thwarted in his dreams of playing the hero by marching to relieve Genoa, he had performed brilliantly. While he attracted Melas' attention by feinting toward Turin, the main army had marched on Milan. Then Lannes marched southeast toward Pavia. The Austrian garrison of this city knew about the French buildup at Milan to the north. Lannes' appearance from the west surprised it. At nine in the evening of June 3, the French swept into Pavia. In addition to seizing 191 Piedmontese artillery pieces, the French secured a large Austrian hospital with 2,000 sick, and most importantly, another valuable bounty of flints, powder, and supplies.

Now the Army of Reserve lay poised for an assault crossing over the Po River. Although the French had captured some pontoons, the army lacked a true pontoon train. Consequently, it had to rely upon the surprise capture of a bridge or an improvised passage utilizing whatever boats were at hand. Bonaparte's plan relied upon both approaches. Lannes would advance southeast from Pavia to the river and cross wherever he could. His objective was to block the Stradella defile and thus sever the main Austrian supply line. Meanwhile, Murat's cavalry supported by Boudet's infantry division would try to seize the bridge at Piacenza further downstream. Bonaparte would remain in Milan, ready to reinforce the first successful crossing.

That an improvised and rapid advance could be a two-edged sword became apparent during the afternoon of June 5. The Austrian General Mosel had about 400 men in Piacenza. When the campaign began in the spring, no Austrian officer had contemplated that the city's bridgehead north of the Po would have military utility. Its works had fallen into decay. Frequent rain and river flood completed the job. When GM Mosel had learned of the French capture of Milan, he set his small garrison to work. His men erected three artillery platforms to elevate the guns above the mire, strengthened the parapet, and deepened the ditch in front. Six guns and one infantry company defended the bridgehead. Mosel placed a detachment of Tyrolese chasseurs as pickets outside the work and sent his entire cavalry force, 30 chasseurs of the Legion of Bussy, to scout toward Milan. On June 5 these horsemen encountered the 11th Hussars leading Murat's advance in mid-afternoon. They and the pickets scampered back to safety and awaited developments.

The French hussars approached to within 500 yards of the bridgehead when the Austrian cannons opened fire. The hussars flitted to safety. Clearly what was ahead was a job for the infantry. Murat conferred with Boudet about how best to advance. They ordered up the single available artillery piece to bombard the Austrians and formed three assault columns. While the 9th Light operated on the flanks, three grenadier companies and a line battalion charged the middle. The plan called for the central column to attract the Austrians' attention while the two flank columns delivered the main assault. The unforeseen flaw in this plan was that the flank advances had to brave fire from across the river as well as canister from the bridgehead itself. The French closed to within short pistol range of the parapet only to be thwarted at the ditch. The assault stalled as the attackers opened up into skirmish order and began firing at the defenders sheltered behind the earthworks. Boudet decided to wait until nightfall and ordered a withdrawal. He had lost 500 men killed and wounded.

Mosel's men had done well. For eight hours they held off a superior force. Having lost 120 casualties, they were now reduced to no more than 280 men and the expected reinforcements had not arrived. At 10 p.m. Mosel withdrew the artillery, abandoned the bridgehead, and severed the pontoon bridge spanning the Po. Although the French later occupied the position they had failed to secure a crossing.

At 4 a.m. the next morning, June 6, Lannes' men began to cross the river upstream. Although they initially encountered no opposition, since they had only a handful of boats it proved slow going. Meanwhile, O'Reilly was on the march toward Piacenza. At 6 a.m., O'Reilly learned that Lannes had crossed the Po behind him. This was the kind of unexpected event that often unsettled Habsburg generals. O'Reilly committed a portion of his force to contain Lannes and pondered what to do. The presence of the reserve artillery on the road further ahead made his choice difficult. If Lannes advanced from the river it was vulnerable to capture. Then O'Reilly's problems increased when he learned that Piacenza had fallen.

After the initial French repulse, Murat had resolved that rather than try to occupy the bridgehead and strike directly at the city he would outflank Piacenza. At 2 a.m. Murat had sent Boudet downstream from the city. Boudet's men collected a few boats and crossed to the far bank. Although Mosel's vedettes detected them, the Austrians could do nothing to oppose Boudet's soldiers. Soon the entire 9th Light was over the Po and marching on Piacenza. They occupied the city before the defenders could destroy its magazines.

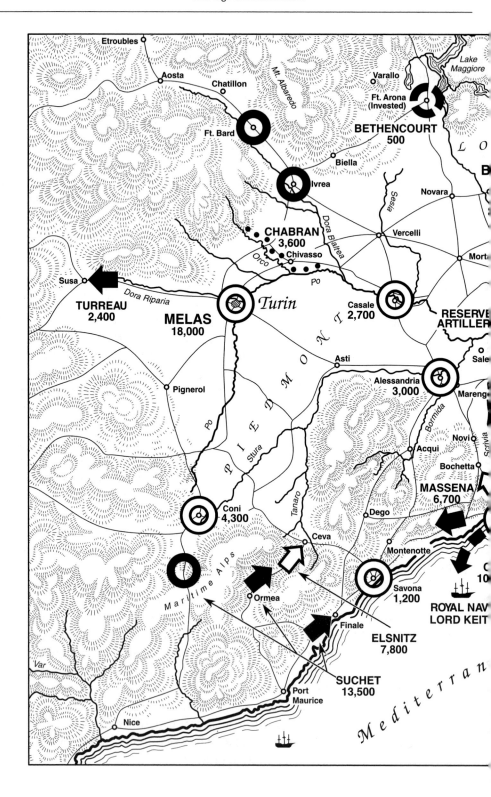

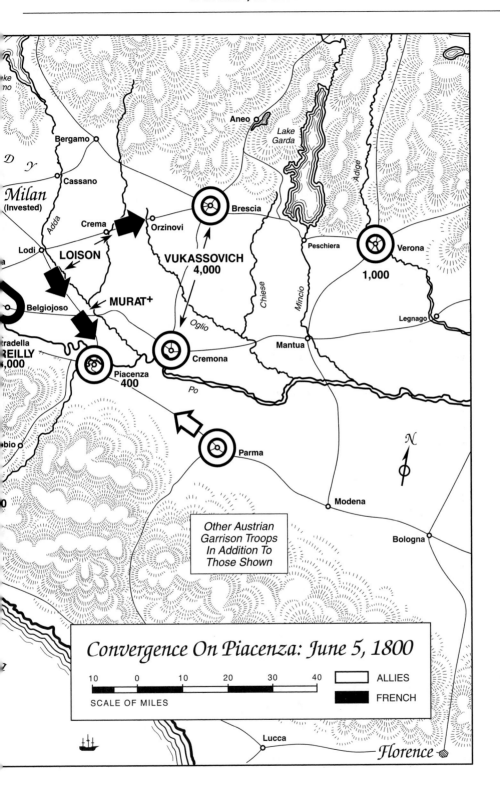

Milan
(Invested)

Bergamo

Cassano

Crema

Orzinovi

LOISON

Lodi

VUKASSOVICH
4,000

Brescia

Aneo

Lake
Garda

Adige

Peschiera

Verona

1,000

Belgiojoso

MURAT+

Chiese

Mincio

Legnago

Oglio

tradella

REILLY+
,000

Cremona

Mantua

Piacenza
400

Po

bio

Parma

N

Other Austrian
Garrison Troops
In Addition To
Those Shown

Modena

Bologna

Convergence On Piacenza: June 5, 1800

| 10 | 0 | 10 | 20 | 30 | 40 | | ALLIES |
| SCALE OF MILES | | | | | | | FRENCH |

Lucca

Florence

So it was that O'Reilly learned that the city he had been sent to secure had already fallen while the slow moving artillery convoy intended to defend the bridgehead was almost trapped between Boudet and Lannes. In the words of the Austrian account, "A great disorder reigned...along the entire road." O'Reilly decided that saving the artillery convoy took precedence over the defense of Piacenza. He was prepared to sacrifice his command to save the artillery. O'Reilly sent a mixed force comprising the Reisky Infantry Regiment and Ottochaner Grenz, the Lobkowitz Dragoons, and two horse batteries to contain Lannes. According to Lannes, the Austrians opposing him fought with great spirit: "They were still proud of their victories [referring to the capture of Genoa]; they fell on us at the bayonet and drove in the center of the line."[5] Fortunately for the French, another 500-man wave had just crossed the Po and they managed to stabilize the center. Because Lannes had neither artillery nor cavalry over the river, a difficult, eleven-hour struggle ensued. When Lannes finally gained the highway, O'Reilly and the reserve artillery convoy had passed safely to the west.

Back in Piacenza, Murat and Boudet learned that an Austrian infantry force was approaching from the southwest. They belonged to Ott's command, the brigade Melas had ordered to march to the city to protect the magazines. Some 600 men of the Klebeck Regiment under the command of a Major Fruhauf composed the column's advance guard. They gallantly charged the Parma gate. Fruhauf's men carried the gate, lost it to a counterattack, and regained it once more. Murat dispatched reinforcements who threatened Fruhauf's flank. However, O'Reilly had sent two squadrons of the Nauendorf Hussars, commanded by Major Grafen, to Piacenza. They providently arrived at this juncture. Major Grafen sized up the situation and charged the French horse. Covered by this charge the remnants of the Klebeck Regiment withdrew east toward Alessandria.

To complete this day of Habsburg blunder, the last of the infantry that Melas had detailed to defend Piacenza approached the city from the southeast. They were a single battalion of the Thurn Regiment, a unit which Melas had ordered brought by sea from Livorno on May 8. They drove in the French pickets until they encountered overwhelming force. In spite of rapidly rising water, French pontonniers had managed to construct a trail bridge connecting the abandoned bridgehead with the city. Horsemen of the 11th Hussars crossed in time to deal with the hapless soldiers of the Thurn Regiment. The hussars hounded the Austrians back the way they had come, capturing some 300 of them.

So ended a swirling 24 hours during which the French experienced initial rebuff followed by twin successes. In exchange for fewer than 1,000 casualties, the French had inflicted more than double that loss. The Austrians were left in no shape to defend Piacenza's citadel, which required a minimum garrison of 600 men. The disjointed Austrian efforts had left only 250 men inside the walls. In spite of adverse weather and in the absence of a bridging train, the French had successfully conducted two crossings over the Po River and captured a major Austrian base at Piacenza. Having secured Melas' last line of communication along the highway between Piacenza and Stradella, the French had accomplished the objective Bonaparte had conceived when he first imagined the creation of the Army of Reserve. By the end of June 6, the noose around Melas was drawing tight.

Part 2.
The Battle of Montebello

At 8 a.m. on June 9 troopers of the Consular Guard escorted Bonaparte and his staff from Milan. The direction was south toward Pavia. The weather had been rainy and the First Consul had a bad cold which put him out of sorts. Nonetheless, the early afternoon found Bonaparte discussing with Marmont how best to utilize the Piedmontese cannons the French had captured in Pavia. It says something about the effectiveness of the Piedmontese Army that among the 191 cannons to choose from, Marmont could find but a handful that met French serviceability standards. In a better mood – gunners always enjoy conversing with fellow gunners about the science of artillery practice – Bonaparte resumed his ride south toward the Po River. He expected to meet with Berthier and Lannes that evening. To his surprise he suddenly began to hear the steady roar of cannon fire. A flaw in the wind had apparently prevented the noise from reaching Pavia. Bonaparte spurred his horse into a fast pace. He arrived at Stradella to find the town full of French wounded. Here he learned that Lannes and Victor had just contested the Battle of Montebello.

Back on June 7, Ott was at Novi, about halfway between Genoa and Alessandria with FML Vogelsang's and FML Schellenberg's divisions comprising some of the best Austrian units in the army. Here he had learned that Lannes had crossed the Po River. Possibly on the basis of the reports from his own spies, he guessed that the French mainbody had yet to cross. Accordingly, he resolved to implement his orders to march to Piacenza. He apparently did not entertain the notion to engage and defeat Lannes' isolated force. Rains and flood delayed him until June 8. By 8 p.m. that evening, Ott's column reached Voghera on the western side of the Stradella defile. Although able to join O'Reilly's command, Ott was in total ignorance of nearby French dispositions. Vogelsang ordered an émigré captain to conduct a cavalry patrol to scout for the French. Exhibiting perhaps more courage than judgment, the captain led the patrol from the front. He located the French outposts by the tactic of having himself shot from the saddle. A lieutenant reported to Vogelsang that the French were present. Ott, in turn, ordered O'Reilly's command, comprising six battalions and four squadrons, to check them at the village of Casteggio near the middle of the Stradella defile.

While conducting his map studies back in Paris, Bonaparte had identified the Stradella defile as an important strategic objective. The major highway linking Mantua and Alessandria ran through the defile. Having attained it on June 6, he became overconfident. Based upon intercepted dispatches, Bonaparte believed he understood Austrian dispositions as of June 5. The First Consul judged that Melas would not have assembled enough men to threaten seriously Lannes' advance guard. Therefore he ordered Lannes to continue his march west: "If troops should present themselves between Voghera and Stradella let them be attacked without caution; they are, certainly, fewer than 10,000 men."[6] In fact, Lannes was dangerously overextended, something that became apparent on the morning of June 9 when he encountered an Austrian force that outnumbered him better than two to one.

Initially it appeared to the French that they faced another routine outpost skirmish. A battalion of the 6th Light drove in the Austrians until they encountered a considerable force occupying a ridgeline position. General Watrin presumed that they were a mere rear guard. He deployed the two remaining battalions of the 6th Light into line and attacked. Unbeknownst to Watrin, when Ott heard the sounds of O'Reilly's combat, he ignored Chief of Staff Zach's advice to shun an engagement. Instead, he announced, "My outposts are attacked; I march to succor them." Consequently, the 6th Light encountered a solid line of Austrian infantry supported by a formidable gun line. These guns initially rebuffed the French.

Watrin's division had been in road column. As each unit reached the front Watrin added it into the battle. He tried to turn the Austrian right

General of division Jean Lannes

flank, which was anchored on the village of Casteggio, but lacked enough men to accomplish this successfully. Although the French gained the village at least twice, Austrian counterattacks reclaimed it. Lannes was in a difficult bind. He had only one infantry division, two batteries, and the 12th Hussars, a force in total numbering about 7,000. Ott commanded a force of 26 battalions and 15 squadrons numbering about 16,000 men.[8]

O'Reilly's successful defense of Casteggio gave Ott time to deploy the balance of his force. He too did not know what he confronted. He decided to defend his ground by stationing one division of nine battalions on the heights south of Casteggio. He maintained a six battalion garrison in the village and arrayed six squadrons of the Lobkowitz Dragoons behind a hedge north of Casteggio. A cavalry battery supported these dragoons. Ott kept his remaining nine squadrons out of the battle line. A five-battalion reserve occupied Montebello while 34 guns deployed among the forward troops.[9]

The fact that the French were so badly outgunned was a legacy of Fort Bard. At the Battle of Montebello, Austrian artillery superiority gave the defenders a big tactical advantage. In the words of an eyewitness, "the Austrians disposed a numerous artillery that shot canister while the republicans charged with the bayonet."[10] When Watrin's men tried to work their way around the Austrian left, the Lobkowitz Dragoons erupted through gaps they had cut in the hedge and drove them back. The only available French cavalry, the 12th Hussars, heroically countercharged to extricate the infantry. Over time, some additional French artillery including the guns of the Consular Guard reached the field. They were too few to suppress the Habsburg fire. For five hours the unequal combat raged. Throughout the contest the piecemeal arrival of French forces, few as they were, confused Ott. From his perspective it seemed that fresh enemy troops were continuously entering the field and that he was outnumbered. On a tactical level, tall fields of rye prevented rivals from distinguishing one another clearly until at point blank range.

Still, the Austrians were clearly getting the best of it. Even Berthier's official report acknowledged that "one battalion of the 40th which allowed itself to make a retrograde movement gave the enemy some advantage"![11] In fact, the entire division was close to breaking when finally a significant number of French reinforcements did enter the battle.

They belonged to General Victor's command and numbered about 5,000 men. At about 1 p.m., when he heard the sounds of battle, Victor ordered his leading brigade, infantry commanded by General Olivier

Rivaud, to accelerate its march. For nearly an hour, at something approaching a trot, Rivaud's men hastened forward. Arriving on the field, Victor ordered the 43rd Demi-brigade to charge the heights to the left of Casteggio. Rivaud put his left and right battalions in open order while retaining the middle battalion in column and sounded the advance. A horde of disordered units belonging to three different demi-brigades obstructed his front. Rivaud's men breasted the tide while the general rallied four of the disordered battalions. He could see that Lannes' men were fought out. They would sullenly follow the fresh troops but could not be relied upon to do much more. Undaunted, Rivaud took position in front of his center battalion and led it up the heights. The Austrians were tired also and they yielded this first position. But overlooking it was a second line of hills on which sat another Austrian battle line. Ordering his battalion in column not to fire a shot but instead to rely upon cold steel, Rivaud pressed ahead.

Meanwhile, Victor's 24th Light attacked the Austrian left while two battalions of his 96th Demi-brigade formed in serried column and attacked parallel to the main road against the Austrian center. The 96th endured heavy Austrian artillery fire until they passed Casteggio. For conscript grenadier Coignet it was his first exposure to fire: "I ducked my head at the sound of the cannons, but my sergeant-major slapped me on the knapsack with his sabre, and said, "You must not duck your head."

"No, I won't" Coignet replied.[12]

After repelling a faint-hearted Austrian cavalry charge, the 96th deployed into open order to reduce its vulnerability to the artillery. The combined pressure from the 96th and 43rd broke the Austrian spirit. Ott ordered a sequential retreat; artillery followed by the infantry. Because most of the guns had to pass over a narrow stone bridge, Ott instructed O'Reilly to shield the withdrawal by defending Casteggio for as long as possible. Shedding prisoners, Ott retired west to Voghera. A lack of French cavalry prevented an effective pursuit.

Lannes had been in the thick of the fighting. A soldier recalls seeing him covered in blood, presumably from nearby victims since he himself was not wounded, and looking dreadful. That evening Lannes returned to Casteggio. He found the village devastated; blood-soaked bodies everywhere. He told Bourrienne, "It was hot, very hot; the bones of my grenadiers cracked under the Austrian balls like a shower of hail falling on a skylight." Precise Austrian tabulation lists 659 killed, 1,445 wounded, and 2,171 prisoners along with two artillery pieces. Vague French reports mention 500 to 600 casualties but they were surely heavier, probably on the order of 3,000 men.[13]

Except when conducting the retreat, Ott exerted little influence on the battle. O'Reilly, on the other hand, defended Casteggio with the same tenacity that the French generals exhibited during their repeated assaults. Ott's command had the recent experience of victory at Genoa. It included the best infantry units that had been involved in the siege. But somehow 17,000 soldiers backed by a superior artillery could barely hold a village and the adjacent heights against half their number and could not retain the position at all when the odds became two French to three Austrians. Something more than Ott's indifferent leadership must account for the Austrian defeat. Clearly in 1800 the Austrians were not a match for the French on a unit for unit basis.

After the fall of Genoa, there was no need to engage the French until the entire Austrian army concentrated. A fluid situation developed and it demanded subordinate initiative. Indicative of the absence of such initiative in the Habsburg army was FML Friedrich Gottesheim's response upon learning of the fall of Piacenza. He halted his march and remained inert pending new orders. Consequently, Melas needed to keep close rein on his subordinates, particularly to ensure they did not unwittingly engage prematurely. Throughout the campaign to date, Melas had tried to be present at the point of decision. He had conducted the battles that led to the investment of Genoa. When affairs there reduced to a siege, he accompanied Elsnitz on the march west to the Var River. Upon receiving reports of a French buildup in his rear, he moved with his reserve to a central position at first Turin and then Alessandria. To be closer to the action, he transferred his headquarters across the Bormida River to Villanova, four miles east of Alessandria. While waiting for Elsnitz and Ott to rejoin him, Melas learned of Lannes' advance over the Po River on June 7. He considered it a feint. He judged that the true French objective was Mantua. To respond, he ordered Haddick's and Kaim's divisions to accelerate their march toward their concentration points.

But Melas could not be everywhere. So, he had sent Zach to advise Ott, and Ott in turn, hearing the sounds of battle, had ignored Zach's counsel. Thus a battle occurred that should not have been fought. It would have been far better if Ott had retired before Lannes' advance in preparation for an engagement elsewhere after the entire army united. Yet the Battle of Montebello did not fatally compromise Melas' situation. His strategy to mass his forces and then attack remained sound.

From the French perspective, General Bonaparte assumed that Lannes would not encounter any substantial enemy force during his westward advance. Lannes, in turn, accepted his chief's rosy view and failed to reconnoiter adequately. He then fought an action where there should have been little to gain and where, against a more able general, there was much risk. That said, once he had clinched with his foe, Lannes clung on tenaciously. In much the same manner as he would do at Friedland in 1807, he fixed his opponent until reinforcements arrived. Everyone agreed he had covered himself in glory. Although the battle hinged on possession of Casteggio, it was labeled Montebello and became, in 1808, the basis of Lannes' title, the Duke of Montebello.

Curiously, the First Consul's contemporary report cites both Victor and Watrin – "General Watrin showed talent and that enthusiasm which carries troops along" – and omits mention of Lannes entirely. It praised the 12th Hussars and attributed ultimate victory to the 96th's bayonet charge that swept past Casteggio. Throughout the battle the French infantry had exhibited a fine variety of tactical formations. They had effortlessly ployed from one formation to another, frequently while under heavy artillery fire. Depending upon tactical dictates, they had charged in column, line, or open order. The French generals from Lannes on down had displayed great energy.

The Battle of Montebello contributed to Bonaparte's growing confidence. It was soon to rise to a dangerous level.

***

On June 10 Ott continued his retreat westward toward Melas. Few Austrian generals ever passed a fortress without seeing the need to garrison it. So it was with Ott when he detached 1,200 men to garrison the citadel of Tortone, a totally useless diminution of his force. With his depleted, dispirited command, Ott crossed the Scrivia River. Meanwhile, for the French who had fought at Montebello, it was a day of rest. Simultaneously, the balance of the Army of Reserve marched to unite with them. Far to the rear, the artillery that had been delayed at Fort Bard also hurried to rejoin the army. But the reinforcement that truly mattered at this moment came in the person of General Louis Desaix.

Desaix was born into an impoverished but noble family. Commissioned into the French army in 1783, he embraced revolutionary ideals. He was a dark complexioned, little man who dressed shabbily and seemed contemptuous of physical comforts. He possessed no interest in riches and pleasures. He had been one of Bonaparte's chosen men for the Egyptian adventure. His upright, honest conduct earned him the title 'the Just Sultan' from the Arabs. During the campaign, Bonaparte gave Desaix several complete sets of field equipment. Desaix contrived to lose them, preferring to wrap himself in a cloak, throw himself under a cannon, and sleep with every appearance of deep contentment. Surprisingly, he did not accompany the general on his return to France. Perhaps Bonaparte feared blunt criticism regarding his abandonment of his army. Desaix had departed Egypt in the late winter and arrived in Toulon about the time Bonaparte began his journey from Paris to join the Army of Reserve. News of Desaix's arrival reached Bonaparte in Switzerland and he immediately summoned the general to join him. Whereas Bonaparte was jealous of some generals, and feared the ambitions of others, he held Desaix in high esteem. Desaix's modest, unassuming disposition had much to do with Bonaparte's attitude. He also recognized in the 32-year-old general a leader of rare talents. During his exile, Napoleon would recall Desaix with fondness, commenting that "Desaix was wholly wrapped up in war and glory."[14] To date his pursuit of glory had cost him three wounds. Four of his horses had been killed beneath him.

It says something about Bonaparte's precarious line of communication that while Desaix descended the Saint Bernard pass, bandits conducted a dawn attack that killed one of his companions, wounded three more, and captured his baggage. When he finally rejoined Bonaparte at Stradella on June 10, the two met for nearly three hours. Bonaparte was not loath to change command structures in order to employ outstanding generals. Just as he was to do with Marshal Ney on the eve of the opening battles in the Waterloo campaign, so it was here. By conversation's end the First Consul had appointed Desaix to corps command. Desaix borrowed a horse from his Egyptian comrade, Bessières, and rode off to join his men.

On June 11 the army's new corps structure became operational. Desaix's corps comprised the divisions of Boudet and Monnier; Victor's, the divisions of Gardanne and Chambarlhac. Detached from the main army were Duhesme's corps comprising the divisions of Loison and Chabran as well as Moncey's corps from the Army of the Rhine. At this time the entire Army of Reserve numbered 55,982 men. During the morning Bonaparte inspected Desaix's corps before sending it west toward the Scrivia River. Beyond lay Alessandria, which Bonaparte identified as the next important objective. By 5 p.m. Desaix had closed on the river. While scouting along the Scrivia, Austrian pickets fired at Desaix. In what his friends believed was a presentiment of his death, he commented, "The Austrian balls have known me in the past, I fear they no longer recognize me."[15]

That evening Toli reported to Bonaparte that Melas was very discouraged by Ott's defeat at Montebello and did not know what to do. His senior generals were telling him to escape while there remained time. It is possible Toli's report was a canard, hatched at Austrian headquarters. Whether the spy was aware of this cannot be determined.[16] Regardless, Toli's intelligence fed the First Consul's confidence. Bonaparte also received welcome news from Suchet. Suchet was marching on Acqui, some 18 miles southwest of Alessandria. The First Consul also knew that Turreau, with 5,100 men, was advancing down the Doire River toward Turin. The vise around Melas was nearly closed. In Bonaparte's mind, all that remained was to determine which route or routes Melas would choose to try to escape. His examination of the map revealed three possibilities: west to Turin; south to Genoa; north to Valenza. The Turin route seemed the least likely. It would actually lead Melas further into the French net. Either of the other two choices would permit Melas to try to regain his line of communication and therefore appeared more probable.

Events now accelerated. On June 11, pontonniers built a trestle bridge across the swollen Scrivia River. At 3 a.m. the next day the army began to cross. That same afternoon, Melas summoned his generals to a conference in Alessandria to brief them on his planned counter-offensive. On June 13, Bonaparte scheduled a reconnaissance in force toward Alessandria to determine Austrian intentions. It fell to the infantry of Victor and Lannes and four brigades of cavalry to conduct this operation. After crossing the Scrivia River in the morning, they entered a flat plain that lay between the Scrivia and Bormida rivers. It was ground perfectly suited to unimpeded cavalry maneuver. Since Melas enjoyed a considerable cavalry advantage, if he intended to offer battle he would do so somewhere on this plain. The French infantry advanced to San Giuliano without meeting resistance. Here they paused to wait for the cavalry. Most of the local people had fled for safety. Victor interrogated a few of the more hardy peasants and learned that an enemy force estimated at 4,000 men occupied Marengo further to the west. If there was to be a battle, surely the Austrians would defend Marengo obstinately. Bonaparte and the cavalry joined the infantry at 3 p.m. at which point a terrific

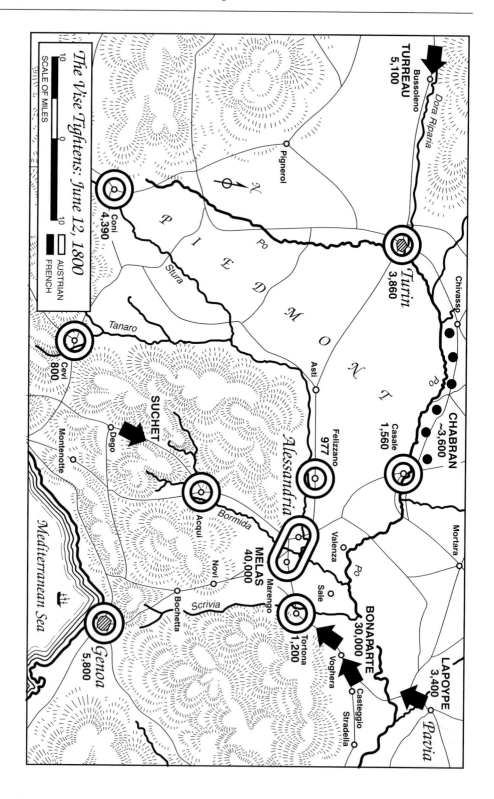

storm began. The rain halted all operations until 4:30, when the reconnaissance resumed. Around 6 p.m. Victor found the Austrians in Marengo. They belonged to O'Reilly's command.

Melas intended O'Reilly to hold hard. His planned offensive was based on the notion that the army could debouch easily onto the Scrivia plain. However, O'Reilly had been unnerved by the Battle of Montebello. There, for the second time in four days, he had fought a sacrificial rear guard action. His defense of Marengo was very different from his defense of Casteggio.

To assault Marengo, Victor divided Gardanne's division into two columns. One column conducted a frontal assault from the east while the other attacked from the south. After a one-hour combat the Austrians yielded, leaving in French hands 100 prisoners and two 4-pounder cannons with their limbers and caissons. O'Reilly's people marched west toward the fortified bridgehead on the Bormida River.

As a punishment for misbehavior at Montebello, the 24th Light received the duty of continuing west to reconnoiter this bridgehead. They were deliberately left exposed to the fire of Austrian cannons mounted behind earthworks. Sullen soldiers exposed to such an ordeal do not make the best scouts. An early dusk descended on the field, a thick mixture of river mist and drizzle. Marmont, who commanded the artillery reserve, brought up eight guns to bombard the bridgehead. It was an unequal contest. Firing from the prepared positions, fourteen Habsburg cannons dismounted three French guns and drove Marmont back. With another storm threatening, the French prepared to call it a day. Most of the cavalry had remained mounted the entire day. They had been soaked to the skin from the frequent showers. Everyone was wet, weary, and hungry.

At this time there was another Austrian pontoon bridge downstream from the fortified bridgehead. It is not certain that the French detected its presence during the evening of June 13. It was sheltered by a river bend that featured high banks. The night was murky and Marmont's artillery duel contributed to the gloom. According to Anne Jean Savary, who it should be noted was absent on a reconnaissance, Bonaparte ordered his aide-de-camp, Jacques Lauriston, to deal with this second bridge. Savary adds that later, when Lauriston reported that he had failed to destroy the pontoon bridge, Bonaparte paid little heed. Only after the battle would Bonaparte rail against Lauriston for bungling the assignment. In fact, Lauriston appears blameless. At all events, if Bonaparte or any other French officer saw the bridge, it caused no particular alarm.[17]

Bonaparte was quite certain that the day's reconnaissance had successfully uncovered Melas' strategy. He personally had spent most of the afternoon scouting. A trooper in the Consular Guard relates, "We saw him almost the whole time...traversing the plain, examining the terrain with attention, by turns profoundly meditating, and giving orders."[18] Melas' abandonment of the field convinced Bonaparte that his opponent was purely intent upon flight. Austrian intelligence agents and 'primed' deserters probably contributed to this impression by relaying misleading tales. Among the likely candidates for this role was a 'prisoner' whom Bonaparte personally interrogated. He was an émigré cavalry officer wearing his Bourbon military medal. His tale of Austrian retreat and ruin perhaps should have alerted the First Consul. Instead, Bonaparte departed the field with the intent of re-crossing the Scrivia River and returning to Voghera. The flooded river thwarted his plan, causing him to establish his headquarters in Torre di Garafoli.

To prevent Melas' escape, the First Consul again had to cast his net wide. He began issuing orders dispersing his hunting pack so as to intercept his quarry's likely escape routes. Given that Bonaparte had entirely misjudged Melas, it was extremely fortunate that the swollen Scrivia forced him to remain with his soldiers. However, on both a strategic and grand tactical level, his army was badly scattered. The troops available for battle included the infantry of the Consular Guard and Monnier's division who were camped around Bonaparte's headquarters. Eight miles to the west were Victor's two divisions at Marengo where they faced the Austrian bridgehead. Echeloned on the plain behind Victor were Lannes and Murat. The cavalry of the Consular Guard occupied a small hamlet in the middle of the plain. To the south lay Desaix, who was on his way to Novi with Boudet's division and was almost beyond recall. Another cavalry brigade was in Sale to the north where it too was just within recall distance.

While still in Paris, Bonaparte had predicted that the campaign's decisive battle would take place west of the Scrivia River. Events on June 13 had persuaded him otherwise. As he went to sleep he had no idea that his original prediction was about to come true.

NOTES

1. Order of the Day, June 6, 1800, in John Howard, ed., *Letters and Documents of Napoleon*, I (New York, 1961), p. 451.

2. "Pièces trouvées sur le courrier intercepté du général Mélas," June 3, 1800,

Jacques Campredon, *La Défense du Var et Le Passage Des Alpes 1800* (Paris, 1889) p. 363. Suchet's report on his captures is in "au Ministre de la guerre," June 6, 1800, Campredon, p. 366.

3. See: "Melas to Count Tige," June 5, 1800, François Roguet, *Mémoires Militaires du Lieutenant Général Comte Roguet*, II (Paris, 1862), pp. 608-09.

4. "Extract from the Austrian Military Review," United States Army Service Schools, *Source Book of the Marengo Campaign in 1800* (Fort Leavenworth, KS, 1922), p. 157.

5. "Lannes to Bonaparte," June 6, 1800, ibid., p. 156.

6. "To General Berthier," June 8, 1800, *Correspondance de Napoléon Ier*, VI (Paris, 1860), p. 351.

7. Jean Baptiste Crossard, *Mémoires Militaires et Historiques*, II (Paris, 1829), p. 283.

8. On June 8 Bonaparte states that Lannes has 8,000 men including his cavalry brigade. Subtracting losses for crossing the Po and the absence of one cavalry regiment yields my estimate. See: "To General Berthier," June 8, 1800, *Correspondance de Napoléon Ier*, VI, p. 350. Regarding artillery, the West Point Atlas claims Lannes had only four guns but Watrin mentions two batteries. See: "Watrin to Dupont," June 10, 1800, *Source Book of the Marengo Campaign in 1800*, p. 166. The Austrian strength is taken from Gaston Bodart, *Militär-historisches kriegs-lexicon 1618-1905* (Vienna, 1908), p. 355.

9. The Austrian order of battle is derived from the Austrian Military Review cited in *Source Book of the Marengo Campaign in 1800*, pp. 168-69.

10. Cited in Édouard Gachot, *La Deuxième Campagne d'Italie* (Paris, 1899), p. 280.

11. Gaspar Jean Marie Rene de Cugnac, *Campagne de l'Armée de Réserve en 1800*, II (Paris, 1901), p. 166.

12. Lorédan Larchey, ed., *The Narrative of Captain Coignet* (New York, 1890), p. 66.

13. Louis de Bourrienne, *Memoirs of Napoleon Bonaparte*, II (New York, 1906), p. 10; and Karl Mras, "Gefchichte Des Feldzuges 1800 in Italien," *Öestereichische Militärische Zeitschrift*, (Vienna, 1822), p. 128. The June 10 Bulletin of the Army of Reserve claims 6,000 prisoners and five guns while acknowledging 600 casualties. Yet the 12th Hussars alone entered battle with about 400 men and three days later had only 245. This, plus Lannes' candid comment, hints at far more severe French losses. Bodart, p. 355, asserts 3,000 French and 4,300 Austrian casualties.

14. J. Christopher Herold, ed., *The Mind of Napoleon: A Selection from His Written and Spoken Words* (New York, 1955), p. 221.

15. Eugène de Beauharnais, *Mémoirs et Correspondance Politique et Militaires du Prince Eugène*, I (Paris, 1858), p. 81. Desaix's comment circulated widely. The Bulletin of the Army of Reserve, June 15, 1800, has it this way: "What a long time it is since I was last fighting in Europe. The bullets have forgotten me, something will certainly happen to me." See: *Correspondance de Napoléon Ier*, VI, p. 363.

16. The Austrian account claims that Melas sent a double agent to mislead Bonaparte. It seems likely that this was Toli. See: Mras, p. 137.

17. Because extensive French historical revision surrounds this incident, all accounts must be read skeptically. For relevant, although contradictory, accounts, see: Anne Savary, *Memoirs of the Duke of Rovigo,* I (Paris, 1901), pp. 172-73, and Bourrienne, II, pp. 12-13. Also note that the Austrians lifted the bridge and moved it upstream at some unknown time. It is possible that this move also deceived the French.

18. Joseph Petit, *Marengo or the Campaign of Italy, by the Army of Reserve Under the Command of the Chief Consul Bonaparte* (Philadelphia, 1801), p. 23.

Right: Bonaparte and his entourage (Josephine seated) anxiously await news on 18 brumaire, the coup's first day.

Below: Although the artist exaggerates the topography, he presents an otherwise realistic depiction of the Battle of Marengo.

While Bonaparte was in Egypt, André Masséna won the pivotal Second Battle of Zurich.

The way Bonaparte wanted history to recall his epic alpine crossing, mounted on a superb charger, following the footsteps of Hannibal and Charlemagne.

Bonaparte and his grenadier escort before the Cinq Cents on 19 brumaire: "I got heated and ended with a silly sentence. The French do not like bad taste; no sooner had I said the words than a murmur made me aware of it."

The climb through the Saint Bernard. A vivandiére dispenses liquid comfort while Bonaparte watches impassively (right) and horses slide toward the precipice (left).

The way Bonaparte ascended the pass; mounted on a humble, but sure-footed mule, led by an experienced guide.

Soldiers improve the bypass around Fort Bard.

The monks at the Hospice greet Bonaparte.

"My conditions are irrevocable... I did not begin to learn the art of war yesterday." Berthier and Melas sign the truce on June 15.

The French 12th Hussars charge to extricate Lannes' infantry at Montebello.

Close combat between French line infantry and Austrian grenadiers at the Battle of Montebello.

Bonaparte said of Louis Desaix that "Desaix was wholly wrapped up in war and glory."

The Mounted Grenadiers of the Consular Guard charge the fleeing Austrian infantry at battle's end.

Consular infantry. Inscribed on the banner of the 32nd Demi-brigade are the words "Discipline" and "Obeissance" to the law. The latter sentiment made many soldiers uneasy about Brumaire.

Triumphal march on the Champ de Mars. Eugène Beauharnais recalls, "It was one of the best moments of my life."

Richepance's column marches through the defile and into a snow squall during its advance against the Austrian rear.

Jean Moreau "did not forget to share his glory with his comrades" and so Hohenlinden became a "celebration of victory in the name of peace and liberty."

Chapter 7

The Battle
of Marengo

PART 1.
THE AUSTRIAN BREAKOUT

"No force should be detached on the eve of a battle, because affairs may change during the night."

NAPOLEON BONAPARTE, MILITARY MAXIM 28

At 10 p.m. on June 13, senior Austrian generals arrived at number 1 *Faa di Bruno* in Alessandria to join their leader for a council of war. Everyone agreed that the situation was critical. Of the 120,000 men who had begun the campaign only about half remained. Twenty-thousand of the survivors occupied various fortresses. This was the usual Habsburg practice. Still, the assignment of 2,816 men to Milan, 5,800 to Genoa, 4,390 to Coni, and 3,860 to Turin, as well as additional thousands to several lesser citadels, was wanton disregard for economy of force. Only 40,000 soldiers remained in and about Alessandria. While opinions about what to do with them were divided, GdK Melas had no doubts. For the past eight days he and GM Zach had been preparing an offensive. They had anticipated it would be based on Piacenza. Instead, it would occur on the plains of the Scrivia. Melas issued orders: the army would risk all and attack at dawn!

The objective was to open the road east so the army could safely move toward Mantua and thus draw closer to Austria itself. The commanding general based his hopes for victory upon "the preponderance and superiority of our artillery and cavalry".[2] He judged that the army was in good spirits. During the past several days he had opened the great storehouses in Alessandria to allow the soldiers to replace worn equipment, clothing, and shoes. He had distributed meat, rice, and wine on a lavish scale. To encourage

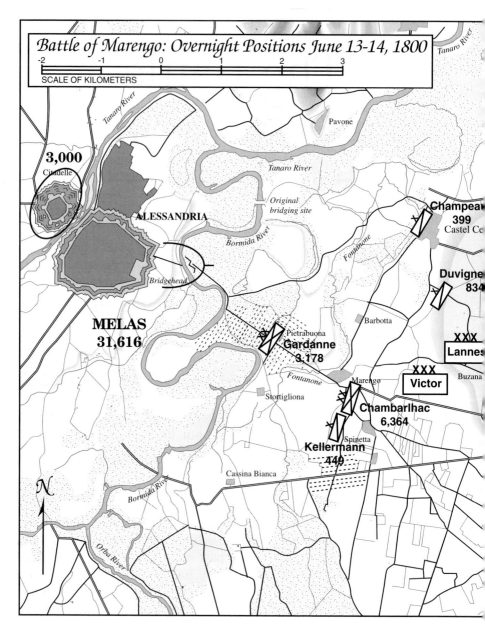

Battle of Marengo: Overnight Positions June 13-14, 1800

SCALE OF KILOMETERS
-2   -1   0   1   2   3

further the soldiers to their duty, Melas issued a stirring proclamation.

Melas and Zach devised a two-prong offensive. As would have been the case at Piacenza, artillery from within the fortified bridgehead would provide fire support. Under its protective barrage, FML O'Reilly would lead the main body out from the bridgehead against Marengo while FML Ott conducted a secondary force across the pontoon bridge that lay downstream from the bridgehead. Ott's

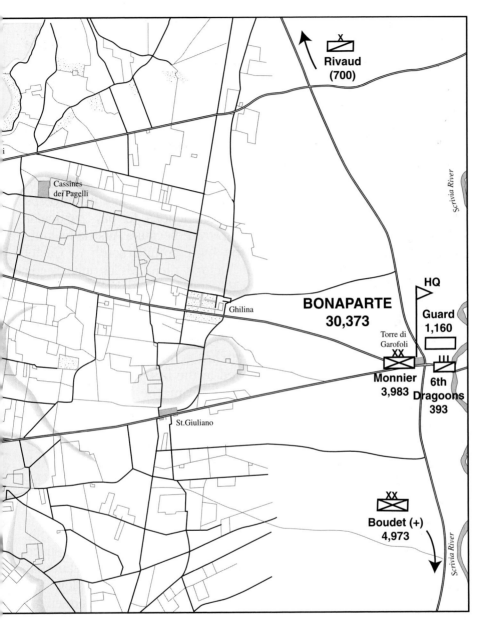

mission was to march on Castel Ceriolo and secure the army's left flank from any French force operating to the north while simultaneously fixing the French center. Meanwhile, the mainbody would move from Marengo to San Giuliano and then turn to its left to roll up the French flank. O'Reilly, who initially would spearhead the breakout from the bridgehead, would turn south to secure the army's right flank. If all went according to plan, the offensive would drive the

Army of Reserve northward into a cul de sac formed by the Scrivia and Po rivers. If the attack failed, the Austrians would retreat to Genoa where the garrison was gathering provisions to feed them.

While commendably bold, Melas' plan contained several important flaws. He labored under a misapprehension regarding French dispositions. First Consul Bonaparte's decision to spread his forces wide to prevent an Austrian escape had confused Melas. He believed that a sizeable French force was at Sale whereas in fact only 760 troopers belonging to Jean Rivaud's light cavalry brigade were there. On battle's eve Melas dispatched a hussar regiment north to Casale to check any French advance from Sale. In addition, because of concerns about the Sale force, Ott received instructions to pay particular attention to the army's left flank. Moreover, because Austrian scouts could see Lannes' campfires on the high ground south of Castel Ceriolo but not those of most of Victor's men, Melas incorrectly judged that the French center lay well north of the main highway.

In detail there were also several other errors and omissions. Three thousand men remained inside Alessandria to garrison the citadel, which was an unnecessary waste. Sometime during the night someone worried that the downstream bridge was too vulnerable at its original location and ordered it moved to the bridgehead. Thus, the entire army would have to debouch from the confines of the bridgehead. It is among a chief of staff's duties to take steps to ensure that the commander's strategy can be implemented. Zach badly let Melas down by failing to foresee how slow would be the army's exit from the bridgehead. Whereas gaps might have been cut in the earthworks to permit a more speedy exit, this was not done. The entire army had to march out from the one opening where the highway emerged onto the plain.

The original plan had been formed with the notion that O'Reilly would still occupy Marengo and thus the army would have the space to deploy for battle. When this proved not to be the case, it meant that the army would have to fight for the ground on which to deploy. Yet no one adjusted the plan to the new reality. Three consequences flowed from this omission. First, once the army exited the bridgehead, no particular unit had the mission to capture Marengo. Second, instead of being able to move freely on Castel Ceriolo, Ott would have to wait for the leading units to clear his front before he could being his maneuver. Lastly, the original plan called for the army to begin moving at midnight. Since the French occupied the deployment ground, movement was postponed until 7 a.m. During the night, 24,073 infantry and 7,543 cavalry along with 92 guns* prepared to attack.

---

* Not including regimental guns

Officers circulated among the bivouacs to prohibit camp fires that might reveal their presence. This subterfuge succeeded.³ Although Victor's pickets reported the sounds of movement, everyone assumed it indicated a retreat.

The highway connecting Alessandria with Piacenza along which the Austrian army was to march issued southeast from the Bormida bridgehead to Marengo, and then continued east through San Giuliano, Torre di Garofoli, and over the Scrivia. It was the main axis alongside of which the armies fought. The battle ground was gently rolling farm country. The highest elevations were around the village of Castel Ceriolo. Here was the only truly rough terrain on the entire battlefield. A series of irregular undulations extended southeast from this village to the hamlet of Cassina Grossa, just south of the highway. The remainder of the field appeared generally flat when viewed on a broad scale. However, there were numerous swales that, at the short ranges fire fights occurred, restricted lines of sight. The fields were planted with grape vines and wheat, and these also reduced tactical visibility.

About one mile from the bridgehead, bordering the highway's northern side, was the stoutly built Pietrabuona farm, where would occur the day's first fighting. Six to seven hundred yards further along the highway was the Fontanone Creek. The Fontanone rose from a marsh adjacent to the Bormida River and wound its way sluggishly northward. Its high banks made it a natural barrier, its location made

The Bormida River at the Austrian bridging site

it a natural trench blocking egress from the Austrian bridgehead. On the creek's eastern side was Marengo, site of the ancient villa of the Lombard kings. Marengo contained three significant, highly defensible structures: a large silkworm farm that included a sixty foot high square tower; and two buildings that housed farm workers.

Twice within the past thirteen months France and her enemies had battled on the Marengo plain. On May 16, 1799, Victor had been serving in Moreau's army during its campaign against Suvorov. Victor led his command eastward out of Alessandria, crossed a bridge and ford over the Bormida, and advanced against Russian-held Marengo. His men had driven the Russians from Marengo and continued through San Giuliano until they encountered overwhelming numbers. Victor then conducted a fighting withdrawal back to his bridgehead. Then as now Gardanne served as Victor's subordinate. This experience provided the two with a fine understanding of the terrain, including the defensive advantages of the Fontanone ravine.

On June 20, 1799 came a second battle of Marengo. This time the French and Austrians occupied the same relative positions they were to occupy the following year. In a curious preview of Bonaparte's battle, at first the advantage lay with the Austrians. General Emmanuel Grouchy fought a stubborn battle against superior numbers but his lack of cavalry and artillery told against him. A column of Hungarian grenadiers was on the verge of driving him from the field when fresh French forces arrived to turn the tide of battle. Although he had a horse shot out from under him, Moreau displayed fine energy throughout the day and drove the Austrians back to Alessandria.

On the morning of June 14, 1800, about 26,029 French infantry, 3,851 cavalry, and 493 gunners crewing 35 artillery pieces lay scattered across the countryside between the Scrivia and Bormida rivers.[4] The rank and file of the Army of Reserve spent a miserable night. Supply wagons were well to the rear so they had little to eat. It rained during the night and naturally only the senior officers occupied the few places of shelter. During the night, neither Victor nor Gardanne took measures to ensure security. Given the remarkably short distance from the French picket line to the Austrian bridgehead, the inability to detect Melas' buildup can only be attributed to gross negligence. Dawn found the French army blissfully unaware that battle was imminent. Gardanne's 3,178-man division had its right flank resting on the Fontanone Creek, its left dangling in the air 600 yards short of the Bormida River. His outposts occupied the Pietrabuona farm. Chambarlhac's division lay in its camps about Marengo. Kellermann's three heavy cavalry regiments occupied the hamlet of Spinetta, south of Marengo. Lannes' people, Watrin's division and the Swiss-born General Joseph Mainoni's brigade were in the rear near the Buzana farm some 1,500 yards southeast of Castel Ceriolo. Pierre Champeaux's cavalry brigade was in Castel Ceriolo with general of brigade Bernard Duvigneau's cavalry nearby.

Within the bridgehead, the Austrian position was very cramped. At daybreak, the main column cautiously filed through the bridgehead's only gate. They appeared to be in fighting fettle. "See how cheerful the soldiers are," commented FML Ludwig Vogelsang to an aide.[5] Melas observed his army debouch while chief of staff Zach ordered a cavalry patrol to scout southward to locate the French flank. At the same time, FML O'Reilly led his force toward Marengo. Behind O'Reilly, the balance of the army began to deploy as soon as it exited the bridgehead. FML Karl Haddick's division was in the first line. Behind him was FML Conrad Kaim's division. FML Peter Morzin's grenadiers stood in column in reserve. While some cavalry took station on both wings, FML Elsnitz's cavalry division remained in the rear. The deployment took time. Not until 7 a.m. did the leading Austrian troops commanded by Oberst (colonel) Johann Frimont (832 infantry; 458 cavalry) contact Victor's outposts at the Pietrabuona farm.[6] Unlike French practice, there were few men deployed as skirmishers to screen the advance. In their stead were two artillery batteries which unlimbered next to a mulberry grove with tubes trained in the direction of Marengo.

The Pietrabuona farm

Frimont's men marched across a series of ditches and advanced against the Pietrabuona farm. The startled French fired a shaky volley and withdrew. This served as a signal for the Austrian artillery to open fire. The bombardment caught the soldiers of the 101st Demi-brigade still in their bivouacs. As the French scrambled into battle formation, Frimont's men pressed forward along the highway until staggered by battalion volleys delivered from Gardanne's infantry. They fell back and spent the next thirty minutes deploying into line. This gave Gardanne invaluable time to organize a defense. Meanwhile, O'Reilly – who, recall, had responsibility to protect the Austrian right flank and was not charged with capturing Marengo – deployed his men (2,228 infantry; 769 cavalry) so that their rightmost files touched the willows that bordered the Bormida River. During his deployment, his two batteries continued to savage the French position some 500 paces northwest of Marengo. Austrian batteries positioned across the Bormida added their fire whenever a target became unmasked. It was a killing bombardment to which the French had no answer. Because of the delay at Fort Bard, the army had never received sufficient artillery. Gardanne's division possessed only two artillery pieces. The only reasons the Austrians did not immediately bowl over Gardanne's men were the difficulty of moving out from the bridgehead – it took until 8:30 a.m. for the entire Austrian force simply to cross the Bormida River – and the constricted, half-mile long front that prevented Melas from using his overwhelming numerical advantage.

Displaying admirable battlefield judgement, Victor reacted quickly to the surprise Austrian assault. He ordered Gardanne to stand fast to absorb the initial shock. By delaying the enemy onslaught, Gardanne would buy time to allow Chambarlhac's division (6,564 infantry) to move forward and deploy behind Marengo. Duvigneau's cavalry brigade, which was without the 6th Dragoon Regiment, was the closest mounted support. Unbeknownst to Victor, the brigade was also without its leader. Eight years earlier, Bernard Duvigneau had received a grievous wound at Valmy. Although this earned him a battlefield promotion, it also gave him a shocking introduction to the perils of combat. The next time he was under fire he was wounded again. Marengo was his third battle and the memory of what had happened twice before unmanned him. Pleading illness – in fact he had suffered a severe fall from his horse the previous evening while inspecting his picket line – Duvigneau fled the field. Victor personally took charge and ordered Duvigneau's 8th Dragoons to move to protect Gardanne's left flank. Then Victor scrawled a hasty note reporting the

Habsburg attack and dispatched a cavalry captain to convey it to Bonaparte. It was 8 a.m.

Obeying Victor's orders, Gardanne spread his division's men from near the Pietrabuona farm to a convenient bend in the Bormida River. This was such a narrow front that the Austrians could attack with a deployed line of only some 4,300 men. Around 9 a.m. came the first serious assault. The French line fired platoon volleys that repelled the initial Austrian charges. There were no available rises from which could fire the Austrian artillery. When the whitecoated infantry charged, they masked their own guns. However, in between charges the Habsburg artillery maintained a steady fire. The iron balls bounded along the nearly flat ground, undeflected by natural obstacles, to create a beaten zone deep into the French rear. Since Gardanne's men were in line, they did not suffer unduly from this fire as long as they held their position. Still it took great discipline to endure a bombardment to which they had no reply. However, French tactics relied upon counterattacks to regain lost ground. Showing great spirit, the soldiers cheered and sang *la Marseillaise* while they advanced. When these counterattacks pressed too far forward the men suffered dearly from enfilade artillery fire delivered by Austrian batteries sited on the far side of the Bormida River.[8]

About this time Melas received a misleading report from one of his scouting detachments. As noted, Bonaparte's dispersal of his force up and down the Scrivia River had worried Melas. In addition, Melas feared the pending arrival of Suchet's and Masséna's commands from the southwest. Accordingly he sent a Captain Ceiwrany with a squadron of the Kaiser Dragoons southwest toward Acqui to scout for Suchet. Around 9 a.m., Ceiwrany sent a message to Melas stating that he had been "attacked by a strong column of French cavalry followed by infantry" and that the enemy was driving hard on Alessandria.[9] If true, this was alarming intelligence. Melas sent GM Nimptsch and his cavalry brigade to counter this threat. Although Nimptsch easily drove Suchet's patrols back to Acqui – Ceiwrany's report wildly exaggerated the proximity of the French threat – his departure subtracted 2,341 hussars from Melas' attack.

On the battlefield, FML Haddick (3,677 infantry; 1,362 cavalry) was dissatisfied with the attack's lack of progress. He placed himself at the head of GM Friedrich Bellegarde's brigade and led them toward Marengo. According to Victor, Haddick's line "finally deployed; with flags flying in the breeze, and musical fanfares as if at a triumphant fete: it threatened to destroy the small French division with its enormous superiority."[10] Recognizing that the enemy would soon prevail, at 10 a.m. Victor ordered Gardanne to retreat in echelon across Fontanone Creek. The challenge of disengaging, reforming, and marching across fireswept ground severely tested the French infantry. Some soldiers could not withstand the pressure and broke to the rear. By and large, Gardanne's division performed superbly.

The Fontanone Creek just west of Marengo where Gardanne's men held firm

While serving in Normandy during the campaign against the rebels, Gardanne had written repeatedly to the First Consul begging for a position with the Army of Reserve. His leadership at Marengo justified his brashness. At a cost of nearly half its men, Gardanne's division bought the Army of Reserve an invaluable two hours. And, they were not yet done.

Recalling his previous battle on this ground, Victor positioned Gardanne's remaining soldiers behind the creek to the left of Marengo (see map p.154). From this position their musketry would sweep the right flank of the expected Austrian assault against Marengo. In addition, one of Chambarlhac's battalions from the 43rd Demi-brigade took position in front of the village. To these soldiers it seemed that they alone faced the entire Austrian army. Because French possession of Marengo thwarted a comfortable Austrian deployment, Melas resolved to capture it at all hazards. Accordingly, Haddick hurled wave after wave into the assault. The Fontanone ravine was enough of an obstacle to slow the Austrian advance while the brush along its banks offered the defenders some concealment. A French staff officer related, "The enemy came up and formed within a very short musket range of us. The irregularity of the ravine giving us a flank fire during his deployment we annoyed him a great deal; we could see men fall in his ranks at every discharge."[11] Habsburg officers exhibited unaccustomed front line leadership to urge their men forward.

Although some Austrian soldiers managed to cross the ravine, it was clear to Haddick that for the moment his division was fought out. He had just ordered it to retire when he received what was to prove a mortal wound. While GM Bellegarde reformed Haddick's division, FML Conrad Kaim (4,939 infantry) committed his division to the assault. They too could make no progress. For ninety minutes Gardanne's division, assisted by a single battalion, stopped the Austrian infantry along the creek line. But in between assaults they had to endure the terrible Austrian artillery fire.

Part 2.
Battle of Attrition

Melas issued orders to outflank Marengo from the north and south. While waiting for these flanking maneuvers to take effect, he resumed the frontal attacks with Kaim's division supported by GM Franz Lattermann's 2,116 grenadiers. The Austrians confronted a new set of

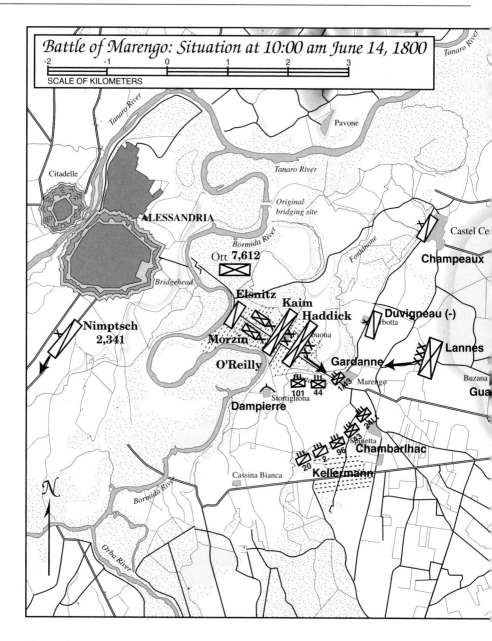

Battle of Marengo: Situation at 10:00 am June 14, 1800

SCALE OF KILOMETERS

defenders. Victor had taken advantage of a lull in the combat to relieve Gardanne's survivors with Chambarlhac's men. Chambarlhac himself was not present. Victor had ordered him to deploy his division behind Marengo while Gardanne contested the Austrian advance. Habsburg gunners spotted the deployment and opened fire. Indicative of the dangers from this bombardment is the fact that a single shell exploded amid the ranks of the 96th Demi-brigade and killed seven soldiers.

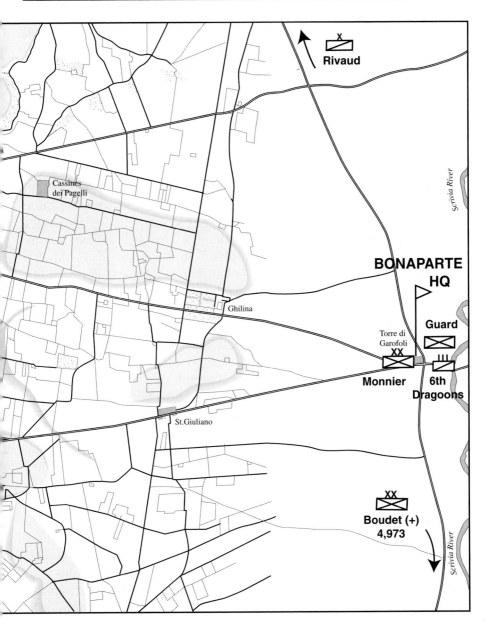

The lethal fire unnerved Chambarlhac who galloped to the rear to be seen no more this day.

Consequently, Victor personally deployed the division. He stationed the 43rd Demi-brigade and the 3rd battalion of the 96th Demi-brigade in or behind Marengo and ordered brigade general Olivier Rivaud to hold at all costs. The division's remaining five fresh battalions lined the creek to the south. Five divisional cannons provided support.

Using regular platoon volleys, Chambarlhac's infantry repulsed Kaim's assault all along the line except where the Erzherzog Josef Regiment charged. A handful of men from this regiment secured a toehold on the east side of the ravine. Their commander, GM Louis de la Marselle, moved up his brigade cannons to sweep the ground in front of his gallant men. Austrian pioneers struggled forward through the beaten zone to begin to build trail bridges so that the artillery could cross the ravine. Simultaneously, an Austrian buildup threatened to envelop Victor's right flank.

At this juncture Lannes moved up to a position north of Marengo. In Victor's words, Lannes thus rendered "to his brother in arms the same service he had received a few days earlier at Montebello."[12] No sooner had Lannes arrived then they too faced a charge. It was led by Friedrich Bellegarde, who had rallied and reformed Haddick's division. Lannes' fresh soldiers, belonging to General Watrin's 6th Light and 22nd Demi-brigade, repulsed them.

A barrage from the Habsburg gun line, which now numbered five batteries with thirty pieces, focused Victor's attention on the defense of Marengo. FML Kaim had added his divisional batteries to la Marselle's guns to try to expand the position conquered by the Erzherzog Josef Regiment. The handful of French guns also concentrated their fire here. Nevertheless, the brave Austrian pioneers completed their bridge. Stimulated by ample supplies of brandy, Lattermann's grenadiers stormed into Marengo. General Rivaud husbanded his resources masterfully, feeding his battalions into the fight one at a time. Three times the grenadiers penetrated into the village. Three times French bayonet charges drove them out. GM Lattermann himself received a severe wound while leading one of these charges. In spite of the grenadiers' efforts, all they could do was continue to cling to a small bridgehead across the ravine. Rivaud's men still denied them Marengo. At some point during the back and forth combat the Austrians drove off the horse artillery gunners who crewed four of Chambarlhac's artillery pieces. Three soldiers in the divisional train battalion risked all to drag the remaining 4-pounder to safety. Here was proof in action of the value of Marmont's reform that had militarized the artillery train.

Meanwhile, outside of the village and along the creek bed the combat continued. Rivaud recalled "an extremely sharp fusillade at close range; it lasted a quarter of an hour; the men were falling like hail on both sides."[13] Mounted men could not survive in this storm of flying lead. Every mounted officer in Rivaud's brigade was hit. Grenadier Coignet, who reports his company lost 156 killed or wounded out of

170 who began the battle, has left us a rank and file's view of this action:

> "We could not see one another in the smoke. The cannons set the wheatfield on fire, and this caused a general commotion in the ranks. The cartridge-boxes exploded; we were obliged to fall back in order to form again as quickly as possible."[14]

Hoping that Rivaud's men were shaken by the carnage, the Austrians tried a cavalry charge. It was a foolish maneuver. The ravine was such an obstacle that it forced the Habsburg charge to slow to a walk. The front rank of troopers withered in the French fire and the survivors recoiled.

Around 11 a.m. a lull descended on the field while the Austrians re-arranged their batteries and brought up fresh troops. On both sides, depending on their wont, men took advantage of the opportunity to help their wounded comrades, pillage the injured and dead, or simply collapse in shock from the noise and bloodshed.

***

At 5 a.m. Bonaparte awoke to receive the day's first reports. Two hours later he heard a heavy cannonade from the direction of Marengo. Initial reports explained that the Austrians were present. Although the firing continued, there were no additional reports to indicate that an attack had begun. The First Consul relaxed. He did not know that this lull resulted from the time-consuming Austrian need to deploy along a cramped front. Consequently, Bonaparte concluded that the bombardment was merely a diversion designed to cover a retreat. He did not intend to play into enemy hands and alter his plan. He ordered division general Lapoype to maintain his vigilance to the north in case Melas tried to escape in that direction and ordered Desaix to continue his march to block escape routes to the south. Around 8:30 a.m. he received Victor's report that Gardanne's division was under attack. At first he refused to credit it. Long after the event he confided to Savary that "he had found it difficult to persuade himself that the Austrians had not attempted to escape him by a road which was not watched."[15] When the noise of the cannonading became too disturbing, he sent the nominal commander of the army, General Berthier, to the front to investigate. The First Consul remained at headquarters to receive reports.

Around 9 a.m. Berthier arrived at the Buzana farm where he

established a field headquarters. He brought with him the 360 horsemen of the Consular Guard. Berthier chose to retain them as a final reserve. The only other available reserve was the 12th Chasseurs à cheval. Left leaderless by Duvigneau's cowardice, this regiment had apparently remained stationary. Having been surprised once already by the Austrian eruption from the bridgehead, Berthier worried about other possible perils. He knew that Jean Rivaud's cavalry brigade should provide warning of any hostile movements from the north. He sent the 12th Chasseurs to protect the army's southern flank along the Orba River. Shortly thereafter he probably informed Bonaparte that the Austrian attack was not a diversion. It appeared to be a serious attempt at breaking out of the French net.

Berthier's report changed everything. Bonaparte immediately recalled his outlying detachments although he held little hope that they could arrive in time. He pinned his faith on his friend Desaix. He dictated an anxious message which read: "I had thought to attack the enemy; they have attacked me; come, in the name of god, if you still can."[16] After ordering the forces that were camped around his headquarters to march to the sound of the guns, the First Consul mounted his favorite horse, the filly 'Styria', and rode toward the front. It was 11 a.m.

About an hour later, the Austrian bombardment resumed. Two new threats emerged to the French position: one to the north and one to the south. A brigade of Habsburg cavalry composed the southern threat. In order to utilize his cavalry superiority, Melas had ordered GM Giovanni Pilati (or Pellati according to the Italian spelling) to move his brigade south along the Bormida and locate a crossing over the Fontanone Creek so as to outflank Gardanne. Around noon, Pilati's troopers found a way across the creek that allowed one man to pass at a time. After crossing in this tedious fashion, the brigade continued through a patch of willows and emerged onto the plain. Pilati saw an alluring target: the open flank of Chambarlhac's infantry. He urged his dragoons onward. He was too impetuous. He had failed to push his scouts out in advance and consequently his leading troopers did not detect a body of French cavalry boring in against their flank until too late.

They belonged to François Kellermann's command. Kellermann served in the shadow of his father, who had commanded at Valmy and earned great renown for saving the infant Republic. The younger Kellermann hardly looked the part of a dashing cavalier – "a little man, of unhealthy and insignificant appearance" – but he was a very capable combat leader.[17] The odds favored the Austrians. Pilati's

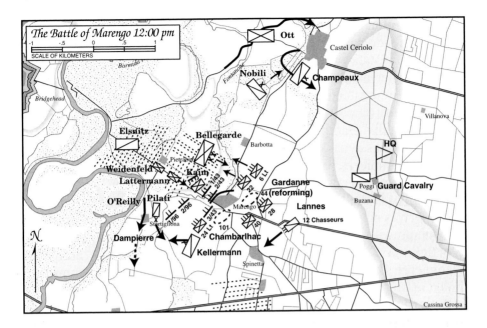

brigade numbered 1,362 troopers. Kellermann's brigade had 449 heavy cavalrymen. Having assumed command of the 8th Dragoons, his entire force numbered 892 troopers. But the Austrians were in poor tactical position with only three squadrons deployed and the balance strung out to the rear. Furthermore, the French had the advantage of surprise.

Initially it was an all-dragoon contest, pitting the 8th Dragoons versus the Kaiser Dragoons. After a brief hack and thrust, the French routed the Austrians. The victors pursued zestfully and lost their order. As was usual in the case of a cavalry versus cavalry encounter, a solid line of troopers could outface a disordered mass. Pilati's second regiment, the Karaczay Dragoons, counterattacked and sent the 8th Dragoons reeling. The 8th retired behind Kellermann's heavy cavalry who then began a steady trot toward the Austrian dragoons. The imposing French formation overawed their foes. At a distance of 50 paces, French trumpeters sounded the charge. The implacable advance of the heavy horse was too much for the Austrians. They broke badly and galloped back to the creek bed. Maddened with fear, many Austrian troopers drove their mounts into the ravine. Like the case of the British 23rd Light Dragoons at the Battle of Talavera, a mass of broken men and horses tumbled into the creek bed. The semi-official Austrian account relates, "Only a few dragoons had the luck to return to the bank."[18] While this exaggerates the extent of the disaster, Pilati's men never recovered from the shock and confusion of this encounter. Profoundly dispirited, for the remainder of the battle Pilati's brigade contributed little to the Habsburg efforts.

Although Pilati was disastrously unsuccessful, he had managed to occupy Kellermann's attention and thereby permit O'Reilly to advance out from the protection of the willows bordering the Bormida River. O'Reilly confronted a scratch force commanded by Victor's adjutant-general, Achille Dampierre. It comprised about 300 to 400 infantry, a platoon of chasseurs à cheval, and one of the division's two cannons. Initially, Dampierre had concealed his force in the ditches adjacent to the Bormida and awaited the enemy. Around 9 a.m. the advance elements of O'Reilly's division had begun to form in a nearby ravine. Dampierre's soldiers opened a destructive fire that toppled numerous opponents with each volley. O'Reilly pressed forward to capture the Stortigliona farm. Isolated and facing overwhelming numbers, Dampierre slowly retired south to Cassina Bianca where his command holed up for a final stand.

With the capture of the Stortigliona farm, O'Reilly stood on Victor's flank. But O'Reilly's orders were to secure the Austrian right flank, not attack the French left flank. Showing no initiative whatsoever, O'Reilly dutifully followed in Dampierre's wake. Late in the afternoon the two forces would fight again at Cassina Bianca. The French were critically short of ammunition, the 4-pounder reduced to a last canister round. Finally, at 7 p.m. the end came when a six-gun Habsburg battery began a point blank bombardment and the Oguliner Grenz prepared an assault. After losing two-thirds his men Dampierre surrendered. Although overshadowed by more dramatic events, Dampierre's prolonged defense against O'Reilly had tied down a sizeable Austrian contingent that would have been more useful elsewhere.

Around the time Pilati's troopers engaged, FML Ott (6,862 infantry; 740 cavalry) finally managed to shake free of the snarl at the bridgehead and march against Castel Ceriolo (see map p.159). Until now, the French had been able to contend with their foes along a limited front where they could almost match the enemy strength. It had been a battle of attrition, but one that the French could endure because of the defensive advantages of their position. Ott's maneuver threatened to upset the equilibrium. Lannes hurled Champeaux's cavalry brigade against Ott in a desperate effort to contain his breakout. The two understrength regiments charged gallantly. Champeaux fell at their head with a mortal wound. In spite of their best efforts, they made little impression against the Austrian infantry squares. When FML Elsnitz brought up the dragoons of GM Johann Nobili's brigade, the surviving French troopers retired.

The heights of Castle Ceriolo viewed from Lannes' position.

According to Melas' original plan, Ott's column was supposed to secure the army's open left flank while engaging the French center. His revised intentions called for Ott to outflank Victor and Lannes. After repulsing the French cavalry, Ott's infantry occupied the hamlet of Castel Ceriolo and the adjacent high ground. Obeying orders to check any French troops coming from the north, Ott sent his cavalry scouting in that direction. He determined that there were no significant numbers of French troops in the direction of Sale. In contrast to O'Reilly, he then exhibited initiative. At about 12:45, Ott faced his infantry south and marched them toward Lannes' flank.

Lannes was alive to Ott's threat. He refaced the 6th Light and a battalion of the 22nd Demi-brigade and aggressively ordered them to advance on Castel Ceriolo. The Gascon also committed his last reserve, Mainoni's 28th Demi-brigade with 1,577 men, to check Ott's advance. During the ensuing confrontation, the Lobkowitz Dragoons, one of the Austrian army's distinguished regiments, delivered a furious charge against the 28th Demi-brigade. Partially sheltered amid the vineyards, the 28th held firm. Thereafter, Ott's infantry attacks degenerated into a series of musketry duels. Here fell General Watrin's brother Lucien, who died of a bullet wound while leading a charge of the battalion of the 22nd Demi-brigade. Although Ott initially failed to outflank the French position, he extended the front onto open ground along which continued the bloody battle of attrition. This was a fight the French could not long endure. While they inflicted more losses then they suffered, the intensified attrition favored the side with more men. For six hours the French had blocked Melas' advance. When Ott's column resumed its sidle past Lannes' open right flank there was nothing the French generals could do. By 1 p.m Victor and Lannes had committed all of their troops to hold their line.

In Marengo, Rivaud's situation also was desperate. In between assaults, the terrific Austrian artillery fire punished the defenders. As casualties mounted, the defenders wavered. French accounts describe 'a handful of skirmishers' who, having run out of ammunition, retired from the field. In fact, it was far worse as numerous soldiers left the ranks, many using the ploy that they were helping wounded comrades to the rear. Even the commitment of Watrin's 40th Demi-brigade into the struggle merely temporarily stabilized the situation. When another Austrian assault loomed, Rivaud ignored the canister round lodged in his thigh, ran to his drummers, and ordered them to beat the charge. The appeal succeeded in rallying enough men to reconquer the streets for one last time. Although Lattermann's grenadiers yielded the village, they clung to their bridgehead over the Fontanone. Whereas the Austrians could summon fresh troops, Rivaud's people were spent. During the defense of Marengo, Rivaud and four battalion chiefs received wounds; 45 other officers and 700 men were killed or wounded.

By 2 p.m., the combination of continual frontal pressure and Ott's advance rendered the position untenable. The Habsburg artillery had dismounted most French guns. Many French had consumed all available ammunition and the reserve supplies were far back near the Scrivia. Worse, scores of soldiers who had fired off their ammunition decided that they had done their duty and ran for the rear. The sight inspired the Austrians. Sensing victory, they cheered loudly and returned to the attack.

Victor and Lannes concurred that the next Austrian assault could not fail. Reluctantly they ordered a retreat. Victor would retire along the main highway while Lannes retreated cross country toward the Buzana farm. Although most of Victor's battered men managed to withdraw in reasonable order, it proved difficult to extricate the skirmishers. The infantry formed column on the highway and retired in echelon. Kellermann's and Champeaux's troopers screened their flanks. Somehow in the confusion the third battalion of the 43rd Demi-brigade did not get the word to retreat. Surrounded, although secure in a walled barn, its leader surrendered his 400-man command to the Liechtenstein Dragoons. His conduct contrasted with Dampierre's defense against O'Reilly and he was later to be court-martialled, with Bonaparte observing caustically, "500 men commanded by a brave man can cut their way out from anywhere."[19]

PART 3.
RETREAT

On the heels of the French withdrawal, the Austrians surged into Marengo in triumph. Soldiers picked up the hats of the fallen French, put them on their bayonets, and raised their muskets in the air. Their cheers proclaimed: here was victory! The elation, the celebration, the inevitable intermingling of units, disordered their ranks. Moreover, many leaders lost control of their men. Scores of soldiers left the ranks to plunder the dead and wounded.

Now was the time to unleash the Austrian cavalry to finish off the defeated French. A level plain extended all the way to the Scrivia River, perfect ground for mounted action. At least 3,000 of the 5,200 Habsburg troopers on the field were fresh. But if an Austrian commander looked to employ them, he looked in vain. According to an émigré staff officer, the cavalry had been dispersed and "squandered" on a variety of secondary missions.[20] At this moment, the pernicious practice of distributing cavalry among multiple formations and the lack of a tactical doctrine that promoted massed cavalry action penalized the Austrian generals. Still, GM Nobili's brigade of dragoons had yet to be employed and it alone numbered over 1,800 troopers. Few Austrian officers were anxious about this wasted opportunity. With the capture of Marengo, everything indicated that the day was won.

Melas shared this view. He directed his staff to organize a pursuit. Laboriously, a battle formation featuring two lines of infantry preceded by a numerous artillery shook loose from Marengo and marched east. Instead of conducting a hell for leather pursuit, the cavalry maintained position on the infantry's flanks. A complacent overconfidence took hold. Now that they had the French on the run, and had suffered severely from prior close combat, no one was eager to close again with the enemy. Leaders preferred to try to fix the French by the threat of a cavalry charge and then let their artillery do its deadly work from a safe distance. Because the French had only five intact artillery pieces with them at this point and were badly outnumbered by the Habsburg cavalry, it was a tactic to which they had no answer.

Time and again the retreating French halted, formed square, and delivered a volley when the Austrian cavalry approached. Having checked their mounted foes, they then resumed the retreat. But to accomplish this the infantry had to retire in closed columns since only this formation permitted an immediate conversion to square. Consequently, they were vulnerable to artillery fire and suffered under "a hail of balls and shells."[21] Lannes particularly praised the coolness of the 28th Demi-brigade as it maneuvered as if on a parade ground in spite of the near proximity of the Austrian cavalry. A French writer noted, "Nothing could shake our battalions. They deployed and went into column with the same composure, under the heaviest fire, as if they were being inspected and reviewed."[22] Likewise, the French cavalry withdrew by platoons at the walk. When the Austrian troopers pressed too close, they faced about to force the Austrians to deploy. Then they nimbly withdrew before the Austrians charged, in order to repeat this process farther east. It was not without cost. Just as was the case of the infantry, Kellermann recalls the cavalry conducting these maneuvers under a "murderous artillery fire."[23]

The retreat from Marengo was testimony to the prowess of the French army. Although a formidable cadre remained with their colors, scores of others did not. They had stood manfully the rigor of combat at Marengo, but become dispirited when facing retreat. In contrast to the official reports full of praise for a difficult fighting withdrawal are the candid accounts from several soldiers. From their perspective, the retreat looked very much like a rout. There was so much abandoned equipment and munitions that the Mounted Chasseurs of the Consular Guard received the task of destroying ammunition-laden caissons to prevent the Austrians from using the munitions.

Lannes' men retired cross country in the direction of the field headquarters at the Buzana farm. At one point two Austrian battalions supported by a pair of guns pressed them too hard. Lannes ordered Colonel Bessières to charge with his cavalry of the Consular Guard. The terrain did not favor cavalry. By the time the horsemen worked their way through the vineyards, the white-coated infantry were ready to receive them. Moreover, a group of opposing cavalry was deploying on the Guard's left flank. Bessières ordered a wheel to the left to confront this threat. The mounted grenadiers and chasseurs suffered from enfilade fire while performing this maneuver. "Every discharge mowed down whole ranks. Their ricochet bullets carried away with them, both men and horses" recalled a guardsman.[25] Still, they managed successfully to redeploy and outface the Austrian horse. The episode angered Lannes, who believed that his orders had been disobeyed. It provided the basis for an epic quarrel that would be played out over the next nine years.

***

Victor's hard-pressed men had retreated a little over a mile when they spied reinforcements. They belonged to Monnier's Division (3,983 infantry), men who had begun the day camped around Bonaparte's headquarters at Torre di Garofoli. Behind them marched the grenadiers of the Consular Guard. Coursing the nearby field was the unmistakable figure of Napoleon Bonaparte.

Apparently much like everyone else, Bonaparte's mood swung with the fortunes of battle. Already he had exerted himself repeatedly to rally troops. While the soldiers in his immediate presence seemed to respond, he was only too aware that his men were near defeat. Coignet reports seeing him seated by the highway, morosely flicking at pebbles with his whip while the nearby troops retreated. The arrival of fresh troops energized him. He galloped alongside the mutilated ranks to call out, "Courage, soldiers, the reserves are coming. Stand firm!"[26] It was the first time most of the soldiers had seen their commanding general this day and they began to cheer.

Judging that Ott's envelopment of the French right flank constituted the most critical of the many threats, Bonaparte sent Monnier's 3,983 men against Castel Ceriolo (see map p.166). While general of division Jean-Charles Monnier remained with the 72nd Demi-brigade in reserve – a decision Bonaparte criticized later – general of brigade Carra Saint-Cyr led the 19th Light in close column toward Castel Ceriolo. Ott had abandoned this village when he marched against Lannes' flank, so the 19th captured it easily. South of the village, general of brigade Schilt maneuvered his 70th Demi-brigade against the flank and rear of Ott's line. Schilt's attack panicked some of Ott's men. They abandoned two 3-pounders and fell back in disorder into the marshes bordering the Bormida. Artillery Lieutenant Douvernelle promptly assigned some horse artillerymen to provide crews for these captured pieces. He also added an 8-pounder and howitzer, two of the six pieces which had run the gauntlet past Fort Bard, to form a four-gun battery that began to pour enfilade fire into Ott's ranks.

The French occupation of Castel Ceriolo and the artillery fire against his flank induced Ott to order FML Ludwig Vogelsang, whose 2,194-man division was in the second line, to countermarch to Castel Ceriolo

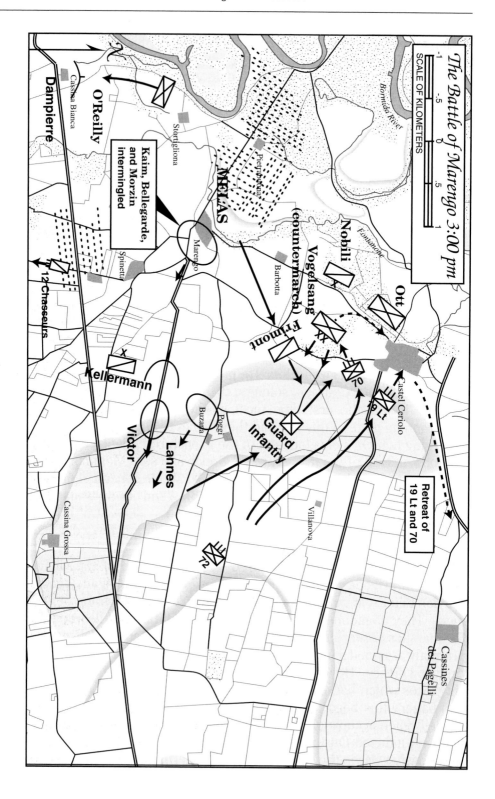

The Battle of Marengo 3:00 pm

SCALE OF KILOMETERS

Castel Ceriolo

with five battalions. Vogelsang's counterattack overlapped Schilt's flank and caused him to retire. This left Douvernelle's gunners without support. An Austrian cavalry charge overran the battery, captured the lieutenant and his men, and secured the guns. Spearheaded by the Stuart Infantry Regiment, the Austrians proceeded to attack the village. The defending French were isolated, well in advance of any supports. They kept looking over their shoulders for reinforcements, but none came. After an hour-long resistance they yielded the village to Vogelsang's men. The two demi-brigades retreated northeast along the highway, effectively removing themselves from the remainder of the battle.

The 800 infantry of the Consular Guard had marched behind Monnier's division and arrived on the field about 2 p.m.[27] Initially they served as ammunition bearers. With pockets stuffed with cartridges, the grenadiers passed behind the infantry to distribute ammunition. Coignet of the 96th Demi-brigade observed simply, "It saved our lives."[28] When Monnier's division marched on Castel Ceriolo, Bonaparte perceived there was a dangerous gap between the 70th Demi-brigade and Lannes' men. To plug this gap he ordered the Consular Guard infantry to advance. We are fortunate to have an eyewitness account provided by cavalryman Joseph Petit of this, the first combat of what was to become one of history's renowned, elite corps:

> "The foot grenadiers of the Consular Guard now came up, in the same state they have always been beheld on the parade. They formed up in the most orderly manner, in subdivisions, and advanced against the enemy, which they met not a hundred paces from our front."

At first the guardsmen drove back their foes. They benefitted from the protection provided by the remaining troopers of Champeaux's dragoon brigade. However, these dragoons had fought a great deal already and had lost their leader. When "a cloud of Austrian cavalry", the Lobkowitz Dragoons, charged toward them, they failed to counter-charge and retired instead. Nearby, Berthier had to gallop for his life to escape. The Guard's skirmishers, who had been 60 paces in front of the battalion columns, ran back to the protection of the grenadiers' hastily formed square. Habsburg artillery opened fire against this vulnerable target. Again Petit describes the scene, the:

> "very first [ball] which struck them laid down three grenadiers and a fourrier [quartermaster] dead on the ground, being in close order. Charged three times by the cavalry, fusilladed by the infantry, within fifty paces, they [the Guard infantry] surrounded their colors, and their wounded, and, in a hollow square, exhausted all their rounds of cartridges; and then, with slow and regular steps, fell back and joined our astonished ranks."[29]

The Consular Guard Grenadiers form square during their attack on Castel Ceriolo.

The Austrian dragoons swarmed around this living citadel but could not penetrate it. According to the Austrian account, the French artillery that accompanied the Guard stopped their charge with point blank canister fire. The dragoons fell back and Champeaux's troopers, showing commendable spirit, rallied to pursue them. Emboldened, the guardsmen deployed out of square and resumed their advance. Exhibiting great spirit of their own, the Spleny Infantry Regiment, although deployed in line, advanced toward Champeaux's troopers. The regiment's battalion guns drove off the French troopers. A musketry duel between the Consular Guard and the two battalions of the Spleny Regiment, supported by one battalion of the Frölich Infantry, ensued. The Austrians outnumbered the French by three to two. In the smoke and confusion this advantage was not decisive. But the Austrians also possessed a considerable artillery superiority and the cannons' fire began to tell. Then, the energetic Oberst Frimont, who had begun the day by leading the advance guard against Victor's outposts, led a cavalry charge against the flank of the Consular Guard. Frimont's four squadrons tipped the balance. After a gallant 30-minute long stand during which time they lost about one-third of their men, the Consular Guard retired. Bonaparte later would say of their fight that they had stood like a "granite redoubt." He added that their action showed "what can be done by a handful of men of spirit."[30]

Now the entire army was in retreat. The only uncommitted soldiers belonged to Monnier's 72nd Demi-brigade. They covered the retirement of Lannes' men until two battalions found themselves suddenly surrounded by hostile cavalry. They were in line and there was no time to form square. While the men in the two front ranks defended themselves with musketry, the soldiers in the third rank faced about and calmly delivered a volley that drove off the horsemen.[31] The two battalions then retired through broken ground and across vineyards to evade the Habsburg cavalry. They encountered the demi-brigade's third battalion, which had remained in reserve. This battalion, in turn, helped cover their withdrawal by forming square to repel three separate Austrian cavalry charges. Then and thereafter, the 72nd's entire performance garnered little credit because of Bonaparte's disgust with Monnier and because the Consular Guard's performance overshadowed it.

Later it could be said that the effort of Monnier's Division and the advance of the Consular Guard worked as a successful diversion by gaining time for additional reinforcements to arrive. At the time, in mid-afternoon on the plain of Marengo, it appeared that the penultimate reserve had been committed to no avail. Victor's people continued their retreat to San Giuliano. They saw the village packed with the wounded and the skulkers. Carts belonging to the vivandières sat jammed beside baggage and equipment wagons. Talk of defeat was in the air.

Perhaps First Consul Bonaparte took solace from an encounter he had with a trumpeter of his mounted guard. About this time a pair of cannons fired and a ball sliced in half the trumpeter's plume. In a bantering, familiar tone Bonaparte asked if anything was wrong. The trumpeter replied, "Nothing general, except the rage in my heart and a damaged plume; but if you would permit me, I will capture those pieces for you."

Bonaparte fixed him with furrowed brow. "Always the same! No, I don't want it, it is too bold."

"Too bold perhaps, general, but if you will give me twenty men, the pieces will be yours."[32]

Although Bonaparte refused to grant permission, such a display of redoubtable fighting spirit must have encouraged him that all was not yet lost. He remained mounted near the highway where bullets and balls kicked up the dirt around him. He encouraged his remaining soldiers to hold hard. In spite of his words, the Austrians continued to advance in an apparently irresistible wave. Habsburg troopers picked up bearskins from the fallen grenadiers of the Consular Guard, fixed them on their swords, and taunted their foes by boldly exhibiting these trophies. It was as if they were saying, 'this too will be your fate.'

Across the lines, on the outskirts of Marengo GdK Melas made a fateful decision. It was about 3 p.m. and had been a hard day with more fighting than he had expected. Like many of his officers, Melas had displayed energetic leadership. But he had paid a price. Two horses had been killed beneath him and during one of his falls he had painfully bruised his left arm. The septuagenarian warrior was sore and tired. As he gazed about him he saw nothing but the backs of his enemies. He instructed FML Kaim to continue the pursuit and gave him orders to use the cavalry and artillery to kill as many as possible before the French repassed the Scrivia River. He cautioned that the infantry should go no farther than San Giuliano. With that, Melas rode back to Alessandria to compose his victory dispatch. In the words of the semi-official Austrian account of the battle, "This sudden departure of the general in chief necessarily produced a bad effect."[33] It could hardly be otherwise. The chain of command was broken with a new officer unexpectedly thrust into a position of supreme responsibility. Furthermore, Zach, who could have provided Kaim important assistance, instead decided to go forward with the advance guard. He was thus unavailable for consultation.

It took time for Kaim to organize the pursuit. A large percentage of the Austrian army had converged on Marengo. This had caused a confusing intermingling of units. It was a hot, humid day and the soldiers had struggled hard to drive the French from the village. Finally officers restored order to the tired rank and file. O'Reilly's column continued with its mission to protect the army's right flank (see map p.172). Frimont, fresh from his success against the Consular Guard, used part of his command to link O'Reilly with the Austrian units advancing east along the highway. Zach accompanied the advance guard. His exact command status is unclear. Probably the brigade officers retained tactical control. The 43-year-old veteran, GM Francis Saint-Julien, led the way with his brigade consisting of the Michael Wallis Infantry. Five grenadier battalions belonging to Lattermann's brigade followed. The Liechtenstein Dragoons advanced along the column's left flank. About 1,000 paces behind the advance guard marched the mainbody led by FML Kaim in the order: GM Bellegarde's brigade with three line battalions; the Tuscan contingent commanded by GM Vinzenz Knesevich; and GM la Marselle's brigade with three line battalions.

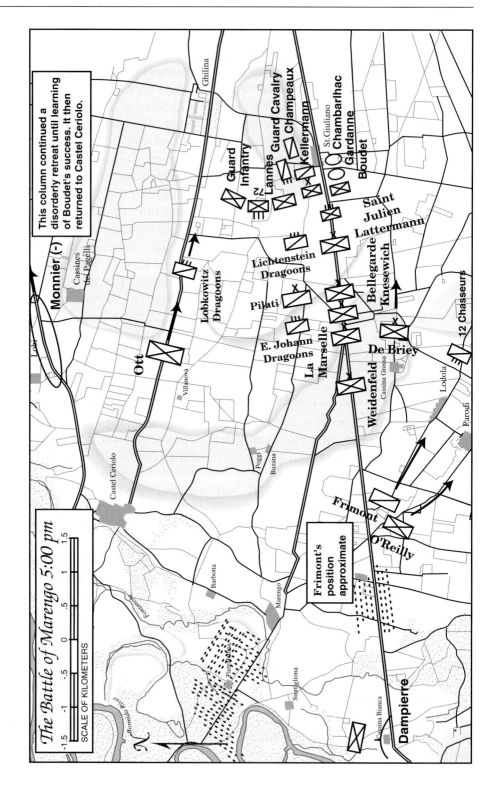

The Battle of Marengo 5:00 pm

SCALE OF KILOMETERS
-1.5   -1   -.5   0   .5   1   1.5

This column continued a disorderly retreat until learning of Boudet's success. It then returned to Castel Ceriolo.

Frimont's position approximate

Another 1,000 paces to the rear were GM Weidenfeld's six battalions of grenadiers. To the south of the highway marched GM De Briey's infantry brigade. Most of the Habsburg cavalry, excluding Ott's troopers, marched abreast of the mainbody just to the north of the highway with Pilati's brigade in the first line and the Erzherzog Johann Dragoon Regiment in the second line.

Further north, Ott's command initially remained near Castel Ceriolo. Sometime around 3 p.m., Ott learned that a force of French cavalry, Jean Rivaud's 700-man light cavalry brigade, was moving against his rear. This was alarming intelligence. Perhaps they were the vanguard of the formation he had been warned about that was occupying Sale. If this was the case, their presence meant a fresh French force was boring in against the Austrian left flank. It took time for Ott to ascertain that the enemy was an isolated cavalry brigade. Reassured, Ott sent the Lobkowitz Dragoons scouting to the fore and followed with his infantry. By the time he resumed his cross country advance, the main column had marched eastward along the highway. Coordination between the columns was lost. If there was to be renewed fighting, it would happen first along the highway and Ott would be unable to provide support.

Neither Zach nor any other Austrian expected to have to fight seriously for the remainder of the day. Everyone knew that the French were beat, an impression confirmed by merely gazing about. The terrain was covered with small knots of flying French soldiers. As the white-coated column marched east its soldiers continued to collect prisoners. About a mile and one-half west of San Giuliano, Zach saw enough of a formed French presence to cause him to order the advance guard to deploy. The enemy he observed belonged to the rallied remnants of the Guard, Monnier, Lannes, and Victor. They occupied a position north of the highway. Probably about one-third of the French forces that had engaged remained with their colors. Another third had fallen or been captured. Skirmishers who had become separated from their parent organization, men busy carrying the wounded from the field, or skulkers simply trying to survive somewhere other than in the front lines composed the remainder.

With their bands playing, Zach's advance guard resumed its march. The ground perpendicular to the highway rose and fell with gentle serpentine undulations. As the soldiers of the Michael Wallis Regiment breasted one of these rises west of San Giuliano, they saw a heretofore undetected and imposing looking French force deploying just to the south of the highway. Desaix and his men had arrived on the field of battle.

Part 4.
Death of a Hero

The early morning of June 14 had found Louis Desaix accompanying Boudet's division (4,856 infantry) as it prepared to march through Rivalta, some five and one-half miles southeast of San Giuliano. The rain-soaked roads were poor, progress slow. Then Desaix heard the sounds of battle off toward Alessandria. He halted his march and sent his aide-de-camp, Anne Savary, to scout toward Serravalle, 20 miles southeast of Alessandria. This was the objective Bonaparte had assigned the division. Two hours later Savary returned to report that there were no Austrians around Serravalle. During the aide's absence, the cannonading had intensified. Desaix resolved to stay put until he learned what the noise meant. He sent Savary galloping off to the First Consul. Savary, in turn, while riding across country encountered a courier, Bonaparte's aide-de-camp Jean Bruyère. Savary told Bruyère where to find Desaix and continued north.

Sometime around 9:30 a.m., Bruyère located Desaix one mile from Rivalta and delivered an urgent recall order. Desaix reversed his column as quickly as he could but, like most countermarches, it proved a time-consuming endeavor. Not until 1 p.m. did the 4,856 infantry belonging to Boudet's division, 120 hussars and 123 heavy cavalry, and 110 artillerists crewing eight cannons truly get under way. They were in fine spirits, "marching as gaily as if they were bound for a ball."[34] Between 4 and 5 p.m. they arrived near San Giuliano to see "the disorder which was beginning to reign in the army, a disorder caused on the one hand by a great number of wounded with the comrades leading them...and on the other by the numbers of carts, and the crowd of servants, with the good for nothing soldiers who usually join them."[35] In other words, like the Austrian soldiers, Boudet's men saw a defeated French army.

Desaix had ridden ahead to reconnoiter the field. He appeared in customary simple garb wearing a plain, all blue uniform without lace or embroidery, a bicorne without feathers, and well-worn, turned down riding boots. He found Bonaparte waiting for him on a small rise west of San Giuliano. Earlier, Bonaparte had climbed the San Giuliano belfry. From its vantage point he had seen Desaix's soldiers moving nearer. Now the First Consul asked Desaix what he made of the situation. "This battle is completely lost," Desaix reputedly responded, but "we have time to win another today."[36] That time began when Boudet's leading unit, the 9th Light, reached the field. Boudet

Wheat field where 9th Light checked Saint-Julien's Brigade

deployed it to the south side of the highway. The 9th's center battalion formed in line while the adjacent battalions formed in column. This was the formation the French labeled 'mixed order', a formation designed to generate firepower from the battalion in line while the battalions in column protected both flanks from cavalry charges.

However, the ground on which this deployment occurred was already within musket range of the advancing Austrians. Accordingly, Boudet ordered a skirmish line to advance and engage the enemy to gain time for the balance of the demi-brigade to deploy. Boudet's arrival encouraged the Army of Reserve. The cry spread rapidly across the field, "Here they are, here they are!" [37] North of the highway, additional soldiers rallied to join the ranks of Victor's, Lannes', and Monnier's commands. For the first time since the retreat from Marengo, the army presented the semblance of a battle line.

The unexpected appearance of Boudet's division caused the leading Austrian unit, Saint-Julien's brigade, to pause. A vineyard and a hedge partially concealed the 9th Light making it difficult for the Austrian officers to judge its strength. Probably it appeared to both Saint-Julien and Zach that they confronted another rear guard like they had been meeting for the past several hours. The Austrian commanders decided to deal with it in the same way they had dealt with the others

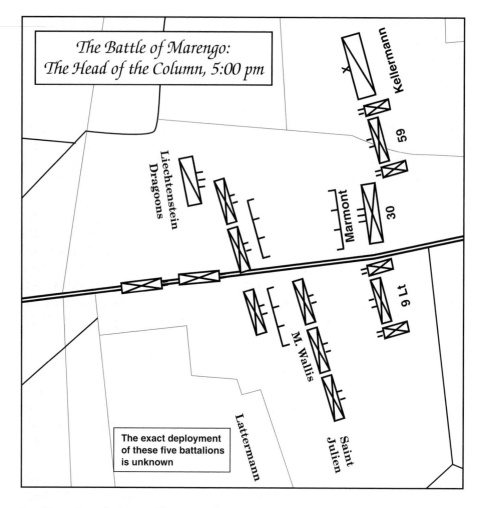

The Battle of Marengo:
The Head of the Column, 5:00 pm

Kellermann

59

Liechtenstein
Dragoons

Marmont

30

9 Lt

M. Wallis

The exact deployment
of these five battalions
is unknown

Lattermann

Saint
Julien

by directing their artillery to eliminate this meddlesome force. As the Habsburg gunners began to pound the 9th Light, Boudet's second brigade, formed from the 30th and 59th Demi-brigades, deployed to the right rear of the 9th Light.

During the time that Boudet deployed his division, Desaix, Marmont, Murat, and Bonaparte conferred. They remained mounted on a nearby swale from where they could see both the approaching Austrians and Boudet's men. According to Marmont, Desaix said, "We need a sharp artillery fire to impress the enemy before attempting a fresh charge; otherwise it will not succeed. We absolutely must have a good artillery fire." Marmont replied that he would establish a battery using the five intact pieces remaining from the previous actions, five more that had been in reserve and just arrived, and the eight assigned to Boudet's division. Marmont arrayed his 18-gun battery along a swale to the north of the highway. Meanwhile, Bonaparte coursed Boudet's lines to harangue the troops. Reputedly his fight talk included the stern reminder to his troops, "Remember it is my custom to sleep on the field of battle."[40] His presence, if not his words, seemed to electrify the men.

Nonetheless, the Austrian infantry and artillery threatened to overwhelm the 9th Light, which remained well forward of the rest of the division. Observing this, Desaix ordered Boudet to withdraw the 9th Light by echelon. Boudet was of two minds. He recognized the need to retire but feared it would sacrifice his skirmish line. Consequently, he relayed the order but commanded that it be executed very slowly. He then rode to confer with Desaix to explain his concerns. Desaix himself had ridden to tell Boudet to inform him that a general attack was imminent and therefore that Boudet should stop the retrograde when the 9th Light came abreast of Boudet's other two demi-brigades. What is notable about these orders and maneuvers is the cool calculation displayed by leaders throughout the French chain of command and the confidence they had in their soldiers' ability to perform complicated maneuvers while under fire.

Still, Desaix worried that his frontal charge would be inadequate. According to Savary, Desaix said, "You see how matters stand. I can no longer put off the attack without danger of being myself attacked under disadvantageous circumstances". Desaix instructed his aide to gallop to the First Consul to inform him that he lacked cavalry and that Bonaparte "must direct a bold charge to be made upon the flank of that column whilst I shall charge it in front."[41]

Across the lines, Saint-Julien's infantry and Lattermann's grenadiers perceived the backward movement of the 9th Light as a sign that once again the French rear guard had recoiled from the artillery fire. A cheer went up and they began to advance. This misapprehension made what was to come all the more shocking.[42]

Marmont's battery opened fire. Firing from a partial enfilade position, its canister tore gaps amid the Michael Wallis Regiment. The Habsburg artillery returned the fire and a cannon ball took off the arm of a Lieutenant Conrad just as he was observing his guns' effect. Ignored and lying on the ground, Conrad saw Savary riding past on his way to deliver Desaix's request. He shouted out to attract Savary's attention. Savary thought the lieutenant was asking for assistance and replied "a little later...have patience."

"It's not this," replied Conrad gesturing toward his gaping wound, "give me the pleasure of telling my gunners to fire a little lower."[43]

With Savary's assistance Conrad's gunners adjusted their fire. It caused the Austrians to hesitate and then halt. After enduring a short bombardment, they heard the stirring cadence of the *pas de charge* and then saw Boudet's division charge. The 9th Light broke the Michael Wallis Regiment. Its men fled rearward toward the grenadiers who calmly opened their ranks to permit passage and then closed up again. The grenadiers had not suffered from Marmont's artillery and consequently held firm against the approaching French infantry. Their professional volleys stopped the charge of the 9th Light. Behind the grenadiers the Michael Wallis Regiment reformed. In the face of an Austrian counter-attack, the 30th Demi-brigade began to retire. The battle's outcome hung in the balance.

When Boudet's division advanced it masked Marmont's guns. Marmont ordered his men to limber the guns and follow the infantry. Instead, to his horror, the gunners continued to fire through the narrow intervals between the infantry. Such ill-disciplined fire risked killing friendly troops. Marmont rode to his left-most guns. These were two 8-pdrs and a howitzer crewed by the Consular Guard. They were positioned next to the highway. Marmont had just ordered them to advance when he saw the 30th Demi-brigade falling back in disorder. Because the gunners had maintained their grasp on the prolonges, they were able to respond quickly to Marmont's command to swing the pieces about and face front. They loaded canister and waited. Fifty paces behind the 30th, Marmont saw a mass of well formed men. At first he could not identify them in the smoke. Then he recognized distinctive bearskin caps. His guns and howitzer discharged four rounds apiece at the charging grenadiers. The grenadiers staggered but replied with a volley.

Meanwhile, Savary had delivered Desaix's request for support to Bonaparte. The First Consul replied, "Have you well examined the [Austrian] column?"

"Yes, general."

"Is it very numerous?"

"Extremely so, General."

"Is Desaix uneasy about it?"

"He only appeared uneasy as to the consequences that might result from hesitation. I must add his having particularly desired I should tell

Kellermann's troopers charged toward the camera as they bore in against the grenadiers.

you that it was useless to send any other orders than that he should attack or retreat – one or the other; and the latter movement would be at least as hazardous as the first."

In fact, by the time this exchange occurred, Desaix had already decided to attack. While Bonaparte rode to Desaix to authorize personally the decision to charge, he sent Savary to explain the situation to Kellermann. Savary carried Bonaparte's order to "charge the enemy without hesitation as soon as Desaix shall commence his attack." [44]

During the time Boudet's division had deployed, General Kellermann had gathered his surviving cavalry, a mere 150 troopers, 400 yards to the right of the highway. A platoon of the 1st Cavalry, two squadrons of the 8th Dragoons and possibly the troopers of the 6th Dragoons joined him. Still, they numbered no more than 400 troopers and were so few that in order to exaggerate their strength Kellermann deployed them in a single line. Given the inequities of the ground, it is doubtful that Kellermann could see much of Boudet's fight. However, before Boudet charged, the field had been relatively silent. Once Marmont's cannons and Boudet engaged, Kellermann could hear them.

Kellermann chose his moment superbly. He ordered an advance by the left flank, thereby converting his battle line into a compact column. Then he had the trumpeters sound the charge. [45]

Many years later an admiring Marmont recalled the moment and observed that if Kellermann had charged three minutes later it would have been too late. Three minutes earlier would have been premature. Instead, his column, spearheaded by the heavy horsemen of the 2nd and 20th Cavalry, struck when the Habsburg grenadiers were unsettled by Marmont's artillery fire and held empty muskets because they had just fired a volley. General Suchet had recently fought against these same grenadiers during his defense of the Var River. He had found that they became discouraged after a setback and at this time they were excessively vulnerable. So it proved when Kellermann struck the flank of Lattermann's grenadiers. According to the Austrian account, "This attack, unlooked for and executed with surprising swiftness, threw the Austrian infantry into disorder and dispersed it after a short resistance. Many men were cut down."[47]

Three grenadier battalions virtually dissolved on contact. Somewhere behind them an artillery caisson blew up with a frightful roar. The explosion unnerved some soldiers and added to the chaos. Most of the Bohemians belonging to the Michael Wallis Infantry Regiment broke to the rear. Trooper Riche of the 2nd Cavalry seized General Zach by the throat and demanded that he surrender. Nearby, another trooper secured GM Saint-Julien. Although Saint-Julien escaped in the confusion, in total, some 2,000 (according to the Austrian account) to 4,000 (according to the French account) officers and men laid down their arms. Reanimated by Kellermann's success, the entire French battle line surged forward. Entire except for the absence of Louis Desaix, whose death went unnoticed in the frenzy of combat.

Such was the state of Austrian morale that Conscript Georges Amptil of the 30th Demi-brigade bayoneted a grenadier standard bearer and captured his standard while the hapless man's entire platoon numbly watched. So far, Kellermann and Boudet had managed only to defeat the enemy advance guard. Now was the time for the Austrian cavalry to counter the French success. They proved wanting. Kellermann rapidly reformed his troopers and led them against the nearest enemy unit. This was the Liechtenstein Dragoons, a unit which should have been providing flank security for the grenadiers. Having failed at that task, they also failed here and broke before contact. Additional French troopers belonging to the Consular Guard and Champeaux's brigade moved forward to join Kellermann's pursuit of the Liechtenstein Dragoons. The army's cavalry commander, Murat, was everywhere and very much in his element. He galloped from the Consular Guard to Kellermann's troopers to coordinate the chase.

The Liechtenstein Dragoons fled in terror. They stampeded through the ranks of Pilati's cavalry brigade. Quite often after a mounted force is defeated once during a day it remains jumpy. So it proved with Pilati's troopers. The morale impact of the routed dragoons and the sight of Kellermann's heavy cavalry and Bessiéres' Consular Guard caused the brigade to dissolve in panic. Trooper Petit describes the scene:

> "The Austrian cavalry, resolving to save the infantry, came up to us in column and their rapid pace obliged us to give loose the reins. We inclined to the left, by obliquing on them. At a distance of about thirty paces, was a ditch, which again separated us. The crossing of it, taking sword in hand, surrounding the two first platoons, all was but the work of five minutes."[48]

During this melee Bonaparte's stepson, nineteen-year-old Eugène Beauharnais, received two saber slashes against his shabraque. However, most of the Austrian troopers ill-defended themselves. The Guard sabered them to the ground, taking no prisoners. While the Guard engaged them frontally, Murat led some dragoons against their flank. Some of Pilati's survivors galloped northward toward Ott's column, most rode for the highway to make their escape.

The Austrian account depicts the situation:

> "Yet no one in the main column could understand the flight of the cavalry. They had heard indeed the sudden growling of the cannon toward San Giuliano but they did not know what had happened; the greater number of the cavalrymen themselves did not know why they were fleeing so precipitately. The main Austrian column, broken by the cavalry fleeing through it, began also to give way."[49]

FML Kaim tried desperately to restore order. He had just managed to deploy an infantry battalion to confront the French when a fresh mob of routing cavalry collided with it. The contagion of fear spread to the infantry and they too became swept up in the torrent streaming rearward. Soon most of the Austrians belonging to the central column along the highway were flying in terror.

Not all of the Austrian cavalry performed poorly. Anticipating that they would confront hostile horsemen, Boudet's division had formed compact battalion columns before continuing to advance. According to Boudet, some Austrian units attempted numerous charges to slow the pursuit while others tried to work around the French columns to charge their rear. Boudet believed that the French ability to maintain order within their serried battalion columns, in spite of the broken terrain, allowed them to repel these charges.

Of the Austrian infantry, apparently only the rearmost brigade, GM Weidenfeld's 2,240 grenadiers who had yet to fight, offered significant resistance. Although unable to stop the fugitives, their rearguard action southeast of Marengo allowed the defeated central column to escape. By nightfall, the bulk of the main column was routing through Marengo. Officers vainly tried to rally them behind the Fontanone Creek. The soldiers had only one thought in mind: to run until they regained the security of the fortified bridgehead. Jammed against the one gate cut through the earthworks, their panic intensified. Horsemen, foot soldiers, gunners, and wagon drivers all wanted to escape through the gate simultaneously. The panic continued across the Bormida bridges. A French officer who had been captured earlier in the day was there: "I have witnessed some defeats in the course of my military career, but I never saw anything that resembled this."[50] The crush to cross the bridges was so great that the officer found himself lifted off of his feet and carried along for some 500 paces.

Impatient with the pace of flight, an artillery driver drove his cannon straight across the river itself. In a scene reminiscent of the Russian flight at the Battle of Friedland in 1807, once other drivers saw that the river could be forded, they too turned off the highway and whipped their teams through the water. Under the weight, the river bottom turned slimy. Soon twenty or so guns with their limbers mired in midstream.

Austrian officers continued to struggle to little avail to rally the routing army. About 7 p.m. Melas learned of the disaster and returned to the bridgehead. Although he exerted himself with all of his remaining energy, his presence did not seem to matter. The soldiers continued to stream past him. However, the French were so weary that they did not pursue closely. Their horses were extremely fatigued, having had nothing to eat during the day and very little the day before. Upon reaching Marengo, the French cavalry reined in when Weidenfeld's grenadiers and artillery opened a hot fire. Their resistance permitted O'Reilly to extricate his command. On the opposite flank, Monnier's division reoccupied Castel Ceriolo at 8 p.m. Two hours later Victor's men reclaimed their original positions near Marengo.

The day's last combat occurred when Ott's column retired toward the bridgehead. Ott's people had not been involved in the general panic. Observing the defeat of the central column, the French émigré and aide to FML Vogelsang, Crossard, had advised that Ott attack the French flank. A ruthlessly determined officer, Bonaparte for example, would have risked this last roll of the dice. Ott may have briefly entertained this idea, but before he could complete his preparations he judged that the opportunity had passed. He sent the Bach Light Battalion to take position in the vineyards south of Castel Ceriolo to secure his flank. They delivered effective enfilade fire that deflected the French cavalry and allowed Ott's men to retire unmolested toward Marengo. The column continued its retreat in the darkness only to learn that some French infantry had regained Marengo and blocked the way. FML Vogelsang placed himself at the head of the Stuart Infantry Regiment and charged the village at the double. Although Vogelsang received a wound, he managed to cleave a passage to safety for Ott's corps. Under cover of O'Reilly's grenzers, the last Habsburg soldiers shuffled to safety within the earthworks. After 14 hours of fighting, the Battle of Marengo was over.

NOTES

1. David G. Chandler, ed., *The Military Maxims of Napoleon* (New York, 1988) Maxim XXVIII, p. 64.

2. "Report of Marshal Melas to the Archduke Charles," June 19, 1800, United States Army Service Schools, *Source Book of the Marengo Campaigne in 1800* (Fort Leavenworth, KS, 1922), p. 215.

3. Savary claims Bonaparte told him that he had spent much of the night on his horse examining the Austrian position and seen no signs of a substantial enemy presence. See: Anne Savary, *Mémoires du Duc de Rovigo*, I (Paris, 1901), p. 204.

4. The French order of battle as duplicated in Gaspard Gourgaud, *Memoirs of the History of France During the Reign of Napoleon, Dictated by the Emperor*, I (London, 1823), following p. 296, gives 23,791 infantry, 3,688 cavalry, and 690 artillery and engineers. Gaston Bodart, *Militär-historisches kriegs-lexicon 1618-1905* (Vienna, 1908), p. 355, gives 24,300 infantry and 3,700 cavalry. My best estimate is in Appendix I. Regarding the number of available tubes: Marmont says each division had a six-piece battery and that he created a five-tube reserve, presumably the same five he mentions selecting from the pieces captured at Pavia. However, we know Boudet had an eight-tube battery. The Consular Guard had three tubes. Thus, a theoretical 35 tubes. Victor captured two more on June 13. Marmont lost three that evening. This leaves 34. However Gardanne asserts in his after action report that his division had only two 4-pounders to support it, yet Berthier, on June 11 assigns two 3-pounders to Gardanne. Major Demarcay, Monnier's chief of artillery, says his division had only two tubes assigned. Édouard Gachot, La *Deuxième Campagne d'Italie* (Paris, 1899), p. 307, n. 2, makes the French total 38.

5. Jean Baptiste Crossard, *Mémoires Militaires et Historiques*, II (Paris, 1829), p. 290.

6. French accounts concur that the battle proper started at 9 a.m., whereas Austrian accounts vary but generally begin the action earlier.

7. One battalion of the 44th demi-brigade did not reach the field until some time around 6 p.m.

8. Writing in 1845, General Quiot, who served as aide-de-camp to Victor, made particular mention of this fire.

9. "Extract from the Austrian Military Review," in United States Army Service Schools, *Source Book of the Marengo Campaign in 1800* (Fort Leavenworth, KS, 1922), p. 222.

10. Claude-Victor Perrin, *Extraits de Mémoires Inédits de feu* (Paris, 1846), p. 168.

11. "Dampierre to General Mathieu-Dumas," June 16, 1800 in *Source Book of the Marengo Campaign in 1800*, p. 193.

12. Perrin, p. 171.

13. "Rivaud to Dupont," June 15, 1800, in *Source Book of the Marengo Campaign in 1800*, p. 195.

14. Lorédan Larchey, ed., *The Narrative of Captain Coignet* (New York, 1890), p. 74.

15. Savary, *Mémoires du Duc de Rovigo*, I, p. 204.

16. Édouard Gachot, *La Deuxième Campagne d'Italie* (Paris, 1899), p. 269.

17. Philip J. Haythornthwaite, *Die Hard! Dramatic Actions from the Napoleonic Wars* (London, 1996), p. 46. The description comes from de Gonneville.

18. Karl Mras, "Gefchichte Des Feldzuges 1800 in Italien," *Öestereichische Militärische Zeitschrift*, V-IX (Vienna, 1823), p. 240.

19. *Source Book of the Marengo Campaign in 1800*, p. 209.

20. Crossard, II, p. 296.

21. See Quiot's account provided in Gaspar Jean Marie Rene de Cugnac, *Campagne de l'Armée de Réserve en 1800* (Paris, 1901), p. 385, n. 1.

22. "French Account of the Battle of Marengo," *The British Military Library*, II:XXV (October 1800) 419.

23. "Kellermann to Victor," June 15, 1800, Perrin, p. 409.

24. For examples, see: F. Grandin, *Souvenirs Historiques du Captaine Krettly, ancien trompette-major*, I (Paris, 1839), p. 150; and Joseph Petit, *Marengo or the Campaign of Italy, by the Army of Reserve Under the Command of the Chief Consul Bonaparte* (Philadelphia, 1801), p. 24.

25. Petit, p. 28.

26. Larchey, p.76.

27. The foot contingent of the guard comprised two grenadier battalions and a company of light infantry.

28. Larchey, p.75.

29. Petit, pp. 24-25.

30. "Bulletin of the Army of Reserve," June 15, 1800, *Source Book of the Marengo Campaigne in 1800*, p. 204.

31. Recall that when the British 28th Regiment did this at the Battle of Alexandria, it was thought so remarkable that men of the regiment were thereafter allowed to wear a special badge on the rear of their shakos.

32. Grandin, I, p. 152.

33. Mras, "Gefchichte Des Feldzuges 1800 in Italien," (Vienna, 1823), p.248.

34. General Lejeune, *Mémoires du Général Lejeune* (Paris, 1896) p. 25.

35. "Extract from the Report of Marches and Operations of the Boudet Division," *Source Book of the Marengo Campaign in 1800*, p. 199.

36. Louis de Bourrienne, *Memoirs of Napoleon Bonaparte*, II (New York, 1906), p. 13.

37. Larchey, p. 77.

38. In addition, about this time a battalion of the 44th Demi-brigade forded the Scrivia and joined its parent unit in Gardanne's Division. See Gachot, p. 304.

39. Marmont's recollections are on pp. 131-35, volume II of his *Mémoires du Maréchal Marmont Duc de Raguse* (Paris, 1857). He provides Desaix's words as

well as the number of guns in his battery and its position. Strength and location are at odds with a variety of secondary sources.

40. "Bulletin of the Army of Reserve," June 15, 1800, *Source Book of the Marengo Campaign in 1800*, p. 205.

41. Savary, I, p. 210.

42. For Boudet's relevant comments see "Extrait du Rapport des marches et operations de la division Boudet," Cugnac, II, p. 398.

43. "Résumé du Rapport du citoyen Duport," Cugnac, II, p. 398, n. 2.

44. Savary, p. 210. Given there was some controversy over who ordered the charge it is important to note that Marmont and Savary mostly concur on the events as described and that Kellermann never claimed credit for conceiving of the charge on his own.

45. "Kellermann to Victor," June 15, 1800, Perrin, p. 409. For a thorough examination of the details of Kellermann's formation changes see the footnotes on pp. 404-407 in Cugnac. It may be that some of the cavalry were already in column because of the difficulty of maneuvering amid the vineyards.

46. Recall "Suchet au Premier Consul," May 30, 1800, Jacques Campredon, *La Défense du Var et Le Passage Des Alpes 1800* (Paris, 1889), p. 347, previously cited in Chapter III.

47. "Extract from the Austrian Military Review," *Source Book of the Marengo Campaign in 1800*, p. 224.

48. Petit, p. 30.

49. Mras, "Gefchichte Des Feldzuges 1800 in Italien," (Vienna, 1823), p. 252.

50. C.J., "Other Interesting Particulars respecting the Battle of Marengo," in *British Military Library or Journal*, II (London, 1799-1801), p. 422.

Chapter 8

Resetting
the Pieces

PART 1.
THE CONVENTION OF ALESSANDRIA

*"My dear fellow, if I should die tomorrow, I would not be given more than
half a page in a general history written ten centuries from now."*[1]

BONAPARTE TO HIS SECRETARY AFTER THE BATTLE

While Victor's and Lannes' men returned to their original campsites,
the troopers of the Consular Guard wearily rode along the
highway to San Giuliano. Many dozed in their saddles until their
mounts shied from stepping on a fallen soldier. Jarred awake, they
looked about to see everywhere shadowy figures on the move. Pairs
of soldiers used muskets as improvised litters to carry comrades to the
field hospitals. Others pushed wheelbarrows to convey the wounded.
In spite of their efforts, hundreds of unattended wounded writhed
helplessly in the adjacent fields. Injured horses neighed in pain,
calling out to the passing troopers in hopes of rejoining the herd. The
debris of battle – abandoned cannons, broken wagons, overturned
carts – choked the roadside ditches. In the distance, houses and
barns burned in lurid glow. When Eugène de Beauharnais counted
noses among his company of Guard mounted chasseurs, only 45
remained of the 115 who had begun the day.

Against this backdrop, the First Consul also returned to where he
had begun the day, his headquarters at Torre di Garofoli. During
the evening he held a discussion with his prestigious prisoner, GM
Zach. As head of state Bonaparte possessed complete power to
negotiate treaties. He stressed to Zach his desire for peace and
proposed a temporary truce with the condition that the Austrians

evacuate the Bormida bridgehead. Zach agreed that this was a reasonable basis on which to proceed and dispatched a note to Melas outlining the proposal.

Meanwhile, a conference of a very different sort was occurring ten miles to the east in Alessandria where Melas convened another council of war. The commanding general was demoralized. An Austrian officer observed, "His appearance was as doddering as his physique."[2] Melas and his generals decided that further resistance was hopeless. So shattered was the army that at daybreak the next morning only some 10,000 of the soldiers who had sortied from the bridgehead had rejoined their colors. Consequently, Melas resolved to accept Bonaparte's conditions for an armistice. At 4 a.m. on June 15 the Austrian General Skal and two captains appeared under a flag of truce in front of the French picket line. The French were suspicious. Previously during the campaign Austrian officers had reconnoitered French positions while under a flag of truce. Only after showing Melas' signature on a document requesting a truce were the envoys allowed to proceed.

Bonaparte treated Skal haughtily. According to Austrian reports, he said if the Austrians did not yield immediately he would attack and that when his soldiers captured Alessandria they would sack the city in vengeance for the capitulation of Genoa. Skal returned to Melas bearing Bonaparte's verbal ultimatum. Thoroughly depressed, Melas assigned General Liechtenstein and Count Adam Neipperg the unpleasant task of negotiating terms for a settlement.

Meanwhile, on the battlefield, the French continued the task of collecting the wounded. In order to cross the Alps the army had forsaken most wagons and carts. Consequently there were far too few vehicles available to use as ambulances. Also, the number of wounded overtaxed the available surgeons. While searching for food for himself and his horse around San Giuliano, Joseph Petit found that the wounded were, "heaped one upon another in the yard, in the granaries, in the stables and out-houses, even to the very cellars and vaults,[and they] were uttering the most lamentable cries, blended with the severest curses against the surgeons."[3]

Around noon Berthier left Bonaparte's headquarters along with the prisoner Zach to begin formal negotiations. For Melas the sticking point was Genoa. Having struggled so hard to capture the port, he was loath to relinquish it. Melas dispatched Liechtenstein with a counter-offer. Liechtenstein found that Bonaparte was in no mood to negotiate. In addition, the First Consul was a superb actor, knowing how to play a part to achieve his goals. There was also a latent imperious streak which was already appearing. Thus the First Consul impatiently replied to Liechtenstein, saying his terms were "irrevocable!" He lectured about the hopelessness of the Austrian strategic position and then dismissed Liechtenstein with the words, "Know that I am as well acquainted with your position as your are yourselves. I did not begin to learn the art of war yesterday."[4]

Fearful of what might happen if hostilities resumed, at 10 p.m. Melas signed the Convention of Alessandria. Its terms allowed the Austrian army to march intact eastward beyond the Mincio River. In return, Melas ceded all remaining Habsburg holdings in Piedmont and Lombardy. The Mincio was to serve as the boundary between France and Austria. Hostilities could not resume without a ten day notice and as long as the truce held the Austrians could not detach units from Italy to reinforce the army in Germany. With an eye toward future negotiations, Bonaparte tried to soften Melas' sense of defeat by sending him an Egyptian saber – he claimed he had captured it himself – "as a symbol of the high esteem for the conduct of your army on the field of Marengo."[5] To his cronies, Bonaparte boasted that in one day he had recovered Italy. While not strictly accurate, it was close enough to satisfy most Frenchmen. The Army of Reserve learned about the peace the next day and responded joyfully. Perhaps better still for the long suffering rank and file, the day brought the first supply convoys with food and wine. In Alessandria the mood was far different. According to Crossard, officers and men alike railed against their chief's decision.[6]

At relatively small cost and in three weeks, Bonaparte had regained what the Directory had lost during the preceding year. As one commentator has observed, "This was not the Cannae for which the First Consul had hoped and planned, but it sufficed."[7] That Bonaparte failed to accomplish more may be accounted for by his lack of manpower. His strategy anticipated receiving more support from Moreau. He also expected Genoa to occupy Ott's corps. When Moreau failed to dispatch as many men as promised and Genoa capitulated sooner than expected, Bonaparte confronted stiffer numerical odds than he had hoped. This made overwhelming victory unlikely.

Given the odds, to obtain an overwhelming victory Bonaparte needed to maneuver flawlessly. He did not do this. To some extent his political concerns can explain several oversights that almost compromised the entire campaign. He was in a hurry to return to Paris and his haste contributed to some miscalculations. His worst mistake cannot be excused on this account. Dispersing his army on battle's eve was a major blunder. It is noteworthy that the young general was not yet too grand to learn. Seldom in the future would he fail to concentrate every available man for the decisive battle.

Yet, it is a tribute to his brilliant overall strategy that his army could have endured a tactical setback at Marengo. Had Melas won the day, Bonaparte could have retired to the Stradella position. Recall that his original plan had been to assume a blocking position here and await an Austrian attack. Whereas he would then have summoned divisions from Cremona and Milan to replace losses, Melas had no reserves available. The Austrian general still would have had to fight for his line of communication and he would have had to do this with an army depleted by battle. Bonaparte had to win the Marengo campaign. He did not have to win the Battle of Marengo.

***

Following the battle, both sides calculated the costs. The official French report claimed losses of 700-800 killed, 2,000 wounded, and 1,100 prisoners.[8] This surely understates. For example, the sum of Chambarlhac's incomplete infantry returns alone nearly equals the purported total for the entire army. Likewise with Watrin, who reported that his division lost 13 officers killed and 83 wounded along with 2,000 casualties among the other ranks. Although a final tabulation will remain elusive, merely summing the numbers reported by individual units yields 5,027. This excludes Gardanne, Chambarlhac's 24th Light, Mainoni's brigade, and Boudet. The French historian Édouard Gachot, working with the reports in the French archives on the eve of the battle's centennial, estimated total losses at 7,700, although this too is probably a low figure.[9] It can be safely concluded that about one soldier in four who served with the Army of Reserve at the battle was either killed, wounded, or captured.

Indicative of both the battle's intensity and the French leadership style is the list of generals killed or wounded: corps commander Desaix, killed; divisional general Boudet, wounded; infantry brigade generals Rivaud, Jean-Pierre Malher, Mainoni, and Louis Guénand wounded; and cavalry brigade general Champeaux mortally wounded. After more than a month of suffering, Champeaux died in Milan on July 28. Guénand, on the other hand, was particularly fortunate that his wound did not prove serious. A ball struck his right thigh but was partially deflected by the coins he carried in his pocket!

As always, Austrian reporting practices are more precise but here too are suspicions of undercounting. The semi-official Austrian account recorded 963 killed including 14 officers; 5,518 wounded including 244 officers; and 2,921 prisoners including 75 officers. This total of 9,416 seems low when one observes that Zach's column laid down their arms to avoid being slaughtered by Kellermann's cavalry and their numbers alone exceed the reported prisoner total. Indeed, the French claimed capturing 4,000 men from this column, although the Austrians claimed only 1,665. Gachot estimates total Austrian losses as about 12,000 while the Austrian compiler, Gaston Bodart, provides a figure of 11,000. Melas' army lost about one man in three killed, wounded, or captured. Senior officers had exerted themselves, showing, for the Habsburg army, unusual front line leadership. FML Haddick died from his wound on June 18. Generals Bellegarde, Lattermann, La Marselle, Vogelsang, and Gottesheim all received wounds. However, only fourteen Austrian officers died at the battle, and none higher than captain. In contrast, in the French army the 24th Light alone lost 10 officers killed while Watrin's division lost 13 officers killed. Probably French officer casualties exceeded Austrian totals by fifty percent. Throughout the horse and musket era cavalry mounts and artillery draft animals suffered fearfully in battle. The Austrians report 1,493 horses killed. The army also lost 12 cannons, 1 howitzer, and 13 wagons.[10]

News of Marengo circulated in Vienna on June 24. It filled the people with dismay. The informed public was quick to point the finger of blame. "All the world here knows," wrote the wife of the British ambassador, "that the day was lost by the cavalry all turning tail and falling back on the infantry, who behaved incomparably."[11]

No one had labored harder to defeat France than Chancellor Thugut and the news deeply distressed him. He attributed the defeat to a colossal failure of intelligence. In his view, somehow Austrian agents had missed the French buildup in Switzerland. This had allowed Bonaparte to cross the Alps and achieve a numerical superiority in Italy. If it comforted Thugut to think that numerical inferiority accounted for Melas' defeat, it was the solace of the deluded.

Part 2.
Honor and Glory

Marengo was a pivotal episode in Napoleon Bonaparte's career. Then and thereafter he understood this. He would often say, 'My house began on the field of Marengo.' The Marengo medal he created included the words he purportedly uttered to rally his troops:

"Remember it is my custom to sleep on the field of battle." He named his favorite charger 'Marengo' and his favorite dish *'poulet à la Marengo.'* He refused to share the battle's glory by allowing any marshal to assume a title that referred to it. And he set out to rewrite the battle's history in a far from truthful manner.

Indeed, beginning with his official report Bonaparte shrouded the battle in a tissue of lies. He made small alterations in Berthier's report to add drama and thereby magnify his achievement. Whereas Berthier wrote, "the enemy, fighting desperately," Bonaparte substituted, "The enemy fought like men who wanted to make an opening for themselves and who had only the alternatives of victory or complete loss." Not content with small changes, Bonaparte turned to pure invention. The official report claimed Desaix died in the arms of his aide-de-camp. In fact, Desaix died unnoticed. It was Savary who found his body, already stripped of clothes, in a pile of dead. Bonaparte, who sincerely grieved the death of one of his few friends, recovered to write a patriotic death speech for Desaix: "Go tell the First Consul that I die regretting not having done enough to live in posterity."[12] Later, he would have these words inscribed upon Desaix's memorial medal. In order to deny how close his army had been to defeat, Bonaparte inserted into the official report the claim that the right flank – Monnier and the Consular Guard – held their position throughout the battle. In time, he would expand upon this lie.

Of course Bonaparte was not alone in altering history. Berthier's 16-year old son had served on the staff during the battle. When Berthier wrote his battle report he cited this son five times. It amused Bonaparte, who laughed at the idea of giving this "brat...credit for the victory."[13] Likewise, in later years when the émigré Baron Crossard penned his battle account, it is apparent that his tactical insights benefitted from years of reflection.

In spite of his fabrications, the First Consul keenly remembered who had done what at the battle. Lannes, Victor, Watrin, Gardanne, and Murat received sabers of honor with the inscription "Battle of Marengo, commanded in person by the First Consul." In the coming years, many of the men of Marengo were to rise far. When the Emperor Napoleon announced the first promotions to *Maréchal d'Empire* in 1804, Berthier, Bessières, Lannes, and Murat were on the list as was the heroic defender of Genoa, Masséna.

In addition to honors and promotions for individual leaders, Bonaparte rewarded distinguished units with special tributes. Well could it be said that Gardanne's 44th and 101st Demi-brigades had "maintained their old reputation for steadiness and valor."[14] No unit honor surpassed that earned by the 9th Light, which had stood firm against the surging Austrian advance and thereby gained the time for the devastating French counterstroke. Three days after the battle, Berthier reported to the First Consul that the 9th had been "incomparable by its bravery." Bonaparte conferred upon it the title 'the Incomparable'. As late as 1814, an officer would say of 'the Incomparable 9th Light': "I have a very fine regiment...it has a brilliant reputation." [16]

Bonaparte also awarded his favorite accolade to the 8th Dragoons. They had "covered themselves with glory." [17] There were muskets, sabers, and drumsticks of honor to deserving infantrymen, cavalry troopers, and drummers. Captain Deblou, the officer who had delivered Victor's message to Bonaparte announcing the Austrian attack, had later distinguished himself by capturing an Austrian flag. Deblou received a saber of honor. When the First Consul handed out these awards, he showed a discerning appreciation of which units had fought particularly well. He was most magnanimous to the units who had borne the initial shock. All of Lannes' demi-brigades as well as those in Chambarlhac's division received 15 muskets of honor. A single battalion in the 101st received five, a proportionally equal honor. Ten went to Gardanne's other unit, the 44th Demi-brigade, and to Boudet's 9th Light and 59th Demi-brigade. Boudet's 30th Demi-brigade received five. Twenty carbines of honor went to cavalry troopers.

Of all the future exploits of the Marengo veterans, probably none was more trying than the experiences of a colonel who had distinguished himself at the battle. In 1805 he was aboard the line of battle ship *Intrépide* at Trafalgar. Although he possessed proven valor in combat on land, naval warfare unnerved him. As British cannonballs blasted the ship, he tried to shelter himself behind the captain. This exercise in futility prompted the captain to roar with laughter: "What's the matter, Colonel? Do you think I am wearing armour." [18]

***

On June 16, 1800 the Army of Reserve paraded past General Bonaparte. It was a joyous affair. In the absence of laurel leaves, the soldiers adorned their hats with oak leaves. The soldiers were pleased with their commander and he with them. The next day the First Consul returned to Milan where, on June 18, a grand *Te Deum* was held at the Dôme. In addition there was the ceremony of occupying

Milan's citadel. According to the terms of the Treaty of Alessandria, the Austrians had to surrender this fortress. Among the Habsburg garrison was a Piedmontese unit. Most of them immediately deserted to join the victors. When Rohan's Legion trooped out, many of the native-born rank and file Frenchmen also switched sides, although the émigré officers remained loyal to the Habsburg army. Four days later Masséna arrived in Milan. Bonaparte appointed him commander in chief of the new Army of Italy, which he formed by merging the Army of Reserve with Masséna's old command. So ended the proud but brief 108-day life of the Army of Reserve.

Ever since leaving Paris Bonaparte had closely monitored police reports in case conspirators launched a coup against his government. To keep everyone off balance, he had repeatedly written to his fellow consuls telling them that he was about to return to the capital. According to Fouché, who made it his business to know such things, during Bonaparte's absence, Paris was in a state of political ferment. Everyone, from the extreme parties comprising the Jacobins and the Royalists to the patriotic republicans who worried that the First Consul was more attracted to cannons than to liberty caps, was in a state of high suspense pending news from Italy. After Parisians first learned about Marengo and the subsequent armistice they were "drunk with joy" for two days.[19]

On June 25 the First Consul departed Italy for Paris. His passage was a Caesar-like journey of triumph. In Lyons, an enthusiastic crowd refused to disperse until the First Consul showed himself on the balcony. In Dijon a group of lovely young women dressed like classical Greek maidens and flocked around his carriage to serve as escort. He arrived in the capital at 2 a.m. on July 2, having been gone four days short of two months. Upon his return, political enmities and discords appeared to evaporate. "It seemed," Fouché later wrote, "as if he were less the conqueror of Italy at Marengo than of France." With hindsight, Fouché noted, "He departed in the character of the first magistrate of a nation, still free" and reappeared "in the character of the conqueror."[20]

Bonaparte responded to the nation's cheers with a flurry of decrees celebrating the victory. He ordered a monument built to commemorate Desaix. In the name of France he gave Desaix's mother a pension. To ensure that there was no jealousy on the part of General Moreau's soldiers in the Army of the Rhine, Bonaparte made certain that they too received national rewards. In particular, the sword belonging to Tour d'Auvergne, the 'First Grenadier of France', was placed in the temple of Mars. Bonaparte's personal assessment of how to divide equitably military glory came later in the month. He ordered that the nation's six best painters be chosen to paint representations of important recent battles. Only one, Möskirch, was devoted to the Army of the Rhine and Moreau. The others were all his: Rivoli, the climactic victory of his first Italian campaign; the three Egyptian triumphs at the Pyramids, Mount Thabor, and Aboukir; and, of course, Marengo.

On July 14, the eleventh anniversary of the storming of the Bastille, occurred one of those carefully staged ceremonies that Bonaparte used to promote patriotism and to solidify his standing. After the battle of Marengo, he had ordered the Consular Guard to return to Paris and had timed its marches so it would arrive the evening of July 13. On schedule, the following day the Guard marched onto the *Champ de Mars* in the middle of the ceremony. They wore their dust streaked, battle-torn uniforms and thus stood out amid the dress uniforms of the garrison troops. Their front ranks carried Austrian standards captured at Marengo. When the crowd sighted them, they gave voice to wild enthusiasm. Riding with the mounted chasseurs was Eugène Beauharnais. He records, "It was one of the best moments of my life." [21]

NOTES

1. J. Christopher Herold, ed., *The Mind of Napoleon: A Selection from His Written and Spoken Words* (New York, 1955), p. 48.

2. Georges Lefebvre, *Napoleon From 18 Brumaire to Tilsit* (New York, 1969), p. 100.

3. Joseph Petit, *Marengo or the Campaign of Italy, by the Army of Reserve Under the Command of the Chief Consul Bonaparte* (Philadelphia, 1801), p. 32.

4. Louis de Bourrienne, *Memoirs of Napoleon Bonaparte*, II (New York, 1906), p. 18.

5. Gunther E. Rothenberg, *Napoleon's Great Adversaries* (Bloomington, IN, 1982), p. 63.

6. Petit, p. 32; and Jean Baptiste Crossard, *Mémoires Militaires et Historiques*, II (Paris, 1829), pp. 316-17.

7. Alexander B. Rodger, *The War of the Second Coalition* (Oxford, 1964), p. 244.

8. "Report of the General in Chief, Berthier on the Battle of Marengo," United States Army Service Schools *Source Book of the Marengo Campaign in 1800* (Fort Leavenworth, KS, 1922), p. 211.

9. Édouard Gachot, *La Deuxième Campagne d'Italie* (Paris, 1899), p. 307, n. 3. Bodart calculates 1,100 killed, 5,400 wounded, and 1,500 prisoners. Gaston

Bodart, Militär-historisches kriegs-lexicon 1618-1905 (Vienna, 1908), p. 355.

10. Karl Mras, "Gefchichte Des Feldzuges 1800 in Italien," *Öestereichische Militärische Zeitschrift* (Vienna, 1823), pp. 256-57. The number or prisoners taken from Zach's column is provided on p. 251. Gachot's estimate is on p. 307, n. 4 and Bodart's on p. 355.

11. Gilbert Elliot, *Life and Letters of Sir Gilbert Elliot, First Earl of Minto from 1751 to 1806*, III (London, 1874), p. 141.

12. "Bulletin of the Reserve Army," June 15, 1800, John Howard, ed., Letters and *Documents of Napoleon,* I (New York, 1961), p. 465.

13. Herold, p. 13.

14. "French Account of the Battle of Marengo," in *The British Military Library*, II:XXV (October 1800) 418.

15. "Berthier to Bonaparte," June 17, 1800, Gaspar Jean Marie Rene de Cugnac, *Campagne de l'Armée de Réserve en 1800*, II (Paris 1901), p. 422.

16. "Bugeaud to Madame de Puyssegenez," Marshal Thomas Bugeaud, *Memoirs of Marshal Bugeaud*, I (London, 1884), p. 80.

17. "Bulletin of the Army of Reserve," June 15, 1800, *Correspondance de Napoléon Ier*, VI (Paris, 1860), p. 361.

18. David Howarth, *Trafalgar: The Nelson Touch* (New York, 1969), p. 203.

19. André Miot, *Memoirs of Count Miot de Melito* (New York, 1881). p. 174.

20. Joseph Fouché, *The Memoirs of Joseph Fouché*, I (London, 1846), pp. 132-33.

21. Eugène de Beauharnais, Mémoirs et *Correspondance Politique et Militaires du Prince Eugène* (Paris, 1858), p. 86.

Chapter 9

Moreau
in Germany

PART 1.
THE RHINE FRONTIER

"At the commencement of a campaign, to advance or not to advance is a
matter for grave consideration, but when once the offensive has been
assumed, it must be sustained to the last extremity."[1]

Napoleon Bonaparte, Military Maxim VI

When the spring campaign season of 1800 had begun, the rival armies in Germany were on familiar terrain, having contested the Rhine River line throughout the Revolutionary Wars:

> "The armies on the Rhine had hitherto been on parallel fronts; the Austrians generally on the defensive...The French, breaking out at one or the other of the bridge-heads...would try to press forward into Germany; the Austrians, drawing together on the threatened points, would oppose them: and the result was that, in 1800, the river still formed the frontier line between them."[2]

Unlike times past, in 1800 the French possessed Switzerland. However, neither General Jean Moreau nor FZM Paul Kray fully appreciated its strategic significance.

The Austrian high command had devised an ambitious plan. Because of the weather, the offensive would begin in Italy where Melas' advance would compel Moreau to detach soldiers from his army to buttress the defense of Provence. Then Kray would swing into action, cross the Rhine and advance through the Belfort gap. Thus,

Switzerland could be avoided. Outflanked, south and north, it would fall like a ripe fruit. At that point Melas would march up the Rhone Valley toward Lyon. Later, he and Kray would unite for the triumphal march on Paris. Until Melas' offensive unfolded, Kray intended to remain on the defensive.

The Hungarian born Kray had earned a fine reputation during the Seven Years' War. He enjoyed further success while suppressing various internal revolts and then shared in a successful campaign against the Turks. He was active against the forces of revolutionary France and his great day came in 1799 when he won the Battle of Magnano and recaptured the fortress city of Mantua. This triumph earned him the appointment to Grand Master of the Artillery and independent command on the Rhine front. The 65-year-old veteran commanded a 120,000-man army. However, the raw numbers give a misleading impression about its true power. There were 7,000 Tyrolese militia of limited value. A host of mercenaries hired by British gold included 12,000 Bavarians who were in excess of Bavaria's required contribution as a member of the Holy Roman Empire. Württemberg provided 6,000 mercenaries while the Elector of Mainz dispatched about 5,000 more. Their capabilities ranged from satisfactory for the Bavarians, tolerable for the Württembergers, to dismal for the soldiers from Mainz, who were, in spite of their price tag, essentially militia. To supplement the army in the event Moreau attacked, Austrian authorities also encouraged the peasants of the Black Forest to resist French incursions.

The Aulic Council judged any French presence in eastern Switzerland to be a dagger aimed at Vienna and consequently ordered a shield to be erected. Accordingly, Kray committed 25,000 men to the defense of the Vorarlberg and the Tyrol.[3] Kray deployed the rest of his army in characteristic Austrian fashion by extending it in a cordon defense over a 170-mile long front. This system of war, with its occupation of all prominent points – river crossings, fortresses, defiles, road junctions – had successfully defended the Rhine in the past. Kray had no doubt it would work again. Ignoring the dangers of a French sortie out of Switzerland, he established his magazines at Stockach, a mere day's march from that country. While such a forward base could well support his own advance, it was vulnerable if the French attacked first. Moreover, by the time the campaign began, incessant feuding among the staff had contributed to a collapse of the army's supply system. Morale fell as the men realized that they were being poorly cared for. Desertions, particularly among the Hungarian units, soared.

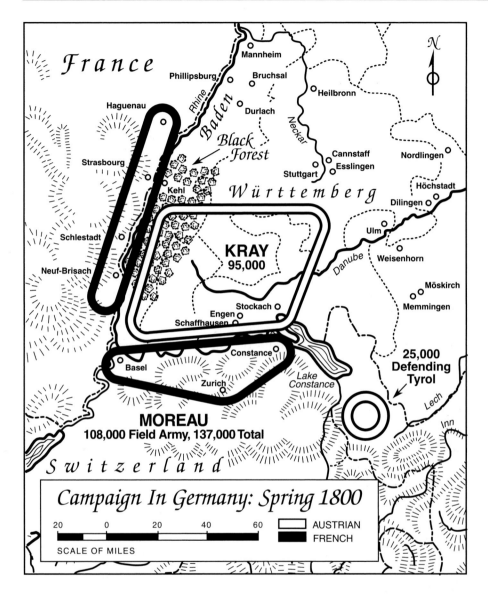

Across the lines, Moreau's Army of the Rhine was in excellent condition. It had received first call on men, equipment, and munitions. It was organized according to an emerging system that forever after altered military science. On March 1, 1800 Bonaparte ordered Moreau to organize his army into four corps. A corps was a self-contained, all-arms organization capable of engaging a larger force for several hours. Meanwhile, adjacent corps could move up to support or to outflank the foe. The corps structure conferred many advantages. It allowed an army to be dispersed, which eased the problems of keeping it fed. Then, when the time came to concentrate, the various corps could utilize all available roads so as to avoid traffic jams. The dispersed corps marched with the confidence that should they encounter the enemy they could contend effectively until reinforcements arrived. The corps structure also simplified command and control, making the army more flexible and quicker to respond. In time, Bonaparte would perfect the corps system and make it "the pre-eminent executive instrument of French conquest and military success during the Napoleonic wars."[4] In 1800 it was still a rough-hewn concept.

On March 20 Moreau organized his army corps: the Ist and IIIrd with three divisions; the IInd and IVth with four. He formed most of the light cavalry – the hussars and chasseurs à cheval – into divisions with two to three thousand men and placed the dragoons and heavy cavalry in a 3,000-man division assigned to the IVth Corps. He nominated the IVth Corps as his Reserve. By virtue of this organization, each division had both organic artillery and cavalry while each corps retained an artillery reserve.

Overall, the field army numbered about 108,000 men with another 29,000 garrisoning Switzerland and occupying the Rhine fortresses.[5] The First Consul's plan called for the Army of Reserve to depart Dijon the day Moreau's army crossed the Rhine. Once Moreau gained an advantage over Kray, he was to detach General Claude Lecourbe's reserve, with a fourth of his infantry and a fifth of his cavalry, to Switzerland where it would operate under the command of the Army of Reserve.

As previously noted, the First Consul and Moreau wrangled about when and where the Army of the Rhine should strike. To Bonaparte, the solution was obvious. The army should concentrate on the south side of the Rhine between Schaffhausen and Lake Constance and attack northward against the flank and rear of the Austrians in the Black Forest region. At a minimum, such an advance would cut the Austrian line of communication. In Bonaparte's mind, it also promised the chance of destroying a considerable part of Kray's army. The scheme was entirely too bold for Moreau. He objected that in order to concentrate his army, he would have to conduct a long flank march south along the Rhine. Kray might advance and maul the French while they were in motion. Alternatively, Kray might match the French concentration near Schaffhausen and defend the Rhine River line in such strength that it could not be pierced. Worse, he might allow the French to cross and then pounce on them and defeat them in detail.

The different outlooks were wholly characteristic of the two different generals. Bonaparte saw the Rhine River as a useful screen to permit the rapid concentration of a superior force. He would then advance to envelop the enemy's rear, natural obstacles be damned. Moreau focused on the difficulties of forcing a passage over one of the continent's major rivers while it was defended by an active foe. He conceived a plan whereby his left would make a powerful feint over the Rhine toward the Black Forest and then retire. Meanwhile, confident that Kray's attention would be focused on the Black Forest, Moreau would cross the Rhine at Basel and march east toward Schaffhausen where, by a complicated series of maneuvers, he would be joined by forces from both his left and right wings. Although doubtful of Moreau's strategy, Bonaparte had yielded when confronted with Moreau's threat to resign. In later years Bonaparte explained his behavior: "I was not yet sufficiently firm in my position to come to an open rupture with a man who had numerous partisans in the army, and who only lacked the energy to attempt to put himself in my place. It was necessary to negotiate with him as a separate power, as indeed, at that time, he really was." After extracting, so he thought, a promise that Lecourbe's corps would cooperate with the march of the Army of Reserve, Bonaparte left Moreau to his own devices.[7] Moreau however, was not known for cooperating with anyone. Consequently, the employment of Lecourbe's reserve remained a contentious issue.

After procrastinating through most of April, Moreau finally began his campaign on April 25. The feint against the Black Forest partially succeeded when Kray sent 7,000 men to reinforce the troops opposing Moreau's left wing. However, this was not economy of force since 49,000 French were occupying the attention of 20,000 Austrians. Next, Moreau managed to mass close to 85,000 men near Schaffhausen, but only after performing a flank march across the Austrian front that was far more dangerous than the one proposed by Bonaparte that Moreau had rejected for being too risky.

Moreau now occupied the same favorable flank position that Bonaparte's strategy had been designed to gain. Kray however began to realize that his immense logistical base at Stockach was imperiled. He resolved to concentrate his forces to defend his magazines. Moreau moved too quickly. He maneuvered so as to concentrate 20,000 men against 12,000 defenders at Stockach. They captured the Austrian base. While this action was occurring, Moreau's and Kray's main bodies locked horns in an intense battle at Engen on May 3. At one point, Moreau placed himself at the head of four infantry companies and led a counterattack to recapture a key village. By day's end the result was a drawn battle with about 7,000 casualties on each side. Stalemate, except that Kray, learning of the fall of Stockach, feared for his communications and retreated toward the entrenched camp at Ulm (see map p.199). This first victory for the Army of the Rhine inspired conscripts and veterans alike and gave the French a morale advantage that persisted for the remainder of the campaign.[8]

Moreau pursued the retiring Austrians who again offered battle to cover their retreat. About 50,000 French fought 40,000 Austrians at Möskirch on May 5. Once more the rival forces sternly contested the field until finally the Army of the Rhine drove the Austrians backward. Kray exhibited soldierly persistence, counterattacked, and sent the French rearward. In a complex series of maneuvers, Kray conceived an outflanking maneuver that was, in turn, outflanked. By day's end about 5,000 Austrians and 3,000 French had fallen. It was this victory that Bonaparte later chose to anoint when he commissioned one battle painting to honor the Army of the Rhine. After Möskirch, Kray realized that Moreau was gaining strength – recall Moreau's plan required his left wing to make its diversion and then send a sizeable detachment to join the main blow – and so he retreated again. He assembled his defeated forces at Ulm and awaited Moreau's attack. Kray's performance had dispirited his army. It had "completely lost" confidence in him.[9]

After such a promising beginning, Moreau hesitated and failed to press his advantage. His behavior annoyed some of his principal subordinates. Among several, Gouvion Saint-Cyr departed the army, using as an excuse poor health. Kray, in turn, did not want to risk battle unless his army occupied favorable terrain or possessed an overwhelming numerical advantage. In the stylized fashion of eighteenth century warfare, Moreau devised a series of feints to cover a march that threatened Kray's line of communication. He hoped that this would force Kray to abandon Ulm. But Kray parried Moreau's tentative thrusts. Ruefully, Moreau wrote the First Consul on May 27 that he and Kray were "fumbling against one another."[10]

The fumbling continued until June 9 when Moreau received a dispatch from the First Consul that informed him of Bonaparte's arrival in Milan. The news that Bonaparte's campaign was progressing satisfactorily re-energized Moreau. He advanced to beat Kray at Höchstadt five days after Marengo on June 19. He proceeded to blockade the fortresses of Ulm and Ingolstadt and managed to catch Kray's rear guard, under the command of Erzherzog Ferdinand, near Landshut on July 7. Ferdinand demonstrated anew that military capacity was not a blood right of the Kaiser's line. He became trapped between converging French columns and lost all of his artillery and much else.

The two sides concluded a truce on July 15, modeled after Bonaparte's post-Marengo truce. From an Austrian standpoint it was an ignoble end to a bungled campaign. Kray had failed to defend eminently defensible ground replete with fortresses and major river lines. It was one thing to explain away prior Habsburg defeats on the basis of mountainous terrain ill-suited to the army's tactics or to a surprise eruption into the army's rear. But it was quite different in Germany where terrain and logistics favored the Austrians. Kray's performance had been so dismal that even the Kaiser recognized that he had to be replaced. Thoroughly discredited and personally demoralized, the once respected general retired to his estates to live out his life in exile. Austrian society could be cruel to its losers. When the Habsburg officer corps shunned him, he was left almost friendless, the memories of his fine service during the Seven Years' War vanished. Later Erzherzog Karl would write Kray a flattering letter explaining that the boorish behavior directed toward him stemmed from envy over his previous victories. Perhaps Karl's kind words partially assuaged the old warrior's despair. FZM Kray died in January 1804.

Moreau also made mistakes during this campaign. He retained personal command of a corps and this compelled him to focus too heavily on events to his immediate front. Consequently, he failed to unite all of his forces. Instead of crushing his foe, he won a series of lesser victories. However, Moreau showed that if he lacked Bonaparte's ability, particularly his driving energy, he possessed strategic skills. His string of victories did nothing to alleviate the First Consul's concern that Moreau was a potentially serious rival.

Part 2.
The Austrian Command Dilemma

In response to defeats in Italy and Germany, Vienna became a hotbed of political intrigue during the summer of 1800. At first, Chancellor Thugut remained the Kaiser's dominant adviser. Defeat had done nothing to soften Thugut's hatred of the French.

His immediate problem at hand was how to respond to Bonaparte's peace overture. This dated back to the evening of June 16 when the First Consul had written to Kaiser Franz. His letter explored conditions for a permanent peace between France and Austria. It informed the Kaiser of the "desire of the French people" to put an end to the war.[11] Whereas the French people were truly war weary, it was disingenuous to suppose that their desires had any influence upon matters of state. However, Bonaparte for his own reasons wanted peace.

Through no fault of his own, the First Consul's timing was poor. His professed good intentions could not compete with raw cash. Once again 'perfidious Albion' had beaten him, for the day before his letter arrived, the Kaiser signed a new accord with Great Britain in which he agreed not to conclude a separate peace with France until February 1, 1801. In return Austria received two million pounds sterling in an interest-free loan to finance the war effort. Thugut persuaded his monarch to honor the accord with Great Britain and to rebuff Bonaparte.

Having received a pledge of money, what Thugut and his hard line clique needed was time to reconstruct the Habsburg military. To gain that time, the Austrian Court dispatched General Joseph Saint-Julien, the brother of the general who had fought at Marengo, and Count Adam Neipperg on an unofficial mission to Paris to explore conditions for a peace. Saint-Julien was a court favorite in Vienna; a cosmopolitan aristocrat whose attainments included membership in the Knights of Malta. Although he was an experienced diplomat and had successfully negotiated the Byzantine intrigues in St. Petersburg, Saint-Julien proved unequal to the challenge of matching wits with Talleyrand and Bonaparte. He signed a preliminary draft of a treaty whereby France gained the entire left bank of the Rhine in return for unspecified compensations in Italy. Saint-Julien and Neipperg returned to Vienna on August 5. The government promptly disavowed the draft treaty, reproached the two officers, and exiled the hapless Saint-Julien to Transylvania. Saint-Julien would be pardoned in 1802. Neipperg would gain delectable revenge for his troubles many years later by accepting the task of seducing Napoleon's second wife.

Following Saint-Julien's rebuff, the debate whether to renew hostilities resumed in Vienna. It pitted Thugut and the ardent Francophobe, the Kaiser's wife, versus the peace party led by Erzherzog Karl. When the decision came to select a replacement for Kray, the Kaiser preferred his brother Karl. Thugut disagreed. He wanted to resume hostilities as soon as possible and he knew that Karl disagreed. As the British ambassador's wife later observed, "Thugut is acknowledged even by his enemies to be the only man capable of being Minister; and the Archduke in the same manner is their only general. Unfortunately they are in high opposition to each other".[12]

The peace current ran deeper than Thugut realized. His single-minded focus on war with France had made him very unpopular. Although the army scrambled to prepare for renewed war, he felt compelled to resign in September. Louis de Cobenzl, who had negotiated the Treaty of Campo Formio with Bonaparte back in 1797, succeeded him. Cobenzl departed for Lunéville, France to negotiate with Joseph Bonaparte. His mission was to stall for time by dragging out negotiations at least until February 1801, at which time Austria could withdraw from its commitment to Great Britain.

Thugut's resignation again opened the door for the Kaiser to offer Karl command of the army. He was clearly the best available man. Yet ever since his first success in 1793, Karl had had to contend with Franz's doubts about his conduct and Thugut's open hostility. These forces had repeatedly undermined Karl. The Erzherzog brought much of this on himself. He believed that Austria's grand strategy had to be based on an accurate assessment of its military strength. Neither the Kaiser nor his principal advisers wanted their vision to be so constrained. They deeply resented Karl's attitude and Karl, in turn, resented how they pushed the army to attain objectives that were beyond its capacities.[13] In the late summer of 1800, Karl was among those who believed that even an unsatisfactory peace was preferable to renewed war. Karl was certain that another campaign had failure written all over it and he wanted no part. Consequently, to his discredit Karl claimed he was too sick – a diplomatic illness if ever there was one – and refused the command. But he was also enough of a patriot and enough of a family man to possess grave doubts that the army's appointed leader, his 18-year-old brother Johann, was equal to the challenge.

The lack of truly able commanders within the Habsburg Empire – a poverty, it should again be noted, that Franz promoted – contributed to Johann's selection. Additionally, the Kaiser judged that dynastic imperatives demanded that a member of the imperial house lead the best remaining Austrian army. The Kaiser also believed, or so he told Johann, that a young man's constitution, his presumed ability to endure hardship and fatigue, would energize the army. The Kaiser instructed Johann that he was to teach the army obedience and discipline. To help the inexperienced youth with the finer points of strategy, logistics, and combat, the Kaiser assigned him as second in command "the most innovative man in the art of war", old Baron von Lauer.[14]

The sixty-five-year-old FZM Franz Lauer had studied at the Engineer Academy and entered army service in 1755. During the Seven Years'

War he received promotion to captain. With peace proclaimed, Lauer resumed his studies and became an expert in fortifications and siege warfare. This served him well at the siege of Belgrade in 1789 where he earned both the order of Marie-Therese and promotion to general. Having seen action on the Rhine in 1795, Lauer went to Italy to serve as Würmser's chief of staff. It was he who devised the overly complex offensive that resulted in Würmser's army becoming surrounded and besieged in Mantua when a young man named Bonaparte responded to the Austrian maneuvers in most unexpected style. To his credit, Lauer thereafter proved the key man during the very stubborn defense of Mantua. He returned to his beloved engineer service until Karl asked for his recall to field operations in 1799.

His appointment as principal adviser to Johann met mixed reaction. Experienced officers deeply doubted that he was the man to inspire confidence in an army suffering low morale after a succession of defeats. Furthermore, the Kaiser had strongly urged Johann to put an end to the pernicious habit practiced by many senior officers of discussing orders and only obeying them if they felt so inclined. He then undermined this commendable imperative by instructing Johann to listen to Lauer and to follow his advice: "your responsibilities will be very easy", the Kaiser wrote, because Lauer will control all military considerations.[15] If Johann obeyed, he would be little more than a figurehead. Given that Johann was to subordinate his initiative to Lauer, it would be most difficult for him to demand subordination from the army's senior officers. By any assessment, internal bickering had produced a ridiculous command structure and caused Austria to fumble the opportunity to develop a coherent strategy during the summer's truce.

***

An undercurrent of intrigue also affected the French command structure during this time. Whereas before Marengo the First Consul had to handle senior generals gingerly, henceforth he possessed the stature to give orders that had to be obeyed. In an effort to simplify the chain of command, on July 24 Bonaparte informed Moreau that the government had entire confidence in his ability. If hostilities resumed, Moreau would command all three armies on the Rhine front. It was a great honor and one that Moreau declined. His response surprised the First Consul who suspected that Moreau harbored a concealed motive.

Regardless, Bonaparte worked to improve Moreau's position. Although he was not a trained lawyer, the First Consul was second to none in his ability to seek advantage within the legal limits of any document. He took advantage of the truce by instructing his old comrade, Pierre Augereau, to march his Franco-Batavian army against the Rhenish princes. This move would secure Moreau's left flank. More importantly, it would be a money making enterprise. Before signing peace accords with the nearly defenseless princes, Augereau was to levy the customary demands for contributions to the French war chest. Simultaneously, Bonaparte ordered Brune to march a new 10,000-man reserve army into Switzerland to relieve the French forces currently in garrison there. This move would secure Moreau's right flank. To ensure that everyone was ready if and when peace talks broke down, Bonaparte sent a circular to his chief subordinates – Moreau, Masséna, Augereau, and Brune – to remain vigilant and be ready to march upon the first warning.

Bonaparte had little doubt that fighting would resume. He had interviewed Chancellor Cobenzl while the Austrian was en route to Lunéville. He immediately grasped that Cobenzl's purpose was to spin out negotiations for as long as possible. Bonaparte concluded that nothing but an overwhelming military victory would force Austria to negotiate seriously. With this insight, he showed that although he had been head of state for only eight months, he already possessed a remarkable and rare combination of talents for both grand strategy and battlefield tactics. He was equally adept at seeing through an experienced diplomat's dissimulations or seeing through a false front offered by a wavering line of enemy infantry.

Thus, just as was the case in Austria, the arrival of autumn brought accelerated French preparations for war. In September the 33rd Demi-brigade paraded before the First Consul in Paris. The wastage of continual war since 1796 had reduced it by more than 90 percent. Over 3,000 men were dead, prisoners of war, or mustered out of service due to crippling wounds. In this latter category were two colonels, six majors, and six captains. The 37 officers and 295 men who survived had not received their clothing distribution before the 1799 campaign. Many were barefoot when they marched past the Tuileries and their tattered uniforms resembled rags. Their plight moved Bonaparte. He circulated among them, recognizing old comrades, remembering old battles.   As ever, his amiability was purposeful. He saw in these veterans the cadre for a new, strong unit. He concluded his inspection by promoting a deserving officer, François Roguet, and instructing him to "reorganize the unit as quickly as possible; I depend on you."[16] In the coming weeks Roguet received refractory conscripts – men who had been caught trying to evade the draft – men dismissed from the cavalry and marine artillery, deserters incarcerated in the Parisian prisons, and reluctant conscripts from the department of the Eure. To feed the war machine, France was scraping the dregs from the barrel.

When it seemed that the diplomats were fast approaching an impasse, Bonaparte instructed his generals to prepare to resume hostilities during the first ten days of September. Moreau complied, after his own fashion, by announcing that he was readying his siege train and his pontoons for a crossing of the Inn River, taking measures to secure his flanks, and arranging his cantonments so as to reassemble his army on the Isar River after eight marches. If this was not quite the dynamic style of Bonaparte, it certainly possessed a methodical acceptability. On September 1, 1800, the Army of the Rhine began its march to is assembly points near Munich.

Five days later, some 215 miles to the east, Kaiser Franz departed Vienna to join his army. He found his advisers, particularly Lauer, deeply divided over the fundamental question of whether to accept Bonaparte's peace terms or to resume hostilities. The disagreement persisted right up to the time the campaign began. The Kaiser joined the army, issued a stirring, eve of battle proclamation in which he pledged to campaign with his troops in order to observe their triumphs, and then accepted Bonaparte's proposal to yield three Bavarian fortresses in order to procure a 45-day extension of the truce.[17] The abrupt about face could not have been good for the army's morale. The new truce, signed at Hohenlinden on September 20, stipulated that either side had to give a fifteen day warning before resuming hostilities.

Most members of the Austrian war faction acknowledged that additional time would be valuable to complete the army's rearmament. On the other hand, former Chancellor Thugut argued heatedly with the Kaiser that it threatened the absolute destruction of the monarchy. However, Thugut was losing his influence. Franz preferred Lauer's counsel, who thought the truce particularly beneficial for Austria since it freed up 20,000 fine infantry who otherwise would be compelled to garrison the fortresses ceded to France. Apparently it never occurred to the Austrian strategists that they could, on their own volition, strip garrisons from fortresses of secondary importance. Their strategic notions remained embedded in an earlier era of positional warfare where entire campaigns were waged for the possession of one or two such fortresses.

The unexpected truce caught the Army of the Rhine rapidly closing in on the Isar River. As Moreau sardonically commented, "In the

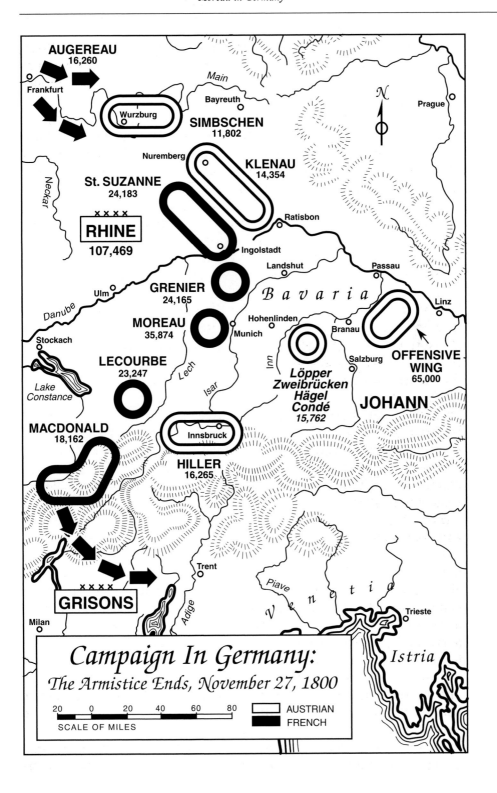

AUGEREAU
16,260

Frankfurt

Main

Bayreuth

Prague

Wurzburg

SIMBSCHEN
11,802

N

Nuremberg

KLENAU
14,354

St. SUZANNE
24,183

Neckar

xxxx
RHINE
107,469

Ratisbon

Ingolstadt

Landshut

Passau

GRENIER
24,165

B a v a r i a

Ulm

Danube

Linz

MOREAU
35,874

Hohenlinden

Branau

Munich

Stockach

LECOURBE
23,247

Lech

Salzburg

OFFENSIVE
WING
65,000

Inn

Isar

Lake
Constance

Löpper
Zweibrücken
Hägel
Condé
15,762

JOHANN

MACDONALD
18,162

Innsbruck

HILLER
16,265

Trent

Piave

xxxx
GRISONS

V   *n*   *t i a*

Milan

Adige

Trieste

Istria

Campaign In Germany:
The Armistice Ends, November 27, 1800

| 20 | 0 | 20 | 40 | 60 | 80 | AUSTRIAN |
| | | | | | | FRENCH |

SCALE OF MILES

French infantry on campaign.

morning, one told the soldiers: prepare your weapons, we are going to fight. Vive la Republique!" That evening, upon the announcement of peace, the soldiers shrugged and said, "Very well! Vive la Republique!" all the same.[18]

Again the diplomats returned to the negotiating table at Lunéville. But an irreconcilable obstacle remained: Bonaparte wanted to treat with Austria and England separately; in spite of his waning influence, Thugut managed to convince the Kaiser to honor his commitment to Great Britain that there be no separate peace with France. By November 5 Bonaparte concluded that negotiations were unlikely to produce the results he desired. Three days earlier he had held a long conference with Moreau. Thus it was no surprise to the commander of the Army of the Rhine to receive once again a warning order to prepare for war.

Moreau's Army of the Rhine, with 107,469 men, would deliver the main stroke (see map p.209). His objective was to drive the Austrians behind the Inn River. Augereau, with a 16,260-man Franco-Batavian Army would operate on his left while Macdonald, with the 18,602-man Army of the Grisons would secure his right by advancing into the Tyrol. In addition, Macdonald would conduct a diversionary attack in favor of the Army of Italy. Simultaneously, in Italy, Brune, who had replaced Masséna, commanded the 55,790-man Army of Italy. He too would take the offensive but had the modest objective of securing the line of the Adige River and laying siege to Peschiera, Legnago, and Mantua. For the winter campaign of 1800, the French host numbered nearly 200,000 men, most of whom were veterans, and all of whom were led by officers who had risen through the merciless meritocracy of revolutionary France.

None of the objectives Bonaparte assigned the armies were decisive. This was so because the First Consul recognized that a campaign begun in November would have to contend with winter weather as well as the Austrians. There is also the suspicion that Bonaparte did not want Moreau to achieve overmuch lest his victory overshadow the First Consul. Accordingly, Bonaparte planned for the French armies to capture an excellent springboard for a decisive campaign the following spring. At that time, Bonaparte anticipated returning to Italy to unite Macdonald's and Brune's armies. Then he would follow the route of his 1797 campaign and march on Vienna from where he would dictate peace.

$$* * *$$

On the evening of November 12, a French cavalry officer delivered a note to Erzherzog Johann that announced the resumption of hostilities. This note set the previously agreed fifteen-day clock ticking toward war. Again the French soldiers emerged from their comfortable south-German cantonments and began to march toward their assembly points. A contemporary French historian wrote that the army was the finest force ever to issue from France:

> "its organization, training, discipline, mobility, at the highest point of perfect; the clothing, the armament having been renewed and repaired; the artillery, commanded by one of the

ablest officers in Europe, General Eblé, was reestablished, almost entirely recast and strengthened in the Augsburg and Munich arsenals." [19]

Divisional General Jean Hardÿ put it more simply: "The army is superb." He assured his wife, "this time, it is certain that we will not sheath our sword until peace is signed." Uninterrupted success during the previous summer's campaign filled the army with great confidence. The army's chief of staff believed that man for man the French were vastly superior to their foes. He observed that even the formerly maligned cavalry now enjoyed a combat advantage over the vaunted Habsburg horse. Moreau sharpened the soldiers' edge in a proclamation that concluded, "The entire Republic has its eyes on the brave Army of the Rhine; she will respond to their attention with new victories!" [20]

Moreau's initial plan was simple. While general of division Gilles Sainte-Suzanne secured his left flank, he would advance toward the Inn River, attacking any enemy he encountered, and then search for a place to force a crossing. [21] As war approached, he had refined his notion. The visits back and forth between emissaries involved in negotiating the truce had allowed some observant French diplomats to provide recent intelligence about Austrian dispositions. Accordingly, Moreau resolved to push his offensive on his left to cover the advance of his right wing as it moved up to the Inn. He did not know whether the Austrians would contest the advance on the west side of the Inn or whether they would choose to defend behind that river. Regardless, the army's first objective was to close up on the Inn River. Moreau and his staff were well acquainted with the local topography and road net. They appreciated that Hohenlinden was a key road hub of essential value "for the offensive and the defensive." [22] Moreau intended to have 77,000 men massed and ready to advance toward Hohenlinden by November 26.

This plan proved overly ambitious. Yet it is a tribute to Moreau's skill that 63,000 well-appointed soldiers were present in position on the designated day. More rare for a French army of this period, the administrative and service departments were in excellent order. In contrast to Bonaparte's methods, Moreau insisted that his army treat the local inhabitants with decency. There were strict orders against promiscuous foraging. Moreau did not intend for the army to live off the land. Instead, each division moved with a convoy carrying seven days' provisions. A powerful military police traversed the line of march to maintain order. In spite of these measures, the campaign's attrition – desertions and a sick list bolstered by cold, damp weather – subtracted 5,097 soldiers from the army's effectives before a shot had been fired.[23]

Like the French, the Austrians had used the succession of truces to reorganize the army. The line regiments were at their authorized strength having received newly raised men, many exchanged prisoners, and recovered invalids from the hospitals. Additional manpower came when Hungry, Transylvania, and Croatia contributed their "insurrection" soldiers. To contend with the French skirmisher tactics, the crown raised a variety of light infantry battalions. The government also called for new levies to be raised locally to defend the Tyrol. Although the monarchy did not truly try to summon Germanic nationalism – that path lay nine years in the future – a variety of volunteer organizations did enlist. Moravia and Bohemia, for example, organized a volunteer legion. Lastly, the British subsidy purchased the services of some 30,000 soldiers raised in Bavaria, Württemberg, and the towns of Mayence and Wurzburg. By the terms of their contract, the Bavarians, who did not much like the Austrians, were not to operate outside the borders of their country. Austrian soldiers heartily reciprocated the Bavarian attitude. Referring to their mercenary status, they called the Bavarians 'beggar soldiers.'

By mid-November, a field army of 49,000 infantry and 16,500 cavalry had assembled east of Inn River (see map p.209). A 15,762-man force built around the Bavarians and Württembergers, but also including 1,800 dubious soldiers commanded by the émigré FML Condé, guarded the Inn River upstream from Branau. FML Johann Hiller protected the Tyrol while to the north, two sizeable forces defended a line from Wurzburg to Ratisbonne. The entire Austrian force numbered about 124,000, which meant that they faced odds of five to three against.

Manpower aside, what really mattered was the senior leadership and its unproven head, Erzherzog Johann. Into the command void stepped an aggressive chief of staff who easily convinced Johann that a brilliant offensive was practical and that it would cement the young man's standing before the entire army. Colonel Franz Weyrother, who had served as Würmser's chief of staff during that officer's ill-fated Italian campaign of 1796-97, proposed concentrating the offensive army on the banks of the Inn River between Braunau and Passau on November 25. Three days later the march west to the Isar River would begin. The army would cross the Isar at Landshut and then wheel south either to crush Moreau's left flank or to sever the French line of communication west of Munich. Johann and Lauer hoped that Weyrother's scheme would permit a rapid advance that would take the

French by surprise. Weyrother's scheme was sound enough strategy. However, it presumed a mobility that Habsburg armies seldom displayed and that the opponent would remain inert.

As the Austrian advance developed, it soon became apparent that a rapid advance would not occur. The soldiers were unaccustomed to hard marching. The movements to concentrate wore them down and involved excessive straggling. Desertions among even the German regiments were frequent. A continual, heavy rain reduced the roads to quagmires and filled streams to overflowing. Bottlenecks and delays ensued. The artillery and trains were unable to keep pace with the infantry. Well before contact with the enemy, the army was wet, weary, and in wretched disorder.[24]

Lauer and Weyrother had ill-served the young Erzherzog. When the offensive began, neither they nor anyone else had a clear idea where stood Moreau's army and what were his intentions. Although compared to Bonaparte, Moreau maneuvered slowly, his rate of advance still surprised the Austrians. When Austrian patrols did detect Moreau's advance, Lauer persuaded Johann – who after all had instructions from the Kaiser to follow Lauer's suggestions – to abandon the plan for a flank march against Moreau's line of communication and to substitute a direct advance toward Munich. The best available road was a highway that passed through Hohenlinden, some 18 miles east of Munich. So the Habsburg army marched blindly toward a collision amid the wooded hills and sodden valleys surrounding the town of Hohenlinden. It was terrain that a Württemberg staff officer later ruefully described as "singularly appropriate to the genius and the tactics of the French infantry".[25]

Yet Austrian strategy had achieved something important. Whereas theater-wide the overall odds were five to three against, Weyrother and Lauer brought the Austrian army to Hohenlinden with a slight numerical superiority. How the army would perform in battle received its first test at Ampfing on December 1.

NOTES

1.David G. Chandler, ed., *The Military Maxims of Napoleon* (New York, 1988) p. 57.

2. Herbert H. Sargent, *The Campaign of Marengo* (Chicago, 1901), p. 115.

3. The numbers here and on the map are taken from Sargent, pp. 93-94. Given the difficulty of ascertaining precise numbers, the totals should be regarded as approximate.

4. David G. Chandler, *Dictionary of the Napoleonic Wars* (New York, 1979), p. 105.

5. Moreau's official returns are in appendix 110 of Laurent Gouvion Saint-Cyr, *Mémoires pour servir a l'histoire militaire sous le directoire, Le Consulat, et l'empire,* II (Paris, 1831).

6. David G. Chandler, *The Campaigns of Napoleon* (New York, 1966), p. 269.

7. For Bonaparte's understanding of Moreau's role see: "To General Berthier," March 1, 1800, *Correspondance de Napoléon Ier,* VI (Paris, 1860), p. 154.

8. Good accounts of the swirling battles between Moreau and Kray are in the chapter "Campagne de 1800 en Souabe," in Saint-Cyr, II, and in *Victoires, Conquêtes, Désastres, Revers et Guerres Civiles des Français,* XII (Paris, 1819), pp. 150-173. Note that Saint-Cyr did not respect Moreau.

9. Thugut's observation to Minto in Minto's dispatch of June 28, 1800. See: Gilbert Elliot, *Life and Letters of Sir Gilbert Elliot, First Earl of Minto from 1751 to 1806,* III (London, 1874), p. 141.

10. "Moreau to Bonaparte," May 27, 1800, cited in H. Bonnal, *La Vie Militaire du Maréchal Ney,* I (Paris, 1910), p. 300.

11. "To His Majesty the Emperor and King," June 16, 1800, *Correspondance de Napoléon Ier,* VI (Paris, 1860) p. 365.

12. "Lady Minto to Lady Malmesbury," December 30, 1800, Elliot, III, p. 183.

13. For a fine discussion of this see: "Command and Staff Problems in the Austrian Army, 1740-1866," in Gordon A. Craig, *War, Politics, and Diplomacy* (New York, 1966).

14. "Kaiser to Erzherzog Jean," August 1800, Ernest Picard, *Hohenlinden* (Paris, 1909), p. 45.

15. Ibid.

16. François Roguet, *Mémoires Militaires du Lieutenant Général Comte Roguet,* II (Paris, 1862), p. 289.

17. All three (Ulm, Ingolstadt, and Philipsburg) were blockaded by French forces.

18. Picard, p. 10.

19. Mathieu Dumas, cited in Picard, p. 36.

20. "Hardÿ to his wife," November 26, 1800, in General Hardÿ de Perini, ed., *Correspondence Intime du Général Jean Hardÿ de 1797 à 1802* (Paris, 1901), p. 225. Moreau's proclamation is on p. 227.

21. Certain authorities including Mathieu Dumas and Jomini have Moreau, on the eve of the campaign, selecting the Hohenlinden field as a place to receive the

Austrian attack. Contemporary documents do not support this view. For a full discussion see Picard, pp. 91-93.

22. "Decaen to Moreau," August 31, 1800, in Picard, p. 26.

23. Compare the army's returns for October 23 and November 22 in Marquis de Carrion-Nisas, *Campagne des Français en Allemagne* (Paris, 1829), p. 430; and Picard, p. 393, respectively.

24. A Bavarian staff officer who summarized the campaign a year later could still not explain how the army had been so mishandled. See: "Relation des Mouvemens de l'Armée Autrichienne" in Carrion-Nisas, p. 378.

25. Ch.-L. Sevelinges, trans., "Précis de la campagne de 1800, la Souabe, la Bavière et l'Autriche," in U. Okouneff, *Considerations sur les Grandes Operations de la Campagne de 1812, en Russie* (Brussels, 1841), p. 444.

Chapter 10

The Battle
of Hohenlinden

PART 1.
THE COMBAT AT AMPFING

"To act upon lines far removed from each other, and without
communications, is to commit a fault."[1]

NAPOLEON BONAPARTE, MILITARY MAXIM XI

The Austrian objective for December 1 was to drive the French from the heights southwest of Ampfing. The army could then continue west and unite around Hohenlinden the next day. The offensive began early. At 5 a.m., twelve battalions and twelve squadrons commanded by FZM Johann Riesch departed Ampfing. An hour later, another nine battalions and 18 squadrons belonging to the Belgian-born corps commander, FZM Maximilien de Baillet, advanced on Riesch's right. The two columns climbed through wooded, broken terrain while additional forces advanced on their flanks. When musket fire broke out, the restricted sight lines prevented the Austrians from realizing that all they confronted were two French divisions. However, one was led by an exceedingly able and stubborn soldier named Michel Ney.

Ney's division numbered 8,245 foot soldiers, 1,105 cavalry, and 14 guns. But Ney had detached a brigade on a reconnaissance toward the Inn River crossing at Wasserburg. His remaining men had barely awakened from their camps when a mass of Austrians drove in their advance posts. Without even taking the time to form proper line of battle, the heavy horsemen of the 19th Cavalry heroically charged the Habsburg cavalry, which outnumbered them twelve squadrons to three. Their self-sacrifice gave Ney's infantry time to rally but the odds remained stiff: twelve Austrian battalions versus 21 companies.

The French grudgingly gave ground while the brigade commander, General Desperrières, sent an appeal for reinforcements. A staff officer returned with Ney's response: hold at all costs as long as possible, even to the point of "extinction".[2] Ney's language was not histrionic. If Desperrières' brigade yielded, the Austrians would cut the road to Haag and with it the French line of retreat.

To hold his position, Desperrières utilized constant maneuver to compensate for his lack of numbers. He stripped manpower from an unengaged sector to meet an Austrian assault, and then hustled the soldiers back to their original position in time to meet a new attack. Eventually, his tactical touch could not contend against overwhelming force. With both flanks turned and a cloud of Habsburg light infantry in his right rear, Desperrières ordered a withdrawal. Just then a squadron of the 13th Dragoons appeared. Noting that the Austrian infantry had outpaced their mounted supports, Desperrières resolved to undertake a bold gamble. He ordered the dragoons to charge while the available infantry, a mere 80 men, supported them. Simultaneously, eight drummers beat the *pas de charge* to simulate an attack by a larger force. The well-executed maneuver – reminiscent of Bonaparte's stratagem at Arcola in 1796 – momentarily drove back the Austrian infantry and allowed the French to disengage. Desperrières used the precious breathing space to reorganize and to find a fresh supply of ammunition. For three more hours his brigade held its ground.

Meanwhile, Ney himself had conducted a very aggressive defense with his other units. At one point a spirited counterattack captured a Habsburg cannon and two caissons. But around noon, superior Austrian numbers told and Ney began to fall back. An Austrian battery pounded Ney's columns as they retired. Up came six French horse guns led in person by an officer who was already making a name for himself as one of Europe's finest artillerists, General Jean-Baptiste Eblé. Eblé served as the army's artillery commander. On this field, he performed as a battery officer. Under his direction, the horse guns engaged in a furious artillery duel. Within 30 minutes, Eblé's battery had dismounted four Habsburg guns and blown up three caissons. French gunners aggressively advanced two cannons to a crest line. Two Habsburg hussar squadrons emerged from a woodline and overran them. This temporary success enraged the surviving French artillerists. Led by a Sergeant Jaziel, they mounted their horses and charged the hussars! During a brief melee in which Jaziel lost his right arm to a saber cut, the horse artillerymen recaptured their guns.

While Ney's men conducted their stout fight, Riesch's corps began to gain ground against general of division Jean Hardÿ's command. Thirty-eight-year-old Hardÿ was an officer who had experienced the roller coaster-like ride characteristic of the revolutionary era. He enlisted at age 21 in the Royalist infantry. The Revolution saw Hardÿ rise from captain to general in a short eighteen months, only to be stripped of command during a political upheaval. Reinstated three months later, he received a promotion and returned to duty. He was a conscientious officer whose division was a powerful mixed arms unit comprising 4,060 infantry, 2,044 cavalry, and 16 cannons. However, the Austrians that appeared at first light grossly outnumbered Hardÿ's division. Although the timely arrival of a brigade belonging to General Claude Legrand's division checked the rightmost of Riesch's flanking columns, Hardÿ lacked the manpower to prevent a tactical envelopment of his left flank. Slowly the Austrians drove him back on Haag. Hardÿ himself had to relinquish command when an exploding shell killed a nearby staff officer and drove a metal fragment into his hand. His senior brigadier, Louis Bastoul, assumed command. Moreau believed that Bastoul had been unjustly passed over for promotion. On this field, Bastoul was determined to take advantage of his opportunity. He dismounted before the 53rd Demi-brigade, seized the colors and led a ferocious counterattack that momentarily restored the position.

By now, Ney's men had been driven back to a final defensive position along a line of trees that bordered the south edge of the Haag road. The wing commander, Lieutenant General Paul Grenier, received a message from Moreau authorizing a withdrawal. This was, of course, easier said than done. Having risen slowly through the ranks of the Royal army, Grenier possessed an unmatched knowledge of complex tactical evolutions. Since he had to funnel two divisions along the narrow road to Haag, Grenier arranged a retreat by echelon. When his artillery needed time to retire through a defile, Grenier ordered a squadron of the 2nd Dragoons to countermarch through the defile and charge the pursuing Austrians. Moreau's brother-in-law, Second Lieutenant Hulot, distinguished himself in this charge that captured some 100 prisoners and regained the far end of the defile.

So Ney and Hardÿ passed through the dark forest and debouched onto the more open plateau near Haag. Here staff officers dispatched by Moreau pointed out new positions for them to occupy. The five mile retreat had been performed masterfully. Ney's aide related how "the columns of different arms occupied successive positions without confusion." In a letter to his wife Hardÿ put it more bluntly, "We fought like lions."[3] The day had cost the French 193 killed, 817 wounded, and 697 prisoners.[4]

If the French generals were content with their fighting withdrawal, Erzherzog Johann, Chief of Staff Weyrother, and the headquarters staff were ecstatic. Johann had appeared on the field at 5 p.m., just in time to see the final French retreat. The experience emboldened him. He boastfully wrote to the Kaiser that after six hours of hard fighting, Austrian bravery had driven the French from a superb defensive position. It had not been done cheaply. Austrian losses totaled 303 killed, 1,690 wounded, and 1,077 prisoners.[5] The fact that an offensive army that drove its foe from the battlefield had lost many more prisoners than its foe was indicative of inferior Austrian morale. Neither had the Austrian attack captured its objective, Haag, nor had the flanking columns kept abreast of the main attack. Furthermore, the Austrian artillery and trains had been unable to maintain the pace of the army's advance. But when considering how to proceed, Johann and Weyrother overlooked most of this. Johann chastised his wing commanders for their lack of progress and told them that he expected a better performance tomorrow. Only General Lauer recommended caution. Lauer appreciated that the heavily wooded terrain to the west would severely restrict the Habsburg cavalry and artillery. Weyrother and his cronies argued that with the French on the run a great opportunity was at hand. Johann listened to them and resolved to continue the attack on the morrow.

Years later, Bonaparte, when on Saint Helena as the imprisoned Emperor Napoleon, observed that given his numerical superiority and the short December days, Johann had no time to waste with deployment and maneuver. "It was necessary to attack...at the pas de charge, heads lowered."[6] Tactically, such a surge would have prevented Desperrières from shifting his limited manpower from an unengaged wing to a threatened sector. Grand tactically, an all out attack would have routed Ney and Hardÿ. Napoleon was also critical of Moreau's strategy. Already by 1800, Bonaparte had acquired vast experience at storming a succession of defended river lines. His prescription for success was to approach the river in echelon formation. If the enemy tried to attack the leading column, the columns echeloned behind would be perfectly positioned to attack the enemy's flanks. Meanwhile, one's light troops ought to cover the river bank so as to prevent the enemy from detecting where the blow was to fall. Then, having determined where to cross, the van column should rapidly advance, build the necessary bridges, and storm the river before the foe knew what was happening. Instead, Moreau had scattered his forces along a 30-mile front and thus exposed Ney and Hardÿ to an Austrian counter-offensive.

Napoleon's critique certainly benefitted from hindsight. After all, Napoleon himself was to suffer his first serious defeat at Aspern-Essling when he tried to force a river crossing.[7] Nonetheless, there is no denying that Johann's offensive was a strategic surprise for Moreau. He had thought he was attacking the Austrians only to learn that they were attacking him. Whether he could regain his balance or whether Johann would be able to capitalize on his initial success would be determined in the coming days.

Part 2.
Plans and Terrain

Erzherzog Johann confidently expected that the campaign's decisive engagement would take place December 2. In all likelihood Moreau would offer battle at Haag, an important road junction eight miles east of Hohenlinden. Instead, to his surprise, patrols reported at dawn that the French had withdrawn. To Johann, this was further proof of the extent of his success at Ampfing. His staff shared his confidence. During the day, the main body of the army marched westward to Haag where Johann established his headquarters. That evening Johann wrote to FZM Michael Kienmayer, who commanded a detached corps operating to the north, instructing him to hasten to rejoin him. Then the united army would attack before Moreau had time to concentrate his army. The rendezvous would occur somewhere west of Hohenlinden. As a Bavarian staff officer at Johann's headquarters later ruefully observed, the success at Ampfing followed by the bloodless occupation of Haag had made the Austrian high command almost giddy with success.[8] They doubted that Moreau would make a stand east of the Isar River. If they encountered any opponents, they were likely to be a rear guard. This erroneous idea prompted Austrian headquarters to ignore all normal precautions in the haste to come to grips. It was exactly for the purpose of cooling hot-headed youth that Lauer had been installed as Johann's adviser. The veteran's presence seems to have had little effect at curbing Johann's ardor. Neither did Chief of Staff Weyrother exert a restraining nor professional influence. Consequently, the army's orders for December 3 were more appropriate for a route march designed to concentrate the army than for a battle.

A sparse road net traversed the region's wooded hills. This contributed to the Habsburg inclination to advance in multiple columns along a broad front. Weyrother divided the army into four

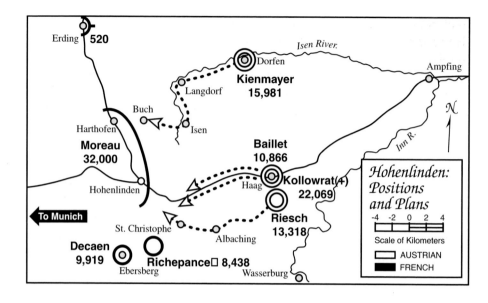

columns. The southernmost, commanded by FZM Riesch (10,186 infantry; 3,132 cavalry), would advance parallel to the Hohenlinden road until it reached Albaching at which point it would turn northwest toward Hohenlinden. The principal column directed by FML Johann Kollowrat (14,987 infantry; 5,109 cavalry) would march along the highway through Hohenlinden and continue westward. To relieve congestion on the highway, Weyrother ordered FZM Baillet, in charge of a third column (8,346 infantry; 2,520 cavalry), to march along secondary roads that ran parallel to and just north of the highway, until he too arrived at Hohenlinden. Kienmayer commanded the fourth column (12,611 infantry; 3,370 cavalry). His mission was to depart Dorfen and march along the Isen valley through Langdorf to Buch.[9]

All movements were to begin no later than 5 a.m. and none of the columns were to pause to allow the artillery to maintain pace. In addition to the normal complement of brigade batteries, each column had a 20-piece artillery reserve. There was also a general army reserve that numbered 48 tubes.[10] Johann informed his subordinates that even if the columns reached their objectives without a single cannon, it would be preferable to hesitating and missing the opportunity to smash Moreau's rear guard. Likewise the cavalry was not to wait for some ideal, flat, and open ground before engaging. Above all else, the enemy was to be pursued vigorously.

When Austrian staff officers examined their maps, it appeared that only Kienmayer's column was truly separated from the balance of the army. The route of march for both Baillet and Riesch varied from one-half mile to no more than three miles distant from the highway. However map distances failed to account for undulating terrain that tended to isolate tactically adjacent formations. More importantly, map study revealed nothing about the next day's weather. At all events, it would be difficult to coordinate the advance of some 64,000 men, many of whom were marching along atrocious, sodden roads and all of whom were passing through an immense forest that lacked lateral communication. In addition, the Austrian columns would be stretched out along the narrow roads. If the van encountered the French, it would take time for the balance of the column to deploy in the woods alongside the road and move forward in support. If there should be a fight, the terrain would negate the Austrian advantage in cavalry and artillery. Battle experience in Italy and Germany had shown that the French infantry enjoyed a considerable advantage over their Austrian counterparts when fighting in such broken terrain.

The giddy optimism emanating from Austrian headquarters might have been dampened had anyone cared to look closely at the rank and file. According to a Bavarian staff officer, in spite of the liberal distribution of drink over the preceding days, "the physical and morale strength of the soldier was spent."[11]

***

The town of Hohenlinden stood at one end of a cleared plateau which was actually a spur of the Tyrolese Alps. At the town, the spur was about a mile wide. Northward, in the direction of Buch, it widened to six miles. When viewed from the higher ground to the east, the direction form which the Austrians approached, the cleared land resembled an open plain. To the southwest of Hohenlinden was the expansive Ebersberg forest; to the east and northeast, a series of wooded ridges. Further east, between the Isen River and the Inn River, was a tangle of small streams flowing into the Isen. It was an undulating land of ridgetop and marsh, full of small woods, isolated farms, and sheepcrofts. The main road from Haag to Hohenlinden was more than 20 feet wide and was the only true all weather road in the region. From the direction of Haag it traversed open ground until it approached the hilltop village of Maitenbeth. Here it entered the open pine woods and continued to climb until it passed a hilltop locally known as the Schimmelberg. Near the Schimmelberg, a network of poor forestry trails extended to the north toward Buch and Isen. To the south was the small village of St. Christoph, which sat in a narrow valley surrounded on three sides by forest. The Haag road continued west until it emerged from the forest and turned northwest toward Hohenlinden. It divided at Hohenlinden with one route continuing north to Erding and the second heading west to Munich.

Moreau was intimately familiar with the terrain. During the truce he had carefully reconnoitered Hohenlinden and its environs. The Austrians, on the other hand, had not availed themselves of past opportunities to study the terrain. The wooded ridges east of Hohenlinden separated the two armies and masked Moreau's dispositions.

Whereas the combat at Ampfing had filled the Austrians with too much confidence, it had taught Moreau prudence. He correctly judged that a major portion of the Austrian army was trying to advance west on the main route from Haag toward Hohenlinden. His patrols also detected Kienmayer's presence in the Isen valley. Moreau deduced that the Austrians were committed to an offensive. He resolved to oppose the Austrian advance and to "benefit from the enemy's movements to seize the offensive."[12] His original notion was to defend along his left and center with Grenier's corps while committing Antoine Richepance's division to a turning movement along his right. Then general of division Charles Decaen arrived at headquarters.

Decaen's appearance underscores the relationship between subordinate initiative and the fog of war. December 1 had found Decaen marching his 10,161-man division through the wooded hills well south of Hohenlinden. His instructions were to explore potential crossing sites over the Inn River. During the day he heard the cannonading associated with the fight at Ampfing, but did not know what it signified. Left without orders, he continued his mission on December 2 until he received a message from Moreau's headquarters. Dated 6 p.m., December 1, it informed him of the Austrian offensive and stated that Moreau had "decided to unite his army to offer battle."[13] Decaen was ordered to concentrate his army around Ebersberg, some six miles southwest of Hohenlinden. Upon reaching the designated assembly point, Decaen resolved to ride to headquarters to learn personally what was afoot.

So, around 7 p.m. on December 2 he arrived at Moreau's headquarters. Moreau greeted him joyfully. Suddenly he had another strong division to add to his forces. He exclaimed, "Ah! Here is Decaen; the battle will be won tomorrow!"[14] He told Decaen to march his division to the Hohenlinden plain to support Grenier. Decaen doubted the wisdom of this. It would require another long march – his men were already tired, the division's rear elements would not go into camp until eleven that night – the road was poor, and at best his division would not reach Hohenlinden until 2 p.m. If the battle began at dawn, as seemed likely, a 2 p.m. arrival would be too late to contribute decisively. Moreau listened carefully and asked if instead Decaen could follow Richepance's turning movement. Decaen replied that his most distant force was within eight miles of Ebersberg, the starting place for Richepance's turning movement, and that the road net favored such a march. "Very good!" concluded Moreau, "I was going to turn the enemy with 10,000 men, it will be done with 20,000." [15]

It was a calculated risk. Grenier, the officer charged with defending the left and center, would have to contain the Austrians until the turning movement took effect. Moreau devised a stratagem to help Grenier. He believed that the Austrians thought his army was in retreat. Moreau encouraged the illusion that he was on the run by relinquishing the wooded ridges east of Hohenlinden. His outposts would yield this seemingly dominant high ground in order to draw the Austrians into his trap. Then he would fight the Austrians when they debouched from the forest onto the open ground. He expected a tough defensive fight along his left and center until his flanking column arrived. But he knew that in contrast to his foe, his defensive forces would deploy on open ground where they would be in sight of one another. Here Moreau himself would be able to exert close control. It would be relatively easy to shift units to the left or right and to engage the Austrian infantry with all three arms as they emerged from the forest. The Habsburg infantry, on the other hand, would have to gain ground in order to provide space for the Austrian cavalry and artillery to deploy.

Moreau's plan in detail required Grenier to establish his headquarters in Hohenlinden. His three and one-half mile long front extended from Hohenlinden, defended by Ney (7,600 infantry, 900 cavalry, 14 guns) to Harthofen, where stood Legrand's division (6,000 infantry, 1,400 cavalry, 12 guns). Between Ney and Legrand was Bastoul's division (formerly Hardÿ, 3,500 infantry, 1,900 cavalry, 16 guns). Legrand was to maintain communication with Erding, on the army's left flank, for as long as possible. A small, 520-man cavalry brigade detached from brigade general Jean d'Hautpoul and commanded by brigade general Jean Espagne held Erding. In reserve behind Hohenlinden were 1,058 troopers and six horse guns belonging to d'Hautpoul's cavalry division along with seven cannons belonging to the artillery reserve. To Ney's right was general of division Emmanuel Grouchy's division (7,039 infantry, 1,399 cavalry, 12 guns). Grouchy deployed his men to defend against any enemy

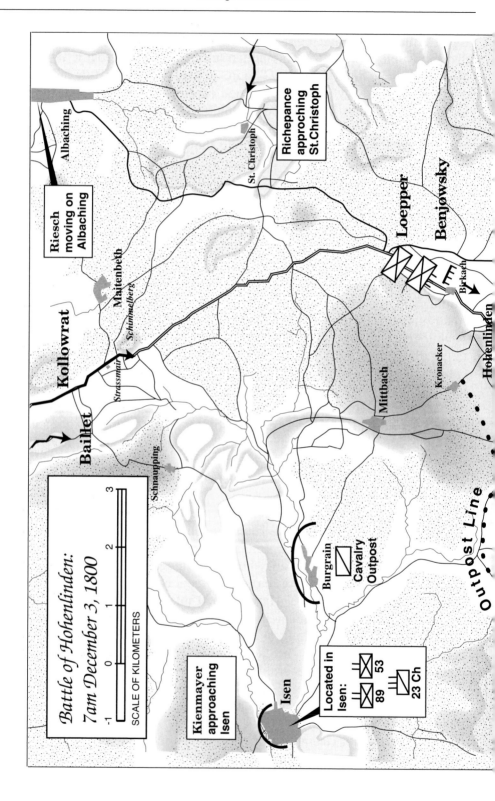

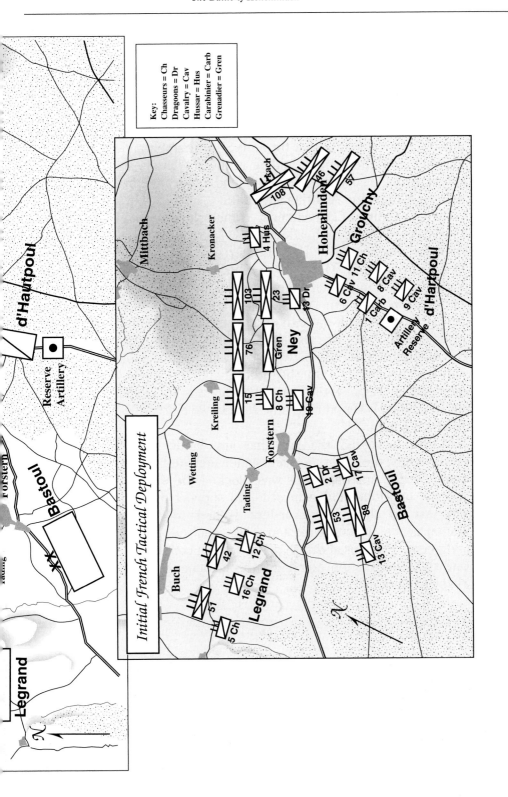

Initial French Tactical Deployment

Key:
Chasseurs = Ch
Dragoons = Dr
Cavalry = Cav
Hussar = Hus
Carabinier = Carb
Grenadier = Gren

thrusts from the east and southeast. When the French generals assembled for a supper at Moreau's headquarters, Decaen told Grouchy, "It will be you, my friend, who will receive the first attack."[16] Off beyond Grouchy's right flank were the forces assigned to the turning movement, generals of division Richepance (7,039 infantry, 1,399 cavalry, 14 guns) and Decaen (7,850 infantry, 2,069 cavalry, 12 guns). They would march through St. Christoph and advance to the highway at Maitenbeth.[17] Adding in the artillerists and engineers, in round terms, 32,000 men would defend a four mile front while 19,000 men enveloped the Austrian left flank.

On the evening of December 2, French patrols brought two Austrian musicians to Moreau's headquarters. Moreau personally interrogated them and they confirmed that Erzherzog Johann intended to attack at first light. From Moreau's perspective, everything hinged upon Richepance. Moreau informed him that he had to have his division in St. Christoph by 7 a.m. Yet Richepance's assignment was fraught with peril. His right flank was exposed to an eruption from the Wasserburg bridgehead. There was also the possibility that while he marched east, the Austrians could slip between him and Decaen, isolate his division, and overwhelm it. On the other hand, he knew he had to act aggressively because the December day was short and even if he met no resistance it would take time to achieve a decisive position on the Austrian flank.

Moreau accepted the fact that any battle involves uncertainty. Accordingly, the orders to Richepance included a contingency: if the route to the Austrian flank was blocked, he should instead march directly on Hohenlinden in order to support the army's center. In contrast to the typical orders issued to Habsburg generals, Richepance's orders expected and required him to exercise his judgment. Perhaps above all of the French commanders on the field – and they were a top notch group – Richepance was equal to the responsibility.

Part 3.
Battle in the Forest

The previous days had witnessed an uncomfortable combination of rain, sleet, and snow. According to a Bavarian officer, in spite of a liberal distribution of brandy, the troops rose from their bivouacs on December 3 with little enthusiasm. There was again the smell of snow in the air. The four Austrian columns began plodding westward.

Kollowrat's column marched along the highway toward the forests of Hohenlinden
(dark area in upper left).

Recent rain rendered the roads nearly impassable. Horses and men skidded through slush and ice. Caissons and wagons bogged in deep mud. At times the snow fell so heavily that visibility reduced to one hundred paces. Because they were marching on the main road, Kollowrat's men outpaced the other columns. Within Kollowrat's column the advance guard, which was without artillery, advanced faster than the formations behind it. Behind the advance guard was an unusual array of units. In echelon from front to rear, were a security detachment made up of two Bavarian light companies and the Erzherzog Ferdinand Hussars, a grenadier division of eight battalions, a Bavarian division also of eight battalions, the reserve artillery, a Bavarian horse battery with a two-company escort, the army trains – a particularly cumbersome mix of caissons, supply wagons, and associated impedimenta – the Bavarian chevau-legers, and a cuirassier brigade serving as the rear guard. Erzherzog Johann and his headquarters staff accompanied this column. The Hohenzollern Cuirassiers remained behind at Haag. A little after 7 a.m., GM Franz Loepper's advance guard reached a point about one mile west of the Schimmelberg. Suddenly, French pickets appeared out of the murk and opened fire. The Battle of Hohenlinden had begun.

The pickets belonged to the 108th Demi-brigade of Grouchy's command. Behind the pickets, the 108th deployed in line along a tree line from where they could control the highway's egress onto the Hohenlinden plain. In echelon to the right of the 108th were the 46th and 57th Demi-brigades. Because the trees concealed the 108th, Loepper could not see what he confronted. In keeping with the high command's preconceptions, he believed he faced a rear guard. Accordingly, he rapidly deployed his 5,341 infantry and 1,319 cavalry. Loepper ordered the Hungarians of the Benjowsky Infantry Regiment, covered by a skirmish line of grenzers, forward to brush the French aside. When they engaged, Kollowrat heard the musketry. He sent a courier to urge Loepper to press the enemy vigorously and promised two grenadier battalions as reinforcements. He also ordered two more grenadier battalions and a hussar squadron to march to St. Christoph to link up with Riesch's column.

Although outnumbered two to one, the 108th Demi-brigade initially held its ground. With assistance from the 4th Hussars and three cannons, Colonel Marcognet conducted a skillful combined arms defense until Kollowrat's reinforcements arrived. Then GM Spannochi skillfully made use of a forest path to position the Sebottendorf Grenadier Battalion on the left flank of the 108th. The ensuing bayonet charge onto the open ground surprised the French and sent them reeling. In their haste, the 108th abandoned the wounded Marcognet to the pursuing Austrians.

Kollowrat reinforced success by committing three Bavarian battalions led by the veteran Bavarian general, Bernhard Deroy. Loepper, in turn, added in a second grenadier battalion. Side by side, the Austrian elite infantry and the scorned Bavarians chased the 108th onto the south end of the Hohenlinden plain. Austrian brigade artillery followed the advancing infantry to take up position at the tree line overlooking the open ground. Soon a deadly canister fire began dropping the exposed soldiers of the 46th Demi-brigade. Faced with the day's first crisis, General Grouchy ordered the 46th Demi-brigade to counterattack. Their charge stopped the Austrian advance. Then, four companies launched a surprise stroke against the Austrian left flank that drove the Habsburg infantry back into the trees. Fighting in the spruce forest, where visibility did not exceed 100 yards, required quick thinking improvisation. The French excelled in this kind of combat. Gliding from tree to tree, Grouchy's line advanced rapidly. Dismayed by the sudden change of fortune, 160 Hungarian grenadiers surrendered.

Now came Grouchy's opportunity. He too reinforced success and added a battalion of the 57th Demi-brigade against the crumbling Austrian left flank. At about the same time, the 11th Chasseurs à cheval advanced to support the 4th Hussars. Together they charged against Loepper's infantry who had become scattered during their

Loepper's advance guard charged out of the forest to attack the 108th Demi-brigade.

advance through the trees. The Austrian advance guard included enough cavalry to match these 1,100 French light horsemen. However, Habsburg tactical control was unequal to the challenge. Loepper failed to utilize his hussars to counter the French. Left to their own devices, the white-coated infantry resisted stoutly. A Hungarian grenadier battalion formed square and repelled a charge delivered by the first squadron of the 11th Chasseurs à cheval. The Chasseurs' colonel placed himself at the head of his second squadron and charged again. When that failed he tried again with his third squadron. Undaunted by three rebuffs, the colonel led his fourth squadron at the charge. Finally the grenadiers collapsed.[18] Emulating the pluck of its sister regiment, the 4th Hussars charged a stubborn Austrian battery three times. Although hit by a canister fragment, second-lieutenant Girod led his platoon in amid the Habsburg gunners. Nearby, trumpeter Plumelin single-handedly captured a cannon and sabered two gunners. A Major Merlin saw that the supporting Austrian infantry looked shaky. He ordered a hussar squadron to charge and was rewarded with the sight of the infantry breaking for the rear.

All across Grouchy's front the tide of battle was against Kollowrat's soldiers. In fairly short order the combination of infantry on their flank and cavalry on their front overwhelmed the

The open ground where Moreau's men deployed looking toward the forest that entangled Kollowrat and Baillet

Austrians and Bavarians. In contrast to the lack of presence by the Austrian and Bavarian leaders, Grouchy played a prominent role during this combat. He rode amid his soldiers to exhort his troops and at one point led a bayonet charge. Grouchy's counterattack captured five cannons and numerous prisoners. Among the prisoners was GM Spannochi.

To stabilize the situation, Kollowrat committed fresh troops including two more grenadier battalions. Although they were successful, his initial misapprehension that he was confronting a rear guard caused him to commit his forces piecemeal. By 9 a.m. he had sent into battle Loepper's advance guard, five of eight Bavarian battalions, and four of eight grenadier battalions. He had sent two more grenadier battalions off toward St. Christoph. In spite of all efforts, the major Habsburg thrust up the highway had petered out.

During this time, at the insistence of Lieutenant General Christian Zweibrücken, two Bavarian battalions had also marched south to probe in the direction of St. Christoph to help secure the flank. Zweibrücken had served with the French army in North America from 1780 to 1783 and this experience had taught him about the perils of open flanks in wooded terrain. He hoped the two battalions would establish contact with Riesch's column. From their position on the Schimmelberg,

Zweibrücken and Kollowrat heard the sounds of musketry to the southwest. They supposed it came from Riesch and that he too was engaging the French rear guard. Kollowrat resolved to hold his ground until Riesch on his left and Baillet on his right could bring up their columns. Then the Austrians could advance along a united front.

***

Although Kollowrat did not know it, if he was going to wait for Baillet, his wait would be long. Baillet had departed his bivouacs just outside of Haag at 5 a.m., the same hour Kollowrat had left Haag. The very poor secondary road so slowed Baillet's march that he could not stay abreast of Kollowrat. Although encountering no opposition, Baillet did not reach Schnaupping until 10 a.m. At this point the difficulties of coordinating multiple columns amidst the wooded ridges emerged. Baillet felt alone. He heard firing on both flanks. To establish contact with Kienmayer to the north, he dispatched a battalion and two cuirassier squadrons toward Isen and four more squadrons toward Burgrain. To link up with Kollowrat, he sent four squadrons of the Lacy Cuirassiers and another infantry battalion marching south. Meanwhile, his patrols learned that the French were to the east at Kronacker on the edge of the Hohenlinden plain. Accordingly, Baillet continued his march west until he arrived at Mittbach. Here he deployed the balance of his column along the heights west of Mittbach. Although he occupied high ground overlooking the Hohenlinden plain, Baillet felt far from secure. The noise of musketry and cannon fire had swollen to alarming proportions, indicating that Kollowrat was engaged in a serious battle. Yet all he did to support Kollowrat was send two more battalions and a battery through the woods south of Mittbach toward Hohenlinden. They arrived in time to see the grenadiers and Bavarians recoiling before Grouchy's counterattack.

When Baillet learned about this he dispatched one more battalion to bolster the two already sent. Completing his half-measures, he then ordered two more battalions and two squadrons to advance against Kronacker to facilitate the deployment of elements of Kienmayer's column onto the open ground. This left Baillet with three battalions and six squadrons unengaged. In sum, Baillet had completely fragmented his column before he had even engaged the foe. He had failed to fix significant numbers of French along his front, thus allowing Grouchy to concentrate his attentions against Kollowrat.

The northernmost Austrian thrust, commanded by Kienmayer, had departed Dorfen in the pre-dawn murk. Its advance guard, GM Karl

Frenel's detachment of 2,250 men, encountered Legrand's outpost line. The French offered little resistance to Frenel's Bohemian infantry. Amid a heavy snowfall, Frenel pressed forward and again the French gave ground easily. No one in Kienmayer's command suspected that this weak resistance was in accord with Moreau's plan. However, the French almost overplayed their hand by ceding terrain too quickly. One element of Kienmayer's column carried Buch on the edge of the Hohenlinden plain and began to deploy on the high ground west of that village.

Meanwhile, FML Karl Schwarzenberg's division had brushed aside the French defenders at Isen. Schwarzenberg continued along a poor forest track that led to Hohenlinden. Just west of Burgrain he detected an Austrian battalion and two cuirassier squadrons belonging to Baillet's column engaged with four French infantry companies and a dragoon squadron. Heretofore the French had stopped their foes cold. Schwarzenberg formed two lines of two battalions, retained a two-battalion reserve, and ordered his drummers to sound the charge. The Austrians easily drove back the badly outnumbered French and pursued them to the heights near Wetting. Here they contacted the left center of the true defensive line occupied by Bastoul and Ney. This position extended along the line Tading, Wetting, Kronacker, and Kreiling.

The ensuing struggle for these hamlets showed what capably handled Austrian troops could accomplish. A battalion of the Gemmingen Regiment carried Forstern. This was a serious enough threat to prompt Moreau to shift d'Hautpoul's cavalry to plug the gap between Bastoul and Legrand. A French counterattack recaptured Forstern. Meanwhile, a battalion of the Brechainville Regiment stormed Tading. Bastoul's French counterattacked, driving the Austrians from the hamlet and continuing the charge all of the way to Loipfing. Here a battalion of the Erzherzog Ferdinand Regiment struck hard at Bastoul's people and blunted the French advance. This type of back and forth combat extended all along Bastoul's and Ney's fronts.

It became clear that whoever controlled Kronacker and its adjacent woodlot controlled egress from the heights onto the Hohenlinden plain. Accordingly, Schwarzenberg sent two battalions of the Murray Infantry Regiment to storm this position. This once-proud Walloon regiment had lost its recruiting area to French expansion and thus its ranks were filled with some of the off scourings of the Habsburg Empire. But it retained a veteran cadre and attacked with spirit. It swept through first Kreiling and then Kronacker only to recoil before a French counterattack organized by Ney. Schwarzenberg, with some help from two battalions belonging to Baillet's command, recaptured Kronacker with a combined arms assault featuring the Hungarians of the Erzherzog Ferdinand Regiment and the Mack Cuirassiers. The difficulty the Austrian cuirassiers experienced in the wooded terrain is reflected by a subaltern who described how "the troopers were suddenly fired upon by enemy chausseurs [sic] stationed in the tree tops" and forced to retire with heavy losses.[19] Still, at the point of its bayonets, the Austrian infantry had secured entry onto the plain within a half-mile of Hohenlinden. Then, Schwarzenberg paused to consolidate and to learn how progressed the main column.

Meanwhile, six miles to the southeast, Riesch's southernmost column had finally arrived at Albaching. It had departed its bivouacs west of Haag at 4:30 a.m. but terrible roads reduced its rate of march to a crawl. It traversed some three and one-half miles in five hours. Patrols contacted French scouts along the forest edge west of Albaching. Some Austrian hussars, who were probing in the direction of St. Christoph, informed Riesch that the French occupied this village and had also established themselves on the high ground two and one-half miles to the south. In fact, by the time Riesch received this intelligence, Richepance's people had departed the high ground, leaving behind a mere outpost line. Lastly, prisoners declared that two French divisions commanded by Richepance and Decaen were at Ebersberg, six miles to the west. This too was outdated information since both French divisions had long since departed their camps. However, unlike the situation confronting the commanders of the other Austrian columns, Riesch had a pretty fair idea of the situation he confronted. He failed to utilize effectively this invaluable intelligence.

Instead, he apparently took counsel of his fears. He correctly judged that Richepance and Decaen badly outnumbered him. The actual odds were about three to two against him. Consequently, Riesch dallied at Albaching until his entire column reassembled. Then, he resolutely decided to proceed with his mission by traversing the forest, driving the French from St. Christoph, and marching on Hohenlinden. Yet having just squandered valuable time concentrating his forces, he proceeded to fragment them into six groups. Excluding his reserve, the largest was not even regimental sized, the smallest included four infantry companies and a cuirassier squadron. Riesch sent five of these detachments along various forest tracks toward St. Christoph while retaining three battalions and 17 squadrons at Albaching. Riesch's strategy, if it may be so honored, invited defeat in detail.

***

Richepance marched along this track leading to Marsmaier.

Like their opponents, Richepance and Decaen began their marches before first light. Since Richepance's orders required him to be in St. Christoph by 7 a.m., his units departed their encampments at 4 a.m. The first phase of the march was uneventful. The van of the division was traversing St. Christoph at 7:15 a.m. when a snow squall descended, reducing visibility to ten paces or less. The guide got lost. The cloying mud grabbed at soldiers' boots and horses' shoes. In an effort to avoid boggy sections, the mounted units frequently had to move cross country. Richepance later reported that it seemed that the cavalry had to take two steps to the side to progress one step forward. Approaching the hamlet of Schützen, about one-half mile north of St. Christoph, at 8 a.m., someone detected an enemy presence on a rise overlooking the column's left flank. They were the two grenadier battalions that Kollowrat had sent on a reconnaissance toward St. Christoph. At short range the grenadiers shot into the middle of Richepance's column. Their fire felled some battery horses at the bottom of a defile. The blockage separated the column into two sections. Worse, the surprise volley caused a small panic. Exhibiting the characteristic front line leadership that was to propel him far, general of brigade Jean-Baptiste Drouet rode amid the men to restore order. Then he sent the 5th Hussars and some infantry to drive back the grenadiers.

The front of the column ignored this uproar and continued its march until once again the guide got lost. This would not do. Richepance, who was with the forward element, halted the column. He sent two infantry companies to assist the 5th Hussars in clearing the flank and dispatched patrols to the neighboring farms to secure a new guide. This guide told Richepance that Maitenbeth was only a fifteen minute walk away. Suddenly, as if to confirm the guide's words, visibility improved and the general could see the base of the hill on which sat his objective. With the 1st Chasseurs à cheval leading the way, the column resumed its march.

At 9 a.m. the forward elements of Richepance's division, those units which had passed the defile before it became blocked, approached Maitenbeth. At this point Richepance faced a decision. He knew an Austrian force had severed his division. The noise of combat continued back at the defile. He did not know how large was the enemy force advancing against his flank. To the north and northwest he could hear the din of battle emanating from the Hohenlinden plain. He believed that the Austrian units involved in this fight had no idea of his presence. What to do? Many, if not most, generals would have given first priority to saving the division by sending a significant force countermarching to clear the division's flank and rear while the remaining units stood on the defensive. To his great credit, Richepance resolved to sacrifice the rear half of his division if necessary in order to use the units at hand to attack the Austrian rear. In the words of a French history written twenty years later, "This sublime decision...came to be regarded as the decisive cause" of the battle's outcome.[20] Richepance sent a courier spurring to Drouet with instructions to hold his ground until relieved by Decaen's division. Then he ordered his available units, which numbered about 5,600 men, to deploy for an assault.

The 8th and 48th Demi-brigades, the 1st Chasseurs à cheval, and a six-gun battery prepared for action. The grenadiers of the 8th Demi-

The grenadiers of the 8th Demi-brigade swept through Marsmaier and toward the camera.

brigade were in a battle frenzy. Screaming 'Kill! Kill!', they spearheaded the advance into the hamlet of Marsmaier, which stood downslope from Maitenbeth. To their surprise, Marsmaier was not defended. Instead, the grenadiers encountered a detachment of Nassau Cuirassiers, many of whom were dismounted and taking their ease. After securing prisoners, the grenadiers continued though the hamlet and then paused to align with their parent unit. The 8th Demi-brigade formed in line parallel to the Haag-Hohenlinden highway. The battery took position to its front while the cavalry secured the right flank. In this position the French were at the base of a knoll. They could see neither the top nor the far side.

Unbeknownst to Richepance, if he advanced over the rise, he would sever Kollowrat's column. Most of Kollowrat's force had already passed to the west where they were engaged with Grouchy. Just over the knoll and extending east from Strassmair, there remained five and one-half squadrons of Bavarian chevau-legers, Kollowrat's trains, the reserve artillery, and GM Christian Wolfskehl's cuirassier brigade. FML Johannes Liechtenstein commanded this group. He and his men were just approaching Strassmair when some fugitives from the cuirassier detachment in Marsmaier arrived with the news of Richepance's presence. Liechtenstein immediately deployed two regiments, the Lorraine and the Albert Cuirassiers, in two lines on the

Richepance's cavalry charged toward the camera while the 8th Demi-brigade deployed in front of the white building.

slope north of the highway. He ordered a battery of eight 12-pounders to cover this deployment (see map p.240).

During this time, Richepance had ridden to the top of the knoll from where he could look east and north and see the highway as it weaved through the forest. More importantly, he saw Wolfskehl's cuirassiers. If the Austrians realized how feeble was his force, Richepance judged his situation hopeless. Without even waiting for the arrival of the 48th Demi-brigade, he resolved to press forward. The 1st Chasseurs à cheval charged in line toward the cuirassiers. Because of a fold in the ground they did not see the nearby Bavarian light horse. Three Bavarian squadrons charged against the Chasseurs' right flank and sent the unit flying back to its original position. Here was a dangerous moment. The retiring chasseurs were intermixed with the divisional battery and with parts of the 8th Demi-brigade. Saber-wielding Bavarian chevau-legers were hot on their heels. Yet the French infantry remained steady and managed to drive off the Bavarians. Because they were not yet deployed, the Habsburg cuirassiers did not participate in the fight.

By this time the 48th Demi-brigade had arrived to take position to the left of the 8th. Undaunted by the near disaster, Richepance retained his resolve to "form in mass on the grand route and march, rapidly like a thunderbolt, against the enemy's rear."[21] He had his infantry form

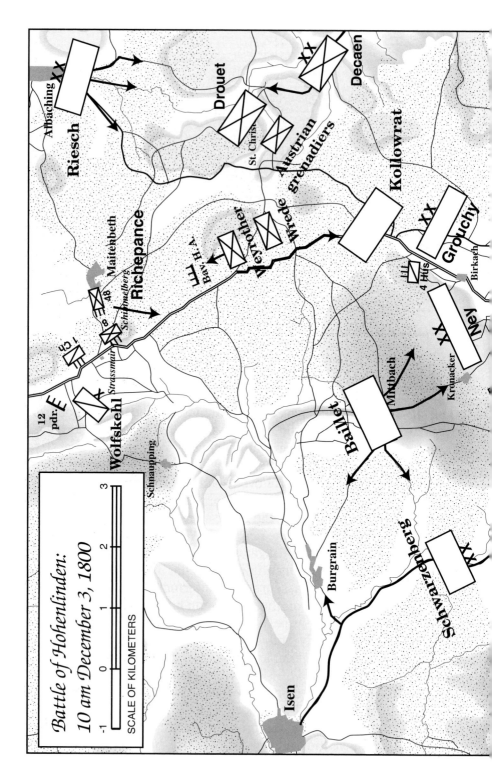

*Battle of Hohenlinden:
10 am December 3, 1800*

SCALE OF KILOMETERS

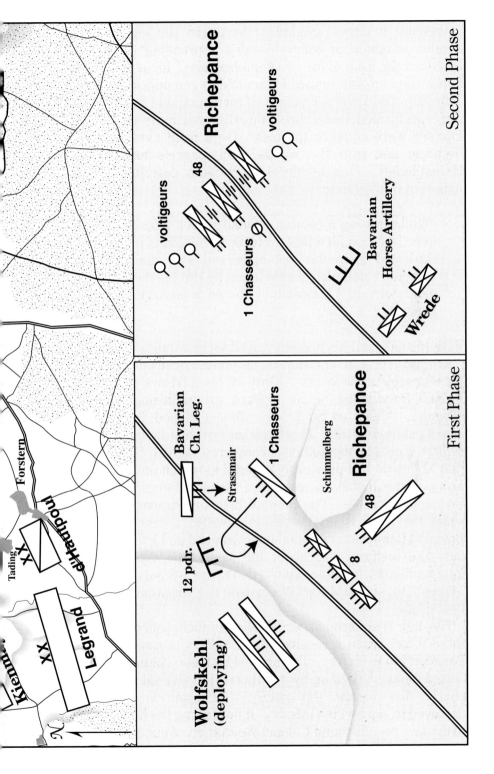

battalion columns with the artillery in the intervals. The 1st Chasseurs à cheval continued to guard the right flank against another eruption of enemy cavalry. Spreading itself thin, it also screened the front of the two demi-brigades. Richepance intended to follow the highway toward Hohenlinden and attack Kollowrat's rear. This required several changes of formation and facing, all of which were performed under fire from the Habsburg 12-pounders. His infantry were equal to the task. On a front extending across the highway and into the woods, Richepance's force marched on Hohenlinden. One of his aides-de-camp described the confused nature of the fighting:

> "While leading a column I found myself attacked at a point here I had no idea that there were Austrians present. I was separated from the mainbody and was alone with three battalions, completely enveloped by the enemy. By hand to hand combat, I successfully forced a passage to rejoin my general."[22]

Both the aide and his horse received saber wounds during the melee.

Around 10 a.m. Erzherzog Johann received a report about Richepance's movements. Most of his advisors believed that this French force must be an isolated group fleeing before Riesch's advance. Chief of Staff Weyrother galloped into the forest to investigate personally. The Bavarian Preysing battalion followed him as best it could. Weyrother encountered the two Bavarian battalions that Kollowrat had previously ordered to march on St. Christoph. He grouped the battalions to form a striking force based around the Preysing battalion. The Stengel battalion supported the left flank while the Schlossberg battalion provided a reserve. A four-gun Bavarian horse battery joined the command and galloped to a position near the highway. At about the same time, Kollowrat, who had independently become alarmed at the sounds of firing about Maitenbeth, sent GM Carl Wrede with two Bavarian battalions toward that village.[23]

The 48th Demi-brigade was the first of Richepance's units to contact these forces when it received three volleys of canister fire from the Bavarian horse battery. The nearest battalion column shuddered and closed ranks. Urged on by its officers, it delivered a spirited bayonet charge that overran the battery. Richepance's divisional battery deployed to support the infantry. It fired along the highway where one of the first rounds found Colonel Weyrother. Wounded, with his horse killed beneath him, Weyrother was knocked out of action at a critical time. Having conquered the battery, the 48th continued west along the highway. On either side the voltigeur companies deployed in the woods in skirmish order. The 48th shouldered its way past numerous caissons and wagons until it encountered Wrede's two Bavarian battalions (see map p.240).

This could well be the decisive engagement and Richepance knew it. He called out to the 48th's grenadiers: "what do you think about those men there?" The grenadiers sternly replied, "General, they are f....d"[24] A fierce, close-range struggle ensued. Perhaps now the Austrians paid the price for having denigrated Bavarian fighting ability by calling them mere mercenaries. Although the Bavarians repulsed the French surge four or five times, in the end they lacked the indomitable spirit to tilt the balance in their favor. Leaving the highway littered with their dead, the Bavarians yielded. It was 10:30 a.m. Colonel Wrede led his battered remnants north where they eventually reached Dorfen. Here they merged into a group of 6,000 badly shaken infantry comprising stragglers, the faint of heart, and leaderless men belonging to the three northernmost Austrian columns.

While this fight was occurring, Weyrother's task force engaged units belonging to Richepance's division who had freed themselves from the combat at the defile. Initially the Preysing and Schlossberg battalions managed to hold their position. However, when the leading elements of Decaen's division intervened, they could do no more. They broke badly, shedding prisoners as they fled. Somehow the Stengel battalion, which had been assigned to provide flank support, managed to avoid the fighting. It fled ignominiously through the woods until it reached friendly lines at midnight.

***

Throughout the anxious morning, General Jean Moreau had maintained his headquarters at Hohenlinden. He had heard nothing from Richepance, nor had he expected to. He had witnessed the Austrian buildup on the heights overlooking Hohenlinden and seen a series of determined assaults against Grouchy and Ney. As noon approached, he perceived that the Austrian assaults against his right had lost momentum. He detected a hesitation in their subsequent maneuvers. In the words of the French historian Ernest Picard, "With a wisdom that does honor to his grasp of the battlefield", he deduced that the Austrian uncertainty was due to Richepance.[25] This was the moment Moreau had been waiting for. He immediately ordered

Grenier's wing to assume the offensive. Ney was to attack directly into the defile where the highway entered the open ground. Grouchy was to crush the Austrian left flank.

Because of FZM Baillet's passivity, Ney was able to strip forces from his left in order to concentrate strength on his right. His divisional horse artillery delivered a punishing preparatory bombardment. Then Ney, exhibiting his renowned front line leadership, conducted a combined arms assault against Birkach and the adjacent wood line. Here the Austrians were tired from their own failed attacks and nervous about the firing they heard to their left and rear. Consequently they offered a feeble resistance. Ney's men drove them through the woods and captured ten cannons and 1,000 prisoners.

Grouchy arrayed his three demi-brigades in battalion column with two forward and one in reserve and advanced eastward. Kollowrat desperately committed his last two grenadier battalions to stem the tide. But here too the Austrians were dispirited. Austrian officers urged them forward but the grenadiers perceived that they were entering a trap with Grouchy to their front, Ney on their right, and Richepance on their left. Their advance lacked conviction and Grouchy quickly repulsed them. To make matters worse for the Austrians, at this juncture the first units of Decaen's division entered the battle.

Decaen's men had been on the march since 5 a.m. From the beginning, Decaen had been very anxious about his line of march. He and Richepance had exchanged messages during the night. They informed Decaen that Richepance was abandoning his outpost line, which was in contact with an Austrian force of unknown size (they belonged to Riesch's column), in order to concentrate manpower for the flank march. However wise from Richepance's perspective, the news distressed Decaen. He worried that the Austrians would enter the void left by Richepance's departure and attack his open right flank. Whereas a Habsburg general might have been rendered inert by his concerns, or at least detached a strong force to address the unknown, after much anxious musing Decaen resolved to carry through with his orders. He ordered his commissary officers to distribute a full measure of gut-wrenching army brandy to the rank and file (one wonders if in order to fortify himself Decaen also partook) and ordered the advance.

By 8 a.m. his column entered Oberndorf, about five miles south of Hohenlinden. Here the division enjoyed a 30 minute rest until Decaen heard the sounds of distant cannons. He interrupted his breakfast, ordered the column to accelerate its pace, and rode to join his advance guard. The track his division followed was so narrow that the column had to proceed on a front of only three men. Decaen laboriously worked his way forward until he passed the men of the Polish Legion. Decaen's lack of Polish prevented him from addressing them. However, their appearance pleased him. And, as he later not immodestly recalled, he believed that his own martial, Gallic appearance pleased them. So inspired, the column labored onward.

As the division approached St. Christoph and the terrain opened up a little, it encountered a fleeing mass of vivandières' wagons and carts as well as ammunition and equipment wagons. Decaen did not know that this was part of the panic triggered by the combat at the defile that had originally severed Richepance's division. Decaen ordered his sappers to the front to clear a path. The leading units, general of brigade Pierre Durutte's French infantry and the Polish Legion, shouldered their way through the snarl and found enough space to deploy in a line of platoon columns. In this formation they proceeded toward St. Christoph.

By 11 a.m. Decaen found Generals Louis Sahuc and Drouet. They told him that the tactical situation was terribly jumbled. A heavy snowfall so reduced visibility that Decaen had to rely upon sound alone to make his dispositions. Hearing a sudden burst of fire to the right he asked Drouet what it meant. "Oh! The enemy is flanking us" came the reply. "Very well!" Decaen responded, "If they are flanking us, we will flank them." Decaen expressed similar confidence moments later when one of Moreau's aides-de- camp rode up and requested information. The general instructed the aide to tell Moreau that the situation was "a little confused" but not to worry because he expected to straighten matters out soon.[26] Decaen had confronted a fast-changing, uncertain situation. Unlike his Austrian counterparts, he reacted confidently and aggressively.

Still, breaking through the first layer of Habsburg resistance proved difficult. A battalion of the 14th Light, accompanied by a cavalry squadron commanded by 'the intrepid Montalon', spearheaded the attack. As the cavalry charged, Montalon's horse fell dead beneath him. He shook himself off and rose to join the infantry. He was subsequently seen leading small knots of men directly at the Austrians during the back and forth fighting. Surprisingly, Montalon survived his infantry service and was alive to witness the tactically decisive intervention of the 2nd Polish Legion. This unit had been raised the previous year in Metz and Strasbourg using veteran cadres from the Italian campaign. When it pitched in, the Austrians ceded their ground for a last time. Just then the sun broke through the clouds as if to celebrate the triumph.

Decaen's division freed Drouet's force from its prolonged struggle around the defile. Drouet reassembled his half of Richepance's division and marched on Maitenbeth. Decaen, in turn, ordered the Polish Legion to assist Drouet. He then focused his attention on securing the army's right flank. While Debilly's brigade advanced northeast toward Albaching, Durutte's brigade marched eastward through the forest against the same objective. Decaen hoped eventually to turn northward to interdict the highway. In the event, Durutte encountered the various columns Riesch had ordered to converge on St. Christoph. It was now that Riesch paid the price for having fragmented his command. Durutte's soldiers methodically defeated the Austrian columns one by one.

Meanwhile, the Polish Legion enjoyed greater glory when it debouched onto the highway near the Schimmelberg. It found itself in the midst of the Austrian artillery park. The Poles' unexpected appearance broke the already wavering Austrians. It seemed to them that the woods contained countless hostile columns that were erupting at will onto the highway. The only avenue to safety and freedom was to the north. Kollowrat's close order formations dissolved into untidy knots of fleeing soldiers running through the woods. The Habsburg drivers cut the traces and abandoned their vehicles to escape. Soon fallen soldiers and overturned cannons littered the highway. The rout was on with the flying soldiers spreading terror and confusion.

The experience of a French chasseur named Côteboeuf and a Polish lancer named Ivisen highlights the collapse in Austrian morale. Côteboeuf galloped ahead of his unit and encountered some 50 Austrian infantry. Undaunted, he glanced over his shoulder and shouted out, "Charge, the 4th!" The Austrians laid down their muskets until they perceived that they faced a solitary rider. They began picking up their weapons when Ivisen appeared. Although this changed the odds to one versus twenty-five, what was more important was that apparently the Austrians belonged to a regiment recruited in Galicia, because Ivisen addressed them in their native Polish. His powers of persuasion were equal to the task and once again the infantry laid down their arms.

Meanwhile, fugitives from Kollowrat's column as well as Riesch's own men came streaming past Riesch's position at Albaching. He dispatched a courier to Erzherzog Johann to report that he had struggled mightily to reach Hohenlinden – a dubious assertion at best – and that he had suffered severely. Nonetheless, Riesch reported the soldierly resolve to hold his ground unless he received orders otherwise. As the courier vanished into the trees, Riesch could not know that Johann was on the verge of having to ride for his life to escape from Decaen's Poles.

Back on the highway, Ney's men continued their drive until they met Richepance's 48th Demi-brigade. Richepance was not yet content with what had been accomplished. His thoughts centered on the scattered Austrian forces which he had bypassed. Accordingly, he turned his men around again, and marched toward Maitenbeth. Near that village the 8th Demi-brigade and 1st Chasseurs à cheval had been charged repeatedly by Wolfskehl's cuirassiers. During these actions the French general of brigade Frederic Walther fell with a grievous wound. On the Austrian side, Colonel Josef Radetzky, the future field marshal, was also knocked out of action. Suddenly some Austrian infantry appeared on the 8th's left flank. They probably belonged to Riesch's column, but at any event their arrival showed that in the forests of Hohenlinden the surprise eruption of hostile soldiers on one's flanks could beset either side. The 8th recoiled from the contact. The Austrians, in turn, freed numerous prisoners who had been held in the hamlet and then continued their retreat.

It was 2:30 when Richepance countermarched the 48th eastward to support the 8th. The two demi-brigades straddled the highway from where they repelled one more charge from the cuirassiers. As the Austrian heavy horsemen left the field, Ney's division closed up on Richepance's left. Together the victorious French marched on Haag. Perhaps only now could Richepance take stock of what he had accomplished. He later paid tribute to his men when he wrote that the memory he would retain for the rest of his life was how his soldiers' conduct gave him a carefree confidence throughout the battle. Because he intimately understood his soldiers' capabilities, Richepance had taken near reckless gambles and won out.

Along the highway, the French reported that they heard terrified cries from the routing Austrians as they abandoned their guns and dropped their muskets. Having lost all order, the fleeing soldiers quickly clogged the few available forest paths. This left those less light on their feet and those who had resisted the longest with a terrible choice: either run through a fire swept gauntlet when Richepance and Ney arrived on their flank and rear; or yield. Many chose to surrender, including General Deroy and eighteen other Bavarian officers. The 47-year-old Zweibrücken narrowly avoided capture by spryly catching an artillery horse and galloping to safety. Erzherzog Johann likewise had to endure a hard gallop for safety. Artillerymen emulated their leaders. They left behind over 60 artillery pieces.

While Richepance, Ney, and Grouchy were sweeping along the highway, Decaen continued his march on Albaching. There were frequent, confused brushes with Austrian columns which were trying to escape from the rapidly closing net. Decaen managed to collect 3,000 prisoners and seven artillery pieces. However, he made no real attempt to storm Riesch's position at Albaching. At dusk Riesch learned of the collapse of Kollowrat's column. He also received a hopelessly optimistic message from Johann suggesting that he renew the offensive. Instead, he led his column back to safety on the heights east of Haag, having lost 900 men but taking with him 500 prisoners.

***

The extreme left flank of Moreau's position had witnessed some stern, but brief fighting between Legrand's division and Erzherzog Ferdinand's command. Ferdinand had tried to advance onto the north end of the Hohenlinden plain in the direction of Harthofen. The combat swayed back and forth until Ferdinand learned that the troops protecting his own left flank had fallen back before a vigorous French counteroffensive. When the 51st Demi-brigade drove Frenel out of Buch, Ferdinand realized that his line of retreat was in peril. The Austrian 13th Dragoon Regiment made a fine charge that drove the French infantry back into Buch. Although a countercharge led by Colonel Jean-Baptiste Corbineau of the 5th Chasseurs à cheval broke the dragoons, they had accomplished their mission of allowing Ferdinand to disengage and retire. When Corbineau went down with a serious wound Ferdinand was able to retreat the way he had come. Legrand's division captured some 500 prisoners and three artillery pieces during its pursuit. It had played its designated role by defending Moreau's left. Indicative of the fact that the division had not faced serious pressure was its casualty list which amounted to only 80 killed and 160 wounded.

Bastoul's division, positioned between Legrand and Ney, also joined the French counteroffensive. Its opponents belonged to Schwarzenberg's command. Schwarzenberg had paused after capturing Kronacker until he learned how progressed the Austrian main column. When Bastoul attacked, the Austrians offered stubborn resistance. Finally the French reclaimed Kronacker but their advance stalled at the woods to the north. Here, the Walloons of the Murray Infantry Regiment, a unit that throughout this day consistently fought well, energetically contested the position. When the 89th Demi-brigade finally cleared the woods, it triggered a bold counterattack. The Erzherzog Ferdinand Regiment and the Mack Cuirassiers surged forward to drive back the 89th and then to capture Kronacker. This counterstroke threatened to overwhelm Bastoul.

To meet this final challenge, Moreau assembled a powerful task force comprising three cavalry regiments commanded by d'Hautpoul, Ney's converged grenadiers, and the 108th Demi-brigade and two battalions of the 57th from Grouchy's division.

After a preparatory artillery bombardment, this force charged Kronacker. Simultaneously, Bastoul's cavalry turned inward against Schwarzenberg's right flank while elements of Ney's division attacked his left. Kienmayer, who about this time learned of Kollowrat's disaster, ordered Schwarzenberg to retreat to Isen. Amid this trying tactical situation, Schwarzenberg retained his balance. He committed several battalions to counterattack and thereby purchase time. When a French officer arrived under a flag of truce to describe the overwhelming French success along the highway and to demand Schwarzenberg's surrender, the Austrian general replied by ordering his artillery to redouble its fire.

Darkness came early on this short December day, and its arrival saved the Austrian army. In order to retire, Schwarzenberg's people had to traverse a poor forest path. Yet they managed to withdraw without losing a single cannon. His successful escape to Dorfen came without any support from the adjacent forces commanded by Baillet. Baillet had remained in position on the heights overlooking Mittbach until he learned of Kollowrat's fate. Without making any attempt to cooperate with Schwarzenberg, he ordered a retreat to Isen. The head of his column reached that village at 4 a.m., the rear arrived four hours later.

Although Legrand and Bastoul experienced limited success, their offensive assured Moreau of victory all along the front. The Army of the Rhine seemed to understand what it had accomplished. From the heights overlooking the Hohenlinden plain to the outskirts of Haag the soldiers cherished their triumph. This army had been among the most republican of all the French armies. They rejoiced in commensurate style: "These patriotic displays, these fraternal embraces on the field of battle, the modesty of their commander who did not forget to share his glory with his comrades, this celebration of victory in the name of peace and liberty."[27] They did not know that it marked the end of an era. In the future, soldiers would march beneath the imperial eagles of Napoleon Bonaparte rather than the banners of the French Republic.

NOTES

1. David G. Chandler, ed., *The Military Maxims of Napoleon* (New York, 1988), p. 59.

2. Desperrières' report cited in Ernest Picard, *Hohenlinden* (Paris, 1909) p. 146.

3. "Bulletin historique de la division Ney," Picard, p. 151; and "Hardÿ to his wife," December 3, 1800, General Hardÿ de Perini, ed., *Correspondence Intime du Général Jean Hardÿ de 1797 à 1802* (Paris, 1901), p. 228.

4. Picard, p. 152. Bodart claims French losses totaled 2,200. See: Gaston Bodart, *Militär-historisches kriegs-lexicon 1618-1905* (Vienna, 1908) p. 357.

5. Picard, p. 152. Bodart, p. 357, places Austrian losses at 3,100.

6. Gaspard Gourgaud, *Memoirs of the History of France During the Reign of Napoleon, Dictated by the Emperor*, II (London, 1823) pp. 55-56.

7. See the author's *Napoleon Conquers Austria: The 1809 Campaign for Vienna* (Westport, CT, 1995).

8. "Relation des Mouvemens de l'Armée Autrichienne," in Marquis de Carrion-Nisas, *Campagne des Français en Allemagne* (Paris, 1829), p. 380.

9. Because there is a Buch, Mittler Buch, and Ober Buch, as well as a nearby Burgrain and Mittbach, there was confusion, with virtually all accounts merely referring to "Buch". The main village of Buch is Buch am Buchrain, referred to hereafter as "Buch".

10. The corps reserve comprised: two 6-pdrs, eight 12-pdrs, four 7-pdr howitzers, four 6-pdr cavalry cannons, two 7-pdr cavalry howitzers. At campaign's start the army reserve comprised: 18 light cannons; 6 howitzers, 24 6-pdrs.

11. "Relation des Mouvemens de l'Armée Autrichienne," Carrion-Nisas, p. 381.

12. Moreau's order cited in Picard, p. 169.

13. Charles Decaen, *Mémoires et Journaux du Général Decaen* (Paris, 1911) p. 134.

14. Ibid., p. 136.

15. Ibid., p. 138.

16. Ibid., p. 139.

17. There was a six-gun artillery reserve attached to Moreau's center corps. I have been unable to find its location at the battle. In all likelihood it followed Decaen or remained behind him.

18. Victor Dupuy, *Souvenirs Militaires* (Paris, 1892), p. 24.

19. Gunther E. Rothenberg, *Napoleon's Great Adversaries* (Bloomington, IN, 1982), pp. 64-65.

20. *Victoires, Conquêtes, Désastres, Revers et Guerres Civiles des Français*, XIII (Paris, 1820), p. 190.

21. Dessolles' report in Picard, p. 210.

22. Lt. General Reiset, *Souvenirs du Lieutenant Général Vicomte de Reiset*, I (Paris, 1899), pp. 96-97.

23. Wrede was born in Heidelberg in 1767. His first name is variously reported as 'Carl', 'Karl' and, according to Picard, 'Charles-Philippe de Wrede'.

24. Antoine Richepance, "Bataille de Hohenlinden," *Le Spectateur Militaire*, XXII (Paris, 1836), 265. Carrion-Nisas relates the same story but substitutes the more genteel "they are dead."
25. Picard, p. 216. The phrase the author employs is the virtually untranslatable "coup d'oeil militaire".
26. Decaen, p. 145.
27. Lanfrey, cited in Picard, p. 234.

Chapter 11

The Security
of Europe

PART 1.
THE LAST REPUBLICAN VICTORY

"When great nations are concerned, peace follows victory." [1]

Napoleon Bonaparte, March 3, 1800

When news of Hohenlinden reached Paris five days after the battle, First Consul Bonaparte "literally danced for joy." [2] In a letter to Moreau he handsomely praised the general, describing his maneuvers as "beautiful and wise". [3] Some time thereafter, he commented that victory came from Moreau's capable pre-battle planning. To his discredit, during his exile on Saint Helena Bonaparte completely altered his opinion. While acknowledging that Hohenlinden was one of the war's decisive battles, he claimed it could be attributed neither to any talent nor to any initiative displayed by Moreau.

Many of the comments he dictated while on Saint Helena are an exercise in selective evidence. They are also the labors of a bored genius. But he rightfully criticized Moreau for fighting Hohenlinden with barely half of his available force. Moreau had campaigned along an overly extensive front and then left Sainte-Suzanne's 24,000 men at Ingolstadt, 66 miles from the battle, and Lecourbe's 23,000 men off to the south 30 miles away. But this does not overshadow the fact that he had devised an elegant plan and stuck to it during the battle's uncertain early hours. Well might General Grouchy later say, in a letter to his wife, "we have won the most complete victory of the war." [4] The great republican armies – the Army of the North, the Army of the Sambre and Meuse, the Army of Italy, the Army of the Rhine and

Moselle – had suffered terrible defeats and earned notable successes. None of their victories rivaled Hohenlinden's combination of overwhelming tactical success with significant strategic results. Moreau appreciated this when he modestly concluded his victory dispatch with the words, "The army is proud of its success, above all with the hope that it will contribute to an early peace."[5]

The casualty lists underscore how one-sided was Moreau's victory. The Austrians lost 798 killed, 3,687 wounded while yielding at least 7,195 prisoners, 50 artillery pieces, and 85 caissons. Throughout its many campaigns since the beginning of the Seven Years' War, the Austrian army had never lost so much artillery. The Bavarians suffered 24 killed and 90 wounded while yielding 1,754 prisoners, 26 artillery pieces, and 36 caissons. The nearly seventeen-fold disparity between men killed and wounded versus those who surrendered proves Bavarian hearts were not in this battle. In round figures, Hohenlinden cost the army 13,500 men.[6]

Typically, it is impossible to tabulate precisely French losses. Summing the totals claimed by those generals who submitted estimates yields 1,839, well above the 1,200 reported by Dessolles, Moreau's chief of staff. The French probably lost nearly 3,000 along with one artillery piece and two caissons.[7] Putting aside the disparity in captured artillery, the Army of the Rhine still enjoyed a favorable casualty ratio verus the Austrians of between four and five to one. Among the French losses was General Louis Bastoul. Eager to justify both Moreau's confidence in him and his worthiness for divisional command, late in the day he had dismounted, seized a standard, and led an attack. The wound he received proved mortal on January 15, 1801.

After the battle, the Habsburg leaders fell into an orgy of blame casting. Bonaparte learned of this and commented, "In this campaign the Austrian generals had a capital plan, but they did not push home their attack on General Grenier when they had beaten him...They are now throwing the blame of the loss of all their artillery on each other."[8] Young Erzherzog Johann had no doubt about what, or rather who, had cost him the battle. First and foremost he blamed Riesch. Johann claimed that Riesch had consumed eleven hours to march from Haag to Albaching and that this slow pace had allowed the French to slip between Riesch and Kollowrat and attack Kollowrat in the rear. In fact, as we have seen, Riesch departed Haag at 4:30 a.m. and arrived at Albaching at 10 a.m. This was not very different from Richepance's rate of march.

When Johann's older brother reviewed the battle, Karl criticized the plan which had Riesch march toward an objective well south of the main column. This invited defeat in detail. Karl's criticism, however, fails to consider the very limited road net available to the Austrian army. Johann also blamed Baillet and Kienmayer for having wasted time and thus failed to cooperate with the main column. Like his brother, Johann did not recognize how poor were the roads. That aside, it is true that Baillet arrived on the fringes of the Hohenlinden plateau and then hesitated. Rather than retain the initiative, he waited to see how fared Kollowrat. As noted, his inaction allowed Ney and Grouchy to concentrate against Kollowrat.

The most acute criticism of the Austrian performance comes from the angry pen of General Zweibrücken. He wrote his liege, the Elector Max-Joseph, that the battle was lost by "ignorance and ineptitude."[9] For Johann's attack to succeed, it was vital to coordinate the movements of the various columns. Instead, none sent out scouts to scour the flanks and to maintain contact with one another. They wandered independently through the forest. None kept an adequate reserve to maintain the front or to cover a retreat. An enormous and useless artillery train cluttered the highway and this thwarted efforts to march units to confront Richepance. History shows that it is nearly impossible for converging columns to arrive on a battle front at the same time and then deliver a coordinated assault. The sad fate of the Austrian army at Hohenlinden is one more contribution to this record.

When the unexpected occurs, many officers behave as did Baillet; they hesitate and are uncertain. At this point, there must be either a well-devised plan to provide a general with guidance so he can overcome obstacles, or the commander-in-chief must rely upon subordinate initiative. At Hohenlinden, the erroneous premise that Moreau was in retreat formed the basis for the Austrian plan. When it became clear that they were not chasing a defeated opponent, that the operational plan was invalid, the Austrian column commanders had to make new decisions. They had to display initiative. The need proved beyond their capacities. In contrast, Moreau's simple, elegant strategy gave his generals a lodestar, a reference point for making tactical adjustments. When Richepance found his column suddenly cut in two, he carried on with his available forces in order to execute Moreau's strategy. The French enjoyed a happy marriage of sound pre-battle strategy and commendable subordinate initiative.

On both sides of the lines, many officers who served at Hohenlinden were to continue to play prominent roles in the subsequent wars of the First French Empire. At the time, the Army of the Rhine had no doubt that Antoine Richepance had been the brightest star amid a shining galaxy that included two future marshals of France, Ney and Grouchy. However, as part of the suppression of prominent officers in the Army of the Rhine, Bonaparte placed Richepance on the inactive list in 1801. Still, had he lived, Richepance would have risen high. Instead, in April 1802 Bonaparte dispatched him to Guadeloupe to serve as Governor-General. Four months later he was dead, a victim of yellow fever.

Many officers who escaped Bonaparte's jealous persecution still suffered from their association with Moreau's Army of the Rhine for the rest of their military service. Two examples demonstrate this legacy. In 1810, when Masséna and his officers debated how to confront the British position atop the Bussaco ridge, the Hohenlinden veteran, General François Fririon, proposed a turning movement. Masséna sneeringly rejected this notion by replying, "You are of the Army of the Rhine, you like to maneuver". Instead, Masséna sent his army climbing the ridge in a clumsy frontal attack. A year later, Napoleon discussed replacing Ney with Marmont. When a staff officer argued that this would not solve the conflict of authority, the emperor explained, "Masséna and Marmont are from the same family; they are of the Army of Italy while Ney is from a foreign army"[10]. He referred, of course, to the Army of the Rhine.

On the Austrian side, the careers of two Hohenlinden veterans dramatically shaped future events. At Austerlitz in 1805, the Russian Czar relied upon Franz Weyrother, who had been Johann's chief of staff, to devise the allied battle plan. Weyrother designed the overly complex maneuver – complete with five columns, two advance guards, and a reserve – that caused the Russian commanding officer, Mikhail Kutusov, to fall asleep while Weyrother explained it. The next day, Weyrother's Hohenlinden-like fragmentation of force contributed enormously to Napoleon's most celebrated victory.

At Hohenlinden, FML Karl Schwarzenberg's leadership towered over that of other Habsburg generals. After participating with distinction in the wars of 1805 and 1809, when Austria entered the lists against France in 1813, he became supreme commander of the allied armies. He acted in an Eisenhower-type role by forwarding grand strategy amid the squabble of rival national goals. He commanded at the great Allied triumph at Leipzig in 1813. Schwarzenberg then enjoyed the satisfaction of leading the invasion of France the following year. He never received much credit for all of this, but his performance was critical to the Allied victory.

***

Although the battle of Hohenlinden did not end the campaign season of 1800, it placed the Austrians in an extreme bind if Moreau vigorously pressed his advantage. No one better appreciated this than Erzherzog Johann. The morning after the battle he wrote that his army was so battered and demoralized that if Moreau advanced, he doubted that he could mount an effective resistance. Johann ordered a series of punishing, forced marches in hopes of retiring behind a river line from where he could organize a defense. However, Moreau chose not to mount an immediate, aggressive pursuit. Instead of maneuvering to exterminate the Austrian army, he selected geographical objectives. With this decision he again showed himself to be a general more comfortable with the prior strategic era than with the new style of war the First Consul was perfecting.

Nonetheless, by any conventional standard Moreau performed very well indeed. His objective was Salzburg. If he occupied that city he would cut off the Austrian units in the Inn Valley and threaten communications between Vienna and Italy. In a skillful series of maneuvers during which Richepance again showed himself to be an exceptional leader, Moreau bounded across the Inn River and marched to within 50 miles of Vienna. He exhibited commendable flexibility by changing plans to take advantage of unexpected opportunity. The Army of the Rhine covered over 200 miles in fifteen days while gathering in 20,000 prisoners and an enormous booty of artillery and wheeled transport. The speed of the advance baffled and alarmed the Aulic Council. The Kaiser warned the citizens of Vienna to prepare for a siege. He and his court made arrangements to flee the capital.

The catastrophe compelled Franz to ask yet again for Erzherzog Karl to assume command of the army. Replying that he "was willing to sacrifice himself for the state," Karl replaced Johann on December 17. [11] He reported to the Kaiser that fewer than half of the men Johann had taken to battle at Hohenlinden remained with the colors. He told a fellow officer that they more resembled an Asiatic "horde" than a disciplined European army. [12] When Karl inspected them he found their condition deplorable and placed seven superior officers under arrest for having abetted their men's misbehavior. But it was impossible to stop the rot. The defeat of the main army affected other formations. Austrian militia levies refused to march to reinforce the army. The Hungarian insurrection soldiers went them one better and refused to even muster. The situation was clearly hopeless. On December 24, the Kaiser authorized Karl to ask for an armistice. Karl obeyed, while noting privately that if Moreau refused "we are lost." [13]

Unbeknownst to the Austrians, Moreau had his own anxieties. He had bypassed several Austrian-held citadels. They imperiled his line of communication. He had heard little from the Army of Italy and worried what might happen if the Austrians in Italy crossed the mountains into the Tyrol and operated against his deep flank and rear.[14] On the other hand, he had done much and if the fighting stopped now, he and France would be well satisfied. Accordingly, the next day Moreau signed the Armistice of Steyer.

He later learned that his concerns about affairs in Italy had been misguided. In that country the slippery General Guillaume Brune had replaced Masséna because, depending upon which source one believes, Bonaparte had become disgusted at his bald-faced thievery or, as seems more likely, he recognized that Masséna had not recovered from the siege of Genoa. Brune's opponent was FML Heinrich Bellegarde. When Melas had learned that he was to be superceded by Bellegarde, the old veteran showed his noble character by cooperating during the transition, sharing all relevant documents, explaining the current position, and introducing Bellegarde to his staff. Only once did he reveal a vindictive side. He introduced Chief of Staff Zach with the comment, "You see this little man, he has a soul as black as his countenance."[15] Within the Austrian army, Bellegarde was a popular choice. However, he seemed to lack confidence in himself and to be too eager to please the court in Vienna. Perhaps his performance was simply another case of an able subordinate becoming indecisive when he ascended to independent command.

The star of the second half of the Italian campaign was General Jacques Macdonald. Macdonald led 7,000 men through the Splügen Pass, a winter march more difficult than Bonaparte's crossing of the Saint Bernard. Through a series of clever maneuvers that revealed a real flair for mountain warfare, he captured Trent on the upper Adige River. Brune had instructions to wait until Macdonald's flank maneuver discomforted the Austrians before advancing in earnest. In spite of his own bungling, on December 25 his army broke the Mincio River line. While defending this line, FML Conrad Kaim – a divisional commander at Marengo and regarded as a brave and true patriot – received a mortal wound. By January 1 the Army of Italy had forced the Adige River and ten days later it passed the Brenta River as well. This series of successful river crossings into the heart of the famed fortresses of the Quadrilateral – Peschiera, Legnano, Mantua, and Verona – made Bellegarde's situation difficult. Coupled with the presence of Macdonald's Army of the Grisons deep on his flank and the need to transfer units to defend Vienna, his situation also became hopeless. He concluded the truce of Trevise on January 16, 1801.

All that remained was for the French to settle with the Neopolitans. A small French force operating in Tuscany ignored the possibility of an allied amphibious landing at Leghorn and marched on Ancona on the Adriatic coast. Its capture on January 27 isolated the Neopolitans from Austrian assistance. The French, under Murat's dynamic leadership, closed on the Neopolitan frontier thereby forcing the Neopolitan leadership to conclude an armistice. In accordance with the formal treaty signed on March 28, a French army of occupation entered Otranto, Brindisi, and Taranto. This left the Royal Navy with no ports on the Italian mainland. All of Italy was again in French control. The Second Coalition had collapsed.

So the diplomats again convened in Lunéville to discuss peace. It was a testament to Habsburg weakness that during the debate over where would be the border of the French-controlled Cisalpine Republic in northern Italy, Chancellor Cobenzl offered the Oglio, the Chiese, and the Mincio rivers, one after the other and each progressively further east. After Marengo, Bonaparte would have accepted the Mincio. After Hohenlinden, he would accept nothing less than the Adige. Many of the other terms merely restated previous agreements. So France cemented her claim to Belgium, Luxembourg, and the German principalities on the Rhine's left bank. This territory improved France's strategic position by providing a bridgehead over the Rhine. Austria also had to accept France's right to impose stiff indemnities on the German princes. In addition, Austria had to recognize the 'independence' of the Ligurian, Cisalpine, Swiss, and Batavian Republics. In fact, as everyone knew, these were French vassal states.

To sign such a treaty Austria had to abase itself before all of Europe. With some satisfaction – during the summer he had told anyone who listened that it was a mistake to resume hostilities – Karl wrote the Kaiser that in normal times the state would risk one or two battles before accepting such harsh terms. But the strategic situation was so bad that another lost battle would ruin the monarchy. Consequently, he advised signing. On February 9, 1801 came the formal peace, the Treaty of Lunéville. By the narrowest, Austria had honored Thugut's pledge to Great Britain not to sign a separate peace any time earlier. Neither then nor later did Bonaparte display the knack of concluding an enduring peace that converted an enemy into an ally or at least into a neutral bystander. In 1801, the sting of profound humiliation prompted the hawks in the Aulic Council to begin immediately preparing for a new war.

The treaty gave France an overwhelming strategic victory unrivaled since the times of Louis XIV. Conversely, it was a terrible setback for Great Britain, who now had but one remaining ally, the Ottoman Empire. Her strategic position had reverted to that which she held at the beginning of 1798. Although there were always foreign hands ready to receive British gold, throughout Europe there were many leaders who were jealous of Great Britain. They believed that as long as war consumed Europe, Great Britain prospered by enjoying a monopoly of trade and specie. The British ambassador to Austria described this sentiment: "We are represented as making war, and inciting all other nations to join us, merely for its profit."[16] Such cynicism, coupled with military necessity, compelled Britain to fight on without allies.

***

When Bonaparte had returned to Paris after Marengo in the summer of 1800, he had written to Tsar Paul in hopes of furthering a Franco-Russian alliance. He disingenuously suggested that if the French were compelled to evacuate Malta – something he well knew was a certainty given the close blockade maintained at sea by the Royal Navy and on land by Maltese insurgents – then he would place the island in the hands of the Grand Master of the Knights of St. John. Since the Tsar was Grand Master, this was an alluring idea to the Russian leader. Bonaparte added bait to the hook. Great Britain had refused to accept an exchange of some 6,000 Russian soldiers, whom the French had captured in 1799, for an equal number of French prisoners who were in British hands. Furthermore, while in winter quarters on the Channel Islands, the Russian remnants who had invaded Holland had received shabby treatment. So, as a mark of his 'esteem for the brave Russian soldier', Bonaparte released his Russian prisoners. To complete this handsome (but wholly calculated) gesture in style, he issued the former prisoners good uniforms and weapons. He omitted any demand for ransom.

The Tsar observed the contrast between French and British behavior toward his soldiers and responded favorably. A potent continental alliance seemed imminent. By the end of 1800, Russian leaders were drawing up plans for a joint operation against British-held India; far fetched but not impossible. Then, high-handed British behavior in the Baltic gave Bonaparte a priceless strategic opportunity to isolate Great Britain from the continent.

The Royal Navy regularly exercised its claim to have the right of search for contraband cargoes. The Baltic states bitterly resented it.

They formed the Second Armed Neutrality, comprising Denmark, Sweden, Russia, and eventually Prussia. It effectively countered the Royal Navy's control of the sea. If it persisted, it allowed France to circumvent the naval blockade of her coast. It also ended the Royal Navy's access to critical naval stores including timber for masts and yards, 'Stockholm tar' – the pitch used for caulking – and hemp for rigging. Moreover, British farmers had suffered through two poor harvests in 1799 and 1800. The Armed Neutrality disrupted grain shipments from the Baltic at a time when, in order to make up the shortfall, 75 percent of British corn imports came from Danzig. The price of wheat trebled, causing social and political unrest, an unrest made more threatening when the government passed oppressive political and labor legislation to control the situation. Cries of 'bread or blood' from the lower class ensued. The landed gentry, who held a dominant position in British politics, appreciated that in the event of insurrection the first blood to be shed would be their own. Consequently they leaned hard on Prime Minister William Pitt to make peace.

Pitt had suffered fierce attacks ever since he had responded to Bonaparte's initial peace overtures by essentially demanding the return of the Bourbons. In the House of Commons one prominent critic queried, "is it out of gratitude to the house of Bourbon that you are lavishing our blood and our treasure?" Referring to the time when the French king had supported the American rebels, he continued, "Recollect the American war!" Recalling the army's need to conduct an armistice in order to flee from Holland, another member said, "It seems that if our government cannot conclude treaties of peace with the French Republic, it can at least conclude capitulations."[17]

Hohenlinden and the collapse of the Second Coalition badly weakened Pitt. He resigned in March 1801. Henry Addington's new government entered negotiations with France immediately. But events that same month altered the strategic landscape.

A powerful British fleet had delivered an ultimatum to the Danish regent demanding that his country detach itself from the Second Armed Neutrality of the North. Its rejection led to the Battle of Copenhagen, won when Nelson literally turned a blind eye to a recall order and pressed matters to a bloody conclusion on April 2, 1801. This victory, coupled with the assassination of "Mad Tsar Paul", caused the collapse of the Armed Neutrality of the North. British naval prestige ascended to a new height. The Armed Neutrality had revealed Great Britain's vulnerability to economic pressure, something the future Emperor Napoleon would recall to his profound detriment. But in the spring of 1801, it was news from Egypt that more concerned the First Consul.

Part 2.
The Peace of Amiens

When a general serves on detached duty and is out of easy contact with headquarters, he will inevitably have to interpret conflicting orders. So it proved for Lieutenant General Ralph Abercromby after he learned of the Austrian defeat at Marengo. The first priority in Abercromby's instructions was to support the Austrians. In July and August of 1800, a formidable group including the Austrians, the Queen of Naples, Admiral George Keith, and British diplomats strongly urged Abercromby to commit his forces to Italy. Abercromby manfully resisted. Instead of reinforcing failure in "an uncertain undertaking on the continent" he wanted to strike in a direction that he believed provided a greater chance for success.[18] With the grudging support of his government, Abercromby resolved to invade Egypt.

In that country, the plague had returned, killing Frenchmen more surely than had Mameluke swords. In General Jean-Baptiste Kléber's words, Bonaparte had seen the fatal crisis fast approaching, deserted, and left the Army of the Orient with "an enormous burden."[19] After Kleber fell, assassinated on the same June day that claimed Desaix, the Army of the Orient passed to its senior officer, General Abdullah Menou. The 50-year-old Jacques-François Menou had taken to the exotic comforts of the Middle East to the extent that he had converted to Islam and acquired the name Abdullah. He had always been prone to laziness and now grew fat from too many lavish feasts and enfeebled by too many dalliances with Egyptian bath girls.

Yet Menou commanded an army that still included Bonaparte's select Italian veterans. They were the men of Lodi, Rivoli, and Castiglione; hardened, confident soldiers accustomed to victory. Although shocked by Bonaparte's desertion, they and their officers retained nothing but contempt for both the Turkish and the British soldier. The former they had trounced repeatedly since landing in Egypt. They knew that the latter had drunk deeply the dregs of defeat ever since losing the American war.

To everyone's suprise, when Abercromby's army invaded Egypt it won the Battle of Aboukir on March 21, 1800. The pivotal encounter occurred when French dragoons charged the rear of the British 28th

Regiment. The regiment's colonel shouted, 'Rear rank 28th! Right about face!'[20] In a performance like that of the 72nd Demi-brigade at Marengo, the rear rank turned, leveled their muskets, and fired a single volley that destroyed the charging dragoons. The regiment thereby earned the unique honor of wearing a commemorative badge on the backs of their caps.

The battle was the British army's greatest victory over the French since the beginning of the French revolution. Egypt, in turn, was the proving ground of David Dundas' tactical system which emphasized superior discipline and weight of fire. Abercromby had firmly adopted Dundas' system. Under his leadership, the British Army began a profound regeneration. The hero of the Battle of Alexandria, General John Moore, appreciated this truth. He wrote, "I have had the satisfaction of seeing the superiority of the British infantry over the French in three successive actions; we have beat them without cavalry and inferior in artillery."[21] During the coming decade Moore and then Wellesley would continue to perfect the army until British foot soldiers became the best infantry in Europe. A difficult, five-month long campaign lay ahead, but eventually Abercromby's successor managed to evict the demoralized French from Egypt. Then it fell to the diplomats to determine what had been won and lost during the war of the Second Coalition.

For the chosen veterans of the Army of Italy who participated in Bonaparte's misguided Egyptian adventure, the human consequences are perhaps best illustrated by the experience of one typical demi-brigade. The 18th Demi-brigade departed Toulon with 2,100 men. A total of 24 officers and 318 soldiers were killed outright in battle. Nine officers and 43 men died of wounds. Eleven officers and 58 men succumbed from the plague while another 8 and 243, respectively, perished from other sicknesses. Five soldiers died from accidents. In sum, 52 of 124 officers died during the campaign along with 667 soldiers.[22] The demi-brigade lost in killed alone about one man in three, with battlefield fatalities only slightly exceeding losses to disease. Then and thereafter Napoleon Bonaparte reflected upon the Egyptian campaign wistfully, calling it the romantic stuff of a novel. The soldiers of the 18th Demi-brigade would not have agreed.

***

The summer of 1801 found France ascendant on the continent but unable to challenge the Royal Navy. Britain's strategic position was more one of stalemate – dominant at sea and in Egypt, unable to intervene on the continent – than of despair. But the new Addington government caved to the strident demands of the propertied class and the selfish views of the mercantile class which equated any sort of peace with a trade revival and profit. A prolonged negotiation ensued, pitting Charles Lord Cornwallis, the veteran of the American war, against Joseph Bonaparte. During numerous conferences at the *Hotel de Ville* at Amiens, Bonaparte won point after point over Cornwallis. Cornwallis showed himself to be no longer the aggressive, persistent general of his younger days but rather a weary landowner, eager to return to his Suffolk estate. By the terms of the Peace of Amiens, signed in March 1802, France retained Savoy, Piedmont, the left bank of the Rhine, and the Netherlands while evacuating the Roman States and the Kingdom of the Two Sicilies. During the war, British forces had conquered the Cape, Egypt, Malta, and numerous important French possessions in the West Indies. The peace dictated that Great Britain relinquish all but Trinidad and the Ceylon settlements. Egypt reverted to the Turks, Malta to the Order of St. John.

The peace left many contentious issues unsettled, yet initially, it proved wildly popular in England. When Bonaparte's aide-de-camp, Jacques Lauriston, brought news from Paris that the treaty had been ratified, a cheering British mob unhitched his carriage and pulled it through the streets while shouting the name 'Bonaparte.' Some observers might sniff that the mob had been paid and liquored by a local radical, but the truth was that the public welcomed peace. Cut off from the continent by long years of war, throngs of British tourists hastened across the channel to visit France. Beneath this gay facade, a wary handful of British strategists understood the perils of a peace with France which relied more upon general assurances rather than formal stipulations. "It is nothing but a frail and deceptive truce", intoned one member of the House of Lords. The men who had directed the failed war effort firmly believed that French diplomacy was synonymous with fraud and falsehood. The only way to treat was with "fleets and armies." [23] Cast into a role akin to that of Neville Chamberlain, Prime Minister Addington declared, "This is no ordinary peace, but a genuine reconciliation between the two first nations of the world." [24]

Had anyone been able to examine the instructions given to the British and French ambassadors as they traveled to Paris and London, respectively, the inevitability of future struggle would have been apparent. The British ambassador was to insist on his country's right to interfere in continental affairs. The French ambassador was to work to block any continental intervention by the British government.

Given incompatible national goals, the Peace of Amiens could not endure. It could but be a truce before another death struggle.

***

The Peace of Amiens allowed Bonaparte to claim justly that he had fulfilled his promise to give France peace and security. The grateful nation responded, in what was probably a rigged national plebiscite, by voting him Consul for Life. Bonaparte's ascension prompted him to recall the battle that had brought him to this exalted level. He knew that the War Department had embarked upon a comprehensive study of Marengo for which it had assembled all relevant documents and interviewed the general officers who had been present at the battle. A topographical officer began the painstaking work of making maps to show troop movements. When Berthier submitted the plans for Bonaparte's review, he scratched out and otherwise 'corrected' the maps so that most of the work had to be redone. Bonaparte accepted the edited work and in 1803 the tedious labor of engraving the printer's plates began.

By the time the work was done, Bonaparte was the Emperor Napoleon I. Berthier conceived the idea of presenting the work to him at a grand review that was to be held on the very field of Marengo. Only five copies had been printed before the historians learned that Napoleon's ideas had changed again. In Bourrienne's words, "The Emperor Napoleon became dissatisfied with what had been said by the First Consul Bonaparte" regarding the battle.[25] He wanted it to appear as if the battle had methodically proceeded according to his master plan. Accordingly, the revised 1805 account described how Bonaparte had 'lured' the Austrians onto the plain by pivoting on Castel Ceriolo. Carra Saint-Cyr had barricaded his division (divisional commander Monnier was purged from the historical record) inside that village. Then, in order to spring his trap, Bonaparte displayed great flexibility by switching his line of retreat from the east to the northeast just as the battle began so that the Austrian eruption onto the plain would not be dangerous. Next, Lannes and Victor led the Austrians into the jaws of the trap by retiring, in great order of course, only as far as San Giuliano. Here they held hard. Then came a Cannae-like double envelopment executed by Desaix and Saint-Cyr. It was all quite brilliant and so much nonsense.

To avoid contradiction, Napoleon ordered the director of the War Depot to burn the five copies of the earlier version along with all of the historical and descriptive documents, to break up the printing forms, and to rub out all the copper engraving plates. Fortunately, a colonel at the depot preserved one copy, which, while containing Bonaparte's first flurry of alterations, at least more closely approximated the truth. [26] This document provided historians with a wedge to peel away the layers of distortion that Napoleon had painstakingly erected around the Battle of Marengo.

At the same time he was improving the history of Marengo, Bonaparte was resolving his relationship with Moreau. After Hohenlinden their chilly association deteriorated. When Bonaparte sent an army on the ill-fated expedition to Santo Domingo in December 1801, people pointed out that most of the selected regiments and their officers (including Richepance) came from Moreau's former command. They said that Bonaparte wished to be rid of them by sending them to perish in the pestilent West Indies. Moreau himself maintained an aloof attitude toward the First Consul while daring to criticize publicly several of his pet projects. According to Madame de Rémusat, one of Josephine's ladies in waiting, after 1802 Moreau never appeared at Bonaparte's court. She adds that Moreau's wife and mother-in-law were ambitious and much given to scheming and Napoleon knew this. He suspected that they controlled Moreau.

Two years after Hohenlinden, at a time when Bonaparte had transformed etiquette and fashion back to regal finery, Moreau appeared at a state dinner dressed in severest republican simplicity. He stood out among the silk suits and gold embroidery and prompted tongues to wag about his apparent protest. At another time, Moreau hosted a splendid dinner in Paris. After his guests pushed back from the table with satisfied bellies, Moreau made reference to Bonaparte's plan to create a Legion of Honor consisting of meritorious citizens. Reflecting upon the meal they had just consumed, he remarked that if he could have his wish he would award a "casserole of honor." [23] Naturally word of his witticism spread and reached Bonaparte's ears. Perhaps only in France – a nation that took its dining seriously while calculating honors with a prickly pride – would such a remark be particularly wounding. Then again, Bonaparte was notably thin-skinned. At any rate, Moreau's remark, and his subsequent bestowal of a collar of honor on his dog, may well have cemented Bonaparte's enmity.

Bonaparte had predicted that Moreau "would one day run his head against the gate of the Tuileries". [28] In early 1804 it appeared that that day had come when police uncovered a Royalist assassination plot implicating General Jean Pichegru and various other high ranking officers. An informer also claimed that Moreau was a participant. The extent of Moreau's actual involvement in the plot is uncertain. In all likelihood the conspirators sounded him out about replacing Bonaparte as head of state and he refused to commit to them while simultaneously declining to expose them to the authorities. Moreau's conduct gave Bonaparte the opportunity he had been waiting for.

Madame de Rémusat recounts Bonaparte's words the day he ordered Moreau's arrest. He acknowledged that there would be a great fuss, that people would claim he was jealous of Moreau or wanted revenge. Bonaparte continued, "Why, he owes the best part of his reputation to me. It was I who left a fine army with him, and kept only recruits with myself in Italy. I wanted nothing more than to get on well with him." Bonaparte elaborated that when Moreau began causing mischief, he had warned him to desist. But Moreau, weak-willed and dominated by women, had not listened. If Bonaparte simply let him fly the country, people would claim that he did not dare to bring him to trial. Bonaparte concluded, "He is guilty; I am the Government; the whole thing is quite simple."[29]

It turned out to be far from simple. Bonaparte had known that Moreau was popular within the army but he misjudged his public popularity. Prominent lawyers refused to share in the prosecution. Throughout the trial crowds thronged the streets to express support for the victor of Hohenlinden. At the theaters veiled allusions of support for Moreau triggered applause. When Bonaparte and his police tried to portray Moreau as a traitor and would-be assassin, the public refused to credit such claims. Sentries at the court respectfully presented arms every time Moreau appeared. In the courtroom, Moreau won the admiration of the jailers themselves. When he stood to speak, his guards rose alongside him and uncovered their heads in a gesture of tribute.

All of this was hard for Bonaparte to swallow. After what can only be described as a show trial, the court deliberated over Moreau's sentence. One judge pressed for a death sentence. A fellow judge replied, "Monsieur, if we condemn him, how shall we be able to acquit ourselves?"[30] The judges compromised by sentencing Moreau to two years' imprisonment. People everywhere ridiculed the sentence, calling it absurd. Bonaparte was well aware that France judged Moreau innocent. Recognizing the need for a strategic retreat, he had the sentence remitted to allow Moreau to emigrate to the United States. So Moreau departed Europe just after Bonaparte ascended to Emperor. It proved the penultimate resolution of a contest between "the two Generals whom France had hitherto looked upon as illustrious rivals."[31]

From Brumaire through Bonaparte's ascent to Emperor, Moreau was the only French general who had enough public support to be considered a rival. Had Moreau possessed more energy and more political acumen he would have presented a true challenge. Bonaparte, in turn, was not jealous of Moreau's military ability; he rightfully recognized his own superiority. Rather, he was jealous of the esteem in which the public held Moreau. He did not want France to divide its affections. His position as head of state, with his total control over the flow of news to the French people, allowed him to ensure that France cherished only himself.

In turn, Moreau's bitterness toward Bonaparte caused him to accept Tsar Alexander's offer to serve as military adviser during the 1813 campaign in Germany. Here a French cannonball inflicted a mortal wound. By all accounts he died bravely. Had circumstances been kinder, Moreau might have enjoyed a long and honorable life in France instead of being remembered as an ignoble traitor.

***

The year 1800 was the last chance to halt Bonaparte before he consolidated his dictatorship. The previous spring, the British Foreign Secretary articulated a clear vision of how to do this: "If I have learned anything by the disagreeable lessons of this war, it is that success in military operations wholly depends on acting *en masse* on one or two chosen points" while avoiding dispersion "by multiplying your points of attack."[32] But the British Army was too small to implement this strategy while the strategists among Britain's coalition partners did not share this profound insight. Britain's most constant ally throughout the long war against France, Austria, conceived plans appropriate to the warfare of an age gone by, but unsuited for war against a Napoleon Bonaparte-led France. During the War of the Second Coalition, Habsburg planners 'multiplied their points of attack'. Austria sought territorial gain in northern Italy, the capture of a fortress on the Rhine, the possible restoration of lands once belonging to the Holy Roman Empire. Austria also worried about Russia and Prussia. It lacked a single-minded focus to concentrate everything to defeat France.

Consequently, in less than a year Bonaparte went from a general under suspicion for deserting his army to ruler of France. To a pedant who asked about his genealogy, Bonaparte replied, "It dates from brumaire."[33] To consolidate Brumaire, Bonaparte needed a military victory. To redeem his pledge to France, he needed a favorable peace.

Marengo and Hohenlinden met these requirements and secured Bonaparte's dictatorship. The failure of the Second Coalition condemned Europe to a fifteen-year struggle to overthrow him.

Given the key role Marengo played in Napoleon's rise to power, it is fitting that the pall placed on his coffin when he died in 1821 was the grey cloak he wore on the battlefield on that memorable June day in 1800.

NOTES

1. "To Citizen Lucien Bonaparte," March 3, 1800, *Correspondance de Napoléon Ier*, VI (Paris, 1860), p. 160.

2. Louis de Bourrienne, *Memoirs of Napoleon Bonaparte*, II (New York, 1906), p. 61. Bourrienne says this incident occurred on December 6 but he misremembers.

3. "To General Moreau," January 9, 1800, *Correspondance de Napoléon Ier*, VI, p. 561.

4. Marquis de Grouchy, *Mémoirs du Maréchal de Grouchy*, II (Paris, 1873), p. 160.

5. "Moreau to the Minister of War," December 3, 1800, Marquis de Carrion-Nisas, *Campagne des Français en Allemagne* (Paris, 1829), p. 414.

6. Ernest Picard, *Hohenlinden* (Paris, 1909), pp. 235-36. Bodart provides Austrian losses at 15,500 and Bavarian losses at 3,600. See: Gaston Bodart, *Militär-historisches kriegs-lexicon 1618-1905* (Vienna, 1908), p. 357. It is a curious anomaly that the Frenchman Picard sets the Austrian losses lower than does the Austrian Bodart.

7. Bodart estimates French losses at 2,500 and makes no mention of lost cannons or caissons. See Bodart, p. 357.

8. Antoine Claire Thibaudeau, *Bonaparte and the Consulate* (New York, 1908), p. 114.

9. "Zweibrücken to Max-Joseph," December 6 or 7, 1800, Picard, p. 252.

10. Jean Jacques Pelet, *The French Campaign in Portugal, 1810-11* (Minneapolis, 1973), p. 175, n. 23 and p. 504.

11. Gunther E. Rothenberg, *Napoleon's Great Adversaries* (Bloomington, IN, 1982), p. 65.

12. "Karl to Bellegarde," December 30, 1800, Picard, p. 374.

13. "Karl to Saxe-Teschen," December 25, 1800, Picard, p. 375.

14. For a sense of how the French perceived their situation see Grouchy's letter to his wife in Grouchy, p. 161.

15. Jean Baptiste Crossard, *Mémoires Militaires et Historiques*, II (Paris, 1829), p. 325.

16. "Minto to Wickham," July 2, 1800, in Gilbert Elliot, *Life and Letters of Sir Gilbert Elliot, First Earl of Minto from 1751 to 1806*, III (London, 1874), p. 145.

17. Cited in: Adolphe Thiers, *History of the Consulate and the Empire*, I (London, 1845), p. 107.

18. Piers Mackesy, *British Victory in Egypt, 1801* (London, 1995), p. 245, n. 3.

19. Cited in: Louis-Jerome Gohier, *Mémoires des Contemporains*, I (Paris, 1824), p. 186.

20. Mackesy, p. 127.

21. Ibid., p. 135

22. The figures are provided by the unit's colonel. See: Pierre Pelleport, *Souvenirs Militaires et Intimes du Général Vte. de. Pelleport*, I (Paris, 1857), p. 188.

23. Elliot, III, p. 166.

24. Anton Guilland, "The Pacification of Europe, 1799-1802," in *The Cambridge Modern History*, IX (New York, 1909), pp. 76-77.

25. Bourrienne, II, p. 14.

26. The details of the fate of the 1803 history were published by the officer charged with drawing the maps in 1828 and are reprinted in "Notes and Addenda," United States Army Service Schools, *Source Book of the Marengo Campaign in 1800* (Fort Leavenworth, KS, 1922), p. 227. David Chandler's essay, "Adjusting the Record: Napoleon and Marengo," examines Napoleon's revisionist history. See: David G. Chandler, *On the Napoleonic Wars: Collected Essays* (London, 1994), pp. 82-98.

27. General Marquis de Bonneval, *Mémoires Anecdotiques du Général Marquis de Bonneval* (Paris, 1900), p. 17. This Legion was not the same as the later Legion announced the day after Bonaparte became emperor.

28. Bourrienne, II, p. 334.

29. Claire Rémusat, *Memoirs of Madame de Rémusat* (New York, 1880), p. 115. For a detailed examination of Moreau's guilt written by one of the investigators, see: André Miot, *Memoirs of Count Miot de Melito* (New York, 1881), pp. 305-308.

30. Bourrienne, II, p. 329.

31. Miot, p. 340.

32. "Grenville to Thomas Grenville," May 17, 1799, Piers Mackesy, *The Strategy of Overthrow 1798-1799* (London, 1974), p. 79.

33. John Holland Rose, *The Life of Napoleon I*, I (London, 1907), p. 233.

Appendix I

French Order of Battle at Marengo

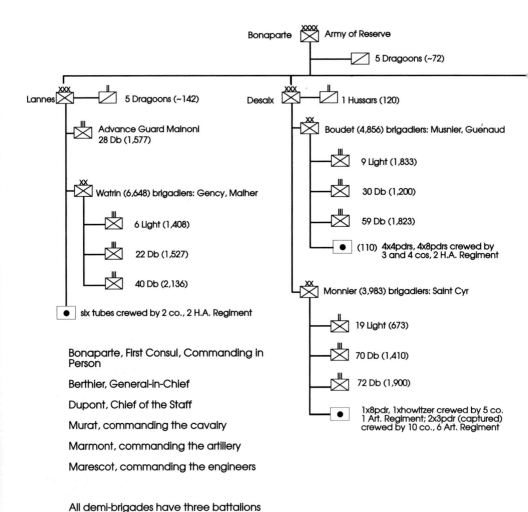

Bonaparte — Army of Reserve

5 Dragoons (~72)

Lannes — 5 Dragoons (~142)

Advance Guard Mainoni
28 Db (1,577)

Watrin (6,648) brigadiers: Gency, Malher

6 Light (1,408)

22 Db (1,527)

40 Db (2,136)

six tubes crewed by 2 co., 2 H.A. Regiment

Desaix — 1 Hussars (120)

Boudet (4,856) brigadiers: Musnier, Guénaud

9 Light (1,833)

30 Db (1,200)

59 Db (1,823)

(110) 4x4pdrs, 4x8pdrs crewed by
3 and 4 cos, 2 H.A. Regiment

Monnier (3,983) brigadiers: Saint Cyr

19 Light (673)

70 Db (1,410)

72 Db (1,900)

1x8pdr, 1xhowitzer crewed by 5 co.
1 Art. Regiment; 2x3pdr (captured)
crewed by 10 co., 6 Art. Regiment

Bonaparte, First Consul, Commanding in Person

Berthier, General-in-Chief

Dupont, Chief of the Staff

Murat, commanding the cavalry

Marmont, commanding the artillery

Marescot, commanding the engineers

All demi-brigades have three battalions

Strengths as of June 11, 1800. Sources: Gachot and the various reports reproduced in De Cugnac. For Murat's reassignment of cavalry, see: "Murat to Dupont", June 12, 1800. For the assignment of captured artillery, see: "Berthier to Dupont", June 11, 1800.

270

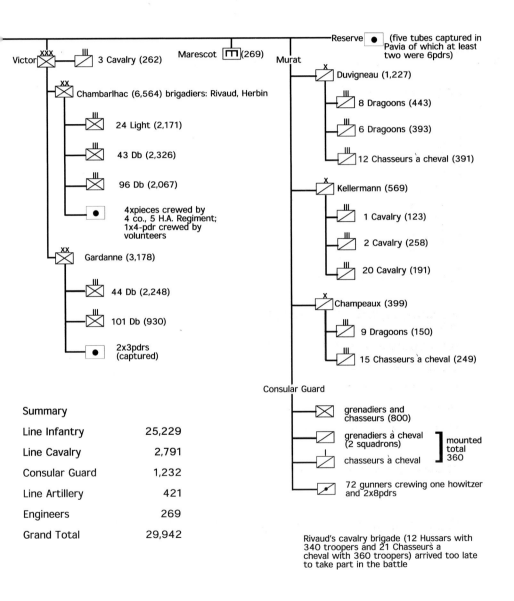

Victor (xxx) — 3 Cavalry (262)   Marescot (269)   Murat

Chambarlhac (6,564) brigadiers: Rivaud, Herbin
- 24 Light (2,171)
- 43 Db (2,326)
- 96 Db (2,067)
- 4xpieces crewed by 4 co., 5 H.A. Regiment; 1x4-pdr crewed by volunteers

Gardanne (3,178)
- 44 Db (2,248)
- 101 Db (930)
- 2x3pdrs (captured)

Reserve (five tubes captured in Pavia of which at least two were 6pdrs)

Duvigneau (1,227)
- 8 Dragoons (443)
- 6 Dragoons (393)
- 12 Chasseurs à cheval (391)

Kellermann (569)
- 1 Cavalry (123)
- 2 Cavalry (258)
- 20 Cavalry (191)

Champeaux (399)
- 9 Dragoons (150)
- 15 Chasseurs à cheval (249)

Consular Guard
- grenadiers and chasseurs (800)
- grenadiers à cheval (2 squadrons) ⎤ mounted total 360
- chasseurs à cheval ⎦
- 72 gunners crewing one howitzer and 2x8pdrs

Summary	
Line Infantry	25,229
Line Cavalry	2,791
Consular Guard	1,232
Line Artillery	421
Engineers	269
Grand Total	29,942

Rivaud's cavalry brigade (12 Hussars with 340 troopers and 21 Chasseurs à cheval with 360 troopers) arrived too late to take part in the battle

Austrian Order of Battle at Marengo

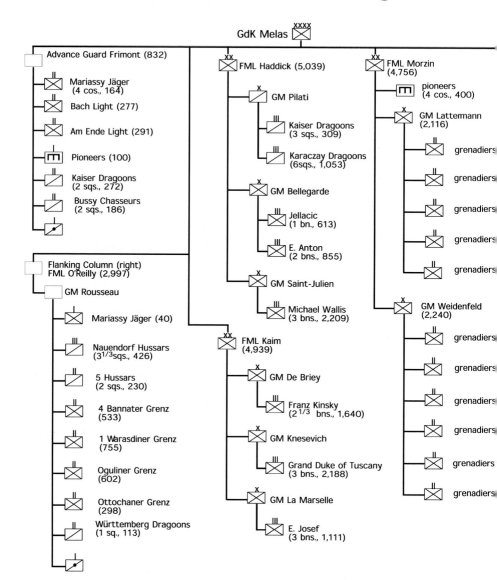

GdK Melas

Advance Guard Frimont (832)
- Mariassy Jäger (4 cos., 164)
- Bach Light (277)
- Am Ende Light (291)
- Pioneers (100)
- Kaiser Dragoons (2 sqs., 272)
- Bussy Chasseurs (2 sqs., 186)

Flanking Column (right) FML O'Reilly (2,997)
- GM Rousseau
  - Mariassy Jäger (40)
  - Nauendorf Hussars (3 1/3 sqs., 426)
  - 5 Hussars (2 sqs., 230)
  - 4 Bannater Grenz (533)
  - 1 Warasdiner Grenz (755)
  - Oguliner Grenz (602)
  - Ottochaner Grenz (298)
  - Württemberg Dragoons (1 sq., 113)

FML Haddick (5,039)
- GM Pilati
  - Kaiser Dragoons (3 sqs., 309)
  - Karaczay Dragoons (6sqs., 1,053)
- GM Bellegarde
  - Jellacic (1 bn., 613)
  - E. Anton (2 bns., 855)
- GM Saint-Julien
  - Michael Wallis (3 bns., 2,209)

FML Kaim (4,939)
- GM De Briey
  - Franz Kinsky (2 1/3 bns., 1,640)
- GM Knesevich
  - Grand Duke of Tuscany (3 bns., 2,188)
- GM La Marselle
  - E. Josef (3 bns., 1,111)

FML Morzin (4,756)
- pioneers (4 cos., 400)
- GM Lattermann (2,116)
  - grenadiers
  - grenadiers
  - grenadiers
  - grenadiers
  - grenadiers
- GM Weidenfeld (2,240)
  - grenadiers
  - grenadiers
  - grenadiers
  - grenadiers
  - grenadiers
  - grenadiers

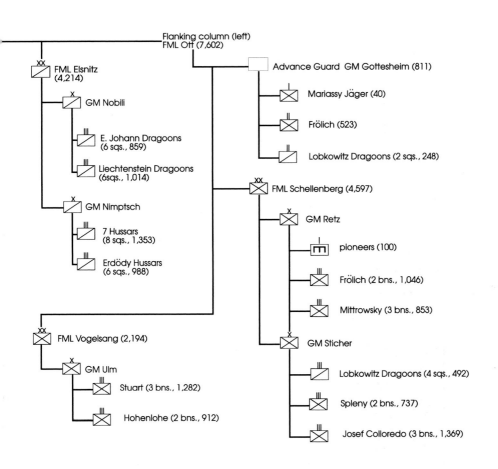

Flanking column (left)
FML Ott (7,602)

FML Elsnitz (4,214)

GM Nobili

E. Johann Dragoons (6 sqs., 859)

Liechtenstein Dragoons (6sqs., 1,014)

GM Nimptsch

7 Hussars (8 sqs., 1,353)

Erdödy Hussars (6 sqs., 988)

Advance Guard GM Gottesheim (811)

Mariassy Jäger (40)

Frölich (523)

Lobkowitz Dragoons (2 sqs., 248)

FML Schellenberg (4,597)

GM Retz

pioneers (100)

Frölich (2 bns., 1,046)

Mittrowsky (3 bns., 853)

GM Sticher

FML Vogelsang (2,194)

GM Ulm

Stuart (3 bns., 1,282)

Hohenlohe (2 bns., 912)

Lobkowitz Dragoons (4 sqs., 492)

Spleny (2 bns., 737)

Josef Colloredo (3 bns., 1,369)

Totals

Infantry	22,836	
Cavalry	7,543	
Artillery	92 pieces	(not including regimental guns)
Total	30,379	

Source: Mras, "Gefchichte Des Feldzuges 1800 in Italien"
Öestereichische Militärische Zeitschrift X (1822) Vienna

French Order of Battle at Hohenlinden

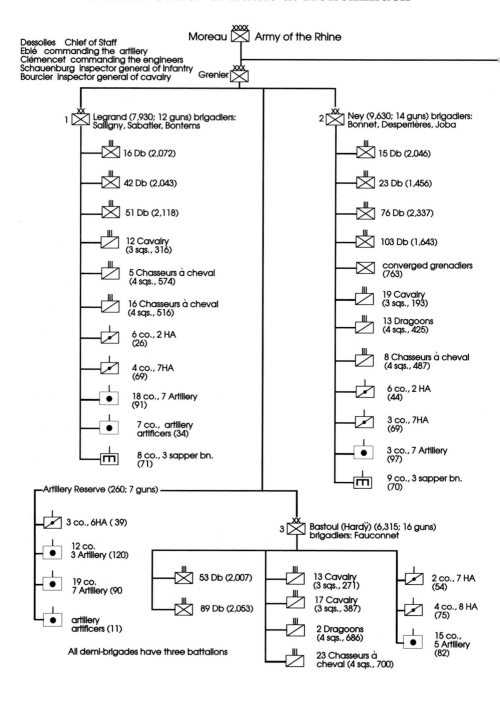

Dessolles Chief of Staff
Eblé commanding the artillery
Clémencet commanding the engineers
Schauenburg Inspector general of infantry
Bourcier Inspector general of cavalry

Moreau — Army of the Rhine

Grenier

1 — Legrand (7,930; 12 guns) brigadiers: Saligny, Sabatier, Bontems

16 Db (2,072)
42 Db (2,043)
51 Db (2,118)
12 Cavalry (3 sqs., 316)
5 Chasseurs à cheval (4 sqs., 574)
16 Chasseurs à cheval (4 sqs., 516)
6 co., 2 HA (26)
4 co., 7HA (69)
18 co., 7 Artillery (91)
7 co., artillery artificers (34)
8 co., 3 sapper bn. (71)

2 — Ney (9,630; 14 guns) brigadiers: Bonnet, Desperrières, Joba

15 Db (2,046)
23 Db (1,456)
76 Db (2,337)
103 Db (1,643)
converged grenadiers (763)
19 Cavalry (3 sqs., 193)
13 Dragoons (4 sqs., 425)
8 Chasseurs à cheval (4 sqs., 487)
6 co., 2 HA (44)
3 co., 7HA (69)
3 co., 7 Artillery (97)
9 co., 3 sapper bn. (70)

Artillery Reserve (260; 7 guns)

3 co., 6HA (39)
12 co. 3 Artillery (120)
19 co. 7 Artillery (90
artillery artificers (11)

3 — Bastoul (Hardÿ) (6,315; 16 guns) brigadiers: Fauconnet

53 Db (2,007)
89 Db (2,053)

13 Cavalry (3 sqs., 271)
17 Cavalry (3 sqs., 387)
2 Dragoons (4 sqs., 686)
23 Chasseurs à cheval (4 sqs., 700)

2 co., 7 HA (54)
4 co., 8 HA (75)
15 co., 5 Artillery (82)

All demi-brigades have three battalions

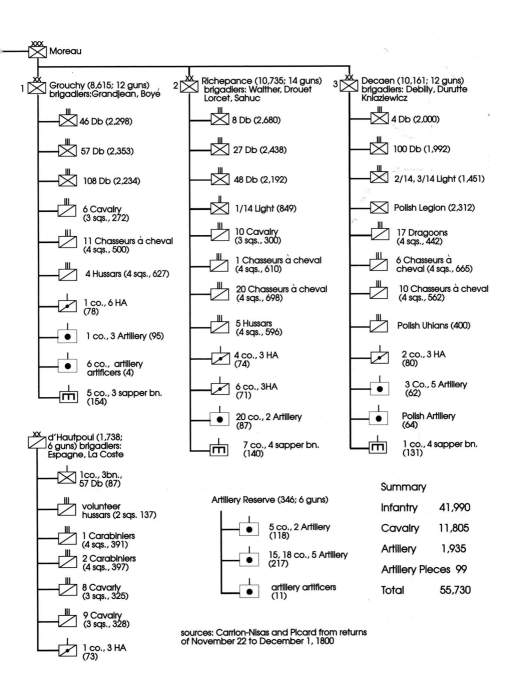

Moreau

1 Grouchy (8,615; 12 guns) brigadiers: Grandjean, Boyé
- 46 Db (2,298)
- 57 Db (2,353)
- 108 Db (2,234)
- 6 Cavalry (3 sqs., 272)
- 11 Chasseurs à cheval (4 sqs., 500)
- 4 Hussars (4 sqs., 627)
- 1 co., 6 HA (78)
- 1 co., 3 Artillery (95)
- 6 co., artillery artificers (4)
- 5 co., 3 sapper bn. (154)

d'Hautpoul (1,738; 6 guns) brigadiers: Espagne, La Coste
- 1 co., 3 bn., 57 Db (87)
- volunteer hussars (2 sqs. 137)
- 1 Carabiniers (4 sqs., 391)
- 2 Carabiniers (4 sqs., 397)
- 8 Cavalry (3 sqs., 325)
- 9 Cavalry (3 sqs., 328)
- 1 co., 3 HA (73)

2 Richepance (10,735; 14 guns) brigadiers: Walther, Drouet Lorcet, Sahuc
- 8 Db (2,680)
- 27 Db (2,438)
- 48 Db (2,192)
- 1/14 Light (849)
- 10 Cavalry (3 sqs., 300)
- 1 Chasseurs à cheval (4 sqs., 610)
- 20 Chasseurs à cheval (4 sqs., 698)
- 5 Hussars (4 sqs., 596)
- 4 co., 3 HA (74)
- 6 co., 3HA (71)
- 20 co., 2 Artillery (87)
- 7 co., 4 sapper bn. (140)

Artillery Reserve (346; 6 guns)
- 5 co., 2 Artillery (118)
- 15, 18 co., 5 Artillery (217)
- artillery artificers (11)

3 Decaen (10,161; 12 guns) brigadiers: Debilly, Durutte Kniazlewicz
- 4 Db (2,000)
- 100 Db (1,992)
- 2/14, 3/14 Light (1,451)
- Polish Legion (2,312)
- 17 Dragoons (4 sqs., 442)
- 6 Chasseurs à cheval (4 sqs., 665)
- 10 Chasseurs à cheval (4 sqs., 562)
- Polish Uhlans (400)
- 2 co., 3 HA (80)
- 3 Co., 5 Artillery (62)
- Polish Artillery (64)
- 1 co., 4 sapper bn. (131)

Summary

Infantry	41,990
Cavalry	11,805
Artillery	1,935
Artillery Pieces	99
Total	55,730

sources: Carrion-Nisas and Picard from returns of November 22 to December 1, 1800

Austrian Order of Battle at Hohenlinden

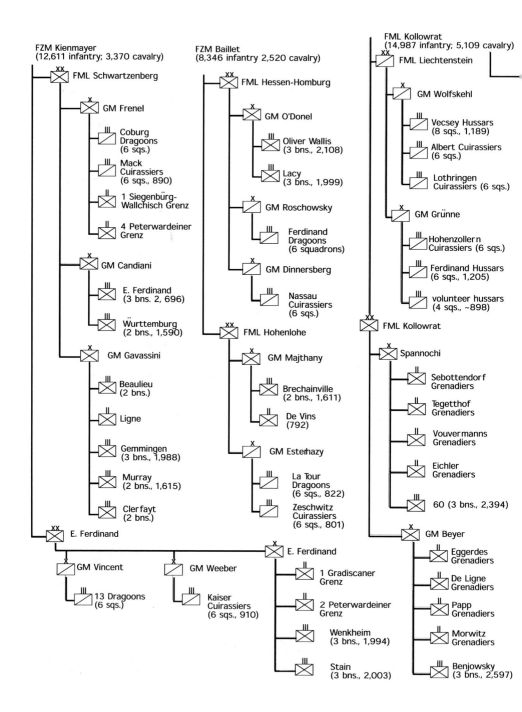

FML Kollowrat
(14,987 infantry; 5,109 cavalry)

FML Kienmayer
(12,611 infantry; 3,370 cavalry)

FZM Baillet
(8,346 infantry 2,520 cavalry)

FML Liechtenstein

FML Schwartzenberg

GM Frenel

Coburg Dragoons (6 sqs.)

Mack Cuirassiers (6 sqs., 890)

1 Siegenbürg-Wallchisch Grenz

4 Peterwardeiner Grenz

GM Candiani

E. Ferdinand (3 bns. 2, 696)

Württemburg (2 bns., 1,590)

GM Gavassini

Beaulieu (2 bns.)

Ligne

Gemmingen (3 bns., 1,988)

Murray (2 bns., 1,615)

Clerfayt (2 bns.)

E. Ferdinand

GM Vincent

13 Dragoons (6 sqs.)

GM Weeber

Kaiser Cuirassiers (6 sqs., 910)

FML Hessen-Homburg

GM O'Donel

Oliver Wallis (3 bns., 2,108)

Lacy (3 bns., 1,999)

GM Roschowsky

Ferdinand Dragoons (6 squadrons)

GM Dinnersberg

Nassau Cuirassiers (6 sqs.)

FML Hohenlohe

GM Majthany

Brechainville (2 bns., 1,611)

De Vins (792)

GM Esterhazy

La Tour Dragoons (6 sqs., 822)

Zeschwitz Cuirassiers (6 sqs., 801)

E. Ferdinand

1 Gradiscaner Grenz

2 Peterwardeiner Grenz

Wenkheim (3 bns., 1,994)

Stain (3 bns., 2,003)

GM Wolfskehl

Vecsey Hussars (8 sqs., 1,189)

Albert Cuirassiers (6 sqs.)

Lothringen Cuirassiers (6 sqs.)

GM Grünne

Hohenzollern Cuirassiers (6 sqs.)

Ferdinand Hussars (6 sqs., 1,205)

volunteer hussars (4 sqs., ~898)

FML Kollowrat

Spannochi

Sebottendorf Grenadiers

Tegetthof Grenadiers

Vouvermanns Grenadiers

Eichler Grenadiers

60 (3 bns., 2,394)

GM Beyer

Eggerdes Grenadiers

De Ligne Grenadiers

Papp Grenadiers

Morwitz Grenadiers

Benjowsky (3 bns., 2,597)

Erzherzog Johann XXXX ⊠

FML Zweibrücken (Bavarian)

GM Deroy X ⊠

- Metzen Light ⊠ ||
- Reuss Grenadiers ⊠ ||
- Minucci ⊠ ||
- Stengel ⊠ ||
- Schlossberg ⊠ ||

GM Wrede X ⊠

- Pompei ⊠ ||
- Preysing ⊠ ||
- Bureck ⊠ ||
- Dallwigk (3 cos.) ⊠ ||
- light infantry (2 cos.) ⊠ ||
- uhlans (5¹/² sqs., 828) |||
- (8 guns) |
- (4 batteries with 18 guns) ●

Bavarian total:
7,017 infantry
828 cavalry
26 guns

Each Austrian
column had
an artillery
reserve consisting
of:
(4x6pdr 2x7pdr howitzer)
● (8x12pdr 2x6pdr 4x7pdr howitzer)

FZM Riesch
(10,186 infantry; 3,132 cavalry)

FML Merveldt XX ⊠

GM Klein X ⊠

- Wenzel Colloredo (3 bns., 2,114) ⊠ |||
- E. Karl (3 bns., 2,090) ⊠ |||

GM Görger X

- Waldeck Dragoons (6 sqs., 888) |||
- Anspach Cuirassiers (6 sqs., 911) |||

FML Gyulai XX ⊠

GM Leuwen X ⊠

- Manfreddini (3 bns., 2,107) ⊠ |||
- Kaunitz (3 bns., 2,105) ⊠ |||

GM Stahel X

- Kinsky Dragoons (6 sqs., 478) |||
- Franz-Mailand Cuirassiers (6 sqs., 855) |||

Army total:

46,130 infantry

14,131 cavalry

3,724 artillery and engineers
(excluding Bavarians)

Grand total: 63,985

Column totals are as of Dec. 2, 180
Individual unit totals as of Nov. 22.
Source: Carrion-Nisas and Picard

Appendix II

Numbers and Losses

Regarding the fighting strengths on the field at Marengo, as noted Melas unwisely detached Nimptsch's entire brigade (2,341 hussars) around mid-morning. Earlier he sent off one squadron of the Kaiser Dragoons to scout to Acqui. These detachments confuse tabulations of Melas' field force. Some accounts include them, some do not. I have not found a wholly reliable tabulation of the artillery in Melas' field army. He seems to have taken 92 tubes (not including regimental guns) onto the field at Marengo while another 23 remained behind the earthworks at the bridgehead or in enfilade position on the west bank of the Bormida. In addition, it should be noted that the compiler for the order of battle provided in the *Öestereichische Militärische Zeitschrift* (Vol.24), whose summary de Cugnac reproduces, was slightly out with his sums for column totals.

The French are better documented, but even here there are some questions. Many arise from the army's on the fly reassignment of cavalry and artillery to various formations. My order of battle utilizes the contemporary documents and post-battle reports. Still, to cite just one example, Victor offers a detailed order of battle in his 1846 *Mémoires* that clearly draws on the army archives and purports to list strengths on June 14. Gachot offers an archival listing for June 11. For the 19th Light, their totals are 914 and 673, respectively. In an October 21, 1800 letter to the War Ministry, Carra-Saint Cyr reports he led 700 men in the attack against Castel Ceriolo, and so my order of battle reproduces Gachot's June 11 total.

Turning to French losses at Marengo, an examination of the incomplete unit returns hints at Marengo's true cost. The six battalions of the 43rd and 96th Demi-brigades lost 82 officers and 1,900 other ranks killed or wounded.[1] The 24th Light lost 10 officers killed and 24 wounded. If the rank and file suffered in the same proportion as did those in its sister units, the 24th Light lost about 788 men. Chambarlhac's artillery chief reports that the horse artillery battery lost 3 killed and 5 wounded and the 1st train battalion lost three men. In other words, as noted, losses for this division alone exceed the official total.

Lannes' report, which includes Watrin and Mainoni's brigade, obviously is misleading since it mentions 14 officers and 300 other ranks killed and 1,800 wounded or prisoners. Since Watrin independently provided figures for his division, one can see that by Lannes' claim, Mainoni suffered virtually no casualties at all! Other infantry reports are Monnier's estimate that he lost 800-900 men and Murat's claim that the grenadiers of the Consular Guard had 121 killed and wounded. In fact, the grenadiers suffered on the order of 300 casualties.[2] Murat placed overall losses in the cavalry at 800. There is a paucity of hard data to support his estimate. In Kellermann's command both the 2nd Cavalry and the 20th Cavalry entered battle with eleven officers. Seven officers in the former and six in the latter received wounds. This too suggests a casualty total higher than Murat's estimate.

For the Hohenlinden campaign, Moreau's Army of the Rhine, as one would expect, maintained a meticulous record of its pre-battle organization and strength. The situation is more confused for the Austrians. For example, Picard, whose detailed analysis seems otherwise very sound, omits the volunteer hussars from his order of battle but then cites the 1836 *Öestereichische Militärische Zeitschrift* for the presence of four squadrons with Loepper's advance guard. Although Carrion-Nisas does not give organizational data for the actual battle, he provides a strength for six squadrons of this unit as 1,194. Thus I derive my order of battle figure of '~898'. When dissatisfied with the quality of the data, I have omitted numerical strengths for individual Austrian and Bavarian units. However, the November 22 returns provide some useful aggregated data regarding the Austrian units for which I do not provide strengths. The average strength of the grenadier battalions was 500; the light and grenz battalions, 600; the cuirassier regiments, 900; the dragoon regiments, 800.

When considering French losses at Hohenlinden, one enters a murky field. Neither Richepance's report nor the division's official bulletin mention losses. Similarly, while Legrand reported about 80 killed 160 wounded, Grenier claimed that the entire left wing – Legrand, Bastoul, and the cavalry – lost only 67 killed. Grouchy provided casualty figures of 500, Ney 350, and Decaen 286. Yet, FZM Riesch maintained that he marched off the field with 500 prisoners, to which must be added 141 more whom Grenier acknowledged losing. Adding Grenier's numbers to those of Grouchy, Ney, and Decaen yields 1,839, well above the 1,200 reported by Moreau's chief of staff. Richepance must have lost more men than Ney and probably more than Grouchy. Merely estimating his losses as equivalent to those suffered by Ney and adding the probable number of prisoners lost, provides a total of nearly 3,000.

NOTES
1. "Rivaud to Dupont," June 15, 1800, Claude-Victor Perrin, *Extraits de Mémoires Inédits de feu* (Paris 1846), p. 408. Note that this is a supplement to Rivaud's report.
2. See: "Murat to Berthier," June 16, 1800, Perrin, p. 417.

Appendix III

Fates Intermingled: Prominent Officers and What Became of Them

(H)= prominent at Hohenlinden
(M)= prominent at Marengo

Maximilien de Baillet (H)
Sixty-three years old at Hohenlinden, Baillet never again commanded troops in battle. In spite of his less than inspiring leadership at Hohenlinden, he became president of the Aulic Council in 1805, but died the following year.

Louis-Alexandre Berthier (M)
On the basis of his performance during the Marengo campaign alone, Berthier was much deserving of being honored at the first promotion of the marshals. As general in chief of the Army of Reserve, he had assumed much responsibility for field operations. While operating under Bonaparte's orders but away from his presence, he had been alert and active, repeatedly riding to the front to make decisions based upon personal reconnaissance. In addition, he had fulfilled many duties of a chief of staff as well as representing Bonaparte while meeting with Moreau before the campaign began and negotiating an armistice to end the campaign. Seldom in the future would he have such autonomy. Years of close work with the Emperor reduced him to a clerk and eroded his self-confidence. In 1809 when Napoleon sent him to Bavaria to reprise his army command role of 1800 he would make a fearful hash of it.

Louis Boudet (M)

Boudet displayed good judgment while operating under Desaix's command, yet he remained a divisional commander. Bonaparte assigned him to the West Indies expedition in 1801, a sure sign he did not hold Boudet in high regard. Boudet survived to return to France in the fall of 1802. From that time until 1809, he had a very active career. He distinguished himself at Aspern but had the misfortune to lose his artillery at the Battle of Wagram. This brought down Napoleon's severe reproach. Deeply shamed, he died that autumn, a death that may have been self-inflicted.

Jean Bruyères (M)

Bonaparte always chose officers whom he believed had high potential as his aides-de-camp. So it was with Bruyères whom he promoted for his gallantry at Marengo. He rose to command a light cavalry brigade in 1808 and distinguished himself at Wagram. Thereafter, Napoleon elevated him to divisional command. Bruyères valiantly served throughout the Russian campaign and died after a cannon ball removed both legs at the thigh during the 1813 campaign in Germany.

Jacques-Antoine Chambarlhac (M)

Curiously, Chambarlhac survived his disgraceful battlefield performance. According to Coignet, when the general reappeared for a grand celebratory parade on June 16, the 96th Demi-brigade fired a volley in his direction! Bonaparte partially overlooked Chambarlhac's June 14 conduct, preferring to recall his gallantry in Italy in 1796. He kept Chambarlhac away from the battlefield by giving him a succession of rear-area commands for the remainder of his career, promoted him in 1803, and named him a baron in 1811. Chambarlhac repaid this faith in 1815 when he refused to serve under the Bourbons and retired instead.

Jean-Baptiste Corbineau (H)

Corbineau recovered from his terrible Hohenlinden wound to play a vital role twelve years later in helping the remnants of the *Grande Armèe* escape over the Beresina River during the Russian debacle. At Brienne in 1814, he saved Napoleon's life from Cossacks.

Achille Dampierre (M)

Serving as Victor's adjutant-general, Dampierre conducted a splendid action in the combats for Stortigliona and Cassina Bianca. Yet Bonaparte sent him on the expedition to the pestilent West Indies where he died in 1802.

Charles Decaen (H)

Victim of the purge of the Army of the Rhine, Bonaparte sent Decaen to the Indian Ocean in 1802. Eight years later he was wounded while defending Mauritius. Decaen returned to France in 1811, served under Suchet in Spain, and had minor assignments thereafter. He was another talented officer whose association with the Army of the Rhine thwarted promotion.

Jean Dessolles (H)

Moreau's former chief of staff remained loyal to Moreau when Bonaparte turned upon that officer in 1804. Because of his refusal to play the role of informer, Dessolles was put on the inactive list. Recalled in 1808, he led a division in Ney's corps during the invasion of Spain. Here he participated in numerous battles until he transferred to the *Grande Armée* for the 1812 campaign. His assignment highlighted the relative importance of seniority versus family in Napoleon's empire. Dessolles served as chief of staff to Eugène Beauharnais, a man who had been a junior cavalry officer back in 1800. After falling gravely ill during the retreat from Moscow, Dessolles received minor rear area commands. In 1815 he remained loyal to King Louis during the Hundred Days. Thereafter, to his eternal discredit, he showed his loyalty to his old Hohenlinden comrade, Ney, by voting for the death sentence during Ney's trial.

Jean-Baptiste Drouet (H)

Drouet recovered from his Hohenlinden wound to receive promotion in 1803. Misfortune plagued his active career. He served with Bernadotte's largely inactive corps at Austerlitz, received another wound at Friedland, and was captured during the siege of Danzig. Posted to Spain in 1810, he participated in numerous battles against the British. After a temporary reconciliation with the Bourbons, he commanded a corps during the Waterloo Campaign. Confused by conflicting orders, he marched and counter-marched, thereby failing to participate in either the Battle of Ligny or Quatre Bras. His bizarre tactical arrangement at Waterloo cost him most of his corps. Condemned to death by the Bourbons after Waterloo, he fled France until pardoned in 1825.

Bernard Duvigneau (M)

Duvigneau had abandoned his command on the field of battle and was relieved on June 21, 1800. In 1811 he applied for reinstatement. Kellermann recalled that his father had promoted Duvigneau on the field at Valmy and apparently interceded on his behalf. Duvigneau served under Kellermann and then Ney during the 1814 Campaign. He lost badly in a combat against the Russians. Routed in his next combat, he thereafter held rear echelon commands. Clearly his reinstatement had been a mistake.

Jean-Baptiste Eblé (H)
The army expected great things of this distinguished gunner, and he did not disappoint. After commanding Masséna's artillery in 1810, he participated in the Russian campaign as commander of the army's bridging train. His greatest day came on the banks of the Beresina where he was instrumental in saving the army. Weakened from exposure, he perished from disease later in 1812.

Johann Frimont (M)
Frimont enjoyed a rapid ascent following his dashing conduct at Genoa and Marengo. By 1809, he carried the rank feldmarschall-leutnant and commanded a division. During the 1813 campaign he commanded the Austrian V Corps while in 1815 he was in charge of the allied army in Italy. He was named President of the Austrian War Council in 1831, a far cry from colonel in command of a 1,290-man advance guard back in June 1800.

Gaspard-Amédée Gardanne (M)
Although Gardanne fought with great distinction at Marengo, Bonaparte apparently assessed him as no more than a divisional commander. He served again in Italy in 1805 and then in East Prussia and Poland in 1807. While on a mission to command Saxon troops he caught a fever and died in August 1807.

Erzherzog Johann (H)
With a small army, Johann received the backwater assignment of defending the Tyrol during the 1805 campaign. In 1809 he assumed command of the Austrian army in Italy. His conduct demonstrated that he had matured as a military commander. He defeated the French, under the command of Eugène Beauharnais, at the Battle of Sacile. Among the French divisional commanders were his Hohenlinden foes: Grenier, Durutte, Grouchy, and Sahuc. Thereafter, Napoleon's drive on Vienna relegated Italy to a backwater. Lacking support, Johann lost the Battle of the Piave and the Battle of Raab. Thereafter, he led a

retiring life and married the daughter of a postmaster, the proverbial 'girl across the lake.' This romance was very much not the done thing: Habsburg archdukes were not supposed to bring commoners into the family. Consequently, when Kaiser Franz died in 1835, the family chose Franz's favorite, and least able brother, Ludwig, to assist the new Kaiser. Ostracized by his family, popular among the people who called him, because of his marriage, 'the Great Commoner', Johann returned to public life in 1848 when the family recalled him to help appease the revolutionaries. Duty done, he retired again. All in all, Johann comes across as an admirable fellow, if not a great general; duty-bound, yet trying and eventually succeeding in escaping from his overbearing family.

François Kellermann (M)

No one was more disgruntled over his lack of recognition than Kellermann. On the evening of June 14, the victors had met for supper at Bonaparte's headquarters. When Kellermann entered, Bonaparte said to him, "You made a pretty good charge." He then turned to Bessières and lavishly praised the cavalry of the Consular Guard. Apparently this rankled with Kellermann. He may have complained around camp that Bonaparte undervalued his achievement. The First Consul's secretary, Bourrienne, claims that later Bonaparte read a letter in which Kellermann wrote, "Would you believe, my friend, that Bonaparte has not made me a general of division though I have just placed the crown on his head?"[1] At any rate, Bonaparte always downplayed Kellermann's brilliant tactical intervention. When he dictated the official report he did not honor Kellermann with a battlefield promotion. Not until July 6, after his return to Paris, did the First Consul elevate him to general of division. Kellermann's subsequent career led to three wounds and several more notable charges including one that almost captured the crossroads at Quatre Bras in 1815. Throughout he remained an independent, prickly fellow. During his campaigning in Spain he earned a reputation for excessive plundering. He responded to this charge with a shrug, "Do they suppose I crossed the Pyrenees for a change of air?" When his misappropriations compelled Napoleon to recall him to Paris in 1811, he tried to justify his conduct. The Emperor replied, "General Kellerman [sic], whenever your name is brought up before me, I can remember nothing but Marengo."

Michael Kienmayer (H)

Kienmayer played an important role at Austerlitz where he

commanded the advance guard of Kutuzov's 1st Column. He served as commander of the II Reserve Corps under Karl during the Eckmuhl phase of the 1809 campaign. Because of his indifferent leadership, Karl replaced him before the battles around Vienna.

Karl Kollowrat (H)
He jointly commanded Kutuzov's IVth Column at Austerlitz where his command sat squarely opposed to Soult's breakthrough on the Pratzen Heights. He served under Karl as a corps commander during the 1809 campaign and was active in the army's offensive on the second day at Wagram. Continuing his unlucky career, here his corps was on the flank of Macdonald's breakthrough assault.

Jean Lannes (M)
Although awarded a saber of honor for his Marengo performance, it did not prevent the Gascon from getting into serious trouble during the autumn of 1800. He spread the word that Bessières had failed to support him properly at Marengo. It did not help that Lannes and Murat were competing for the same woman and that Bessières was one of his rival's dear friends. In 1801, Bessières achieved his revenge when he detected Lannes misappropriating army funds and denounced him. The feud would climax in 1809 when the two narrowly averted a duel on the battlefield of Aspern-Essling the evening before Lannes received a mortal wound.

Claude Legrand (H)
Legrand's career contrasted to the habitual persecution of many of the notable officers who served in the Army of the Rhine. He fought with great distinction with the *Grande Armée* from Austerlitz through the 1812 campaign. Napoleon steadily rewarded him with titles and money. Legrand received a terrible wound during the passage of the Beresina and eventually died from this injury in January 1815.

Jean-Charles Monnier (M)
Monnier's performance at Marengo displeased Bonaparte. He doubted Monnier's wisdom in sending only two demi-brigades into the attack while retaining one in reserve. Far worse, he doubted his courage since Monnier had remained with his reserve. In 1802 Monnier became implicated in a plot against Bonaparte and thereafter never received another command. When Napoleon re-wrote the history of Marengo, he purged all references to Monnier and instead gave credit for the division's qualified success to brigade commander

Saint-Cyr. In 1814, Monnier overtly joined the Bourbon cause and served with them during the Waterloo campaign the following year.

Johann Riesch (H)

Riesch survived Johann's verbal assaults after Hohenlinden to serve with Mack's army in the 1805 campaign. With the vise tightening around the "unfortunate" Mack at Ulm, Riesch participated in a breakout attempt. He conducted a less than brilliant engagement against Ney, the Battle of Elchingen, on October 14, 1805 and then retreated toward Ulm. His defeat at Elchingen seems to mark the end of Riesch's active duty career.

Louis Suchet (M)

Suchet was another officer who believed he deserved far more credit than he received. During his defense of the Var River, a flattering letter from Minister of War Carnot likened his efforts to the Spartans at Thermopylae. This may have gone to Suchet's head. After his successful pursuit of Elsnitz he was full of bold plans. Masséna, perhaps exhausted from the siege of Genoa, reined him in. Displeased, Suchet sent his chief of staff to Bonaparte to explain that if Suchet's men did not arrive in time to share in the First Consul's battles, the fault was not his but rather Masséna's. His message angered Bonaparte and infuriated Masséna. When Suchet met with Masséna a little later, Masséna relayed the First Consul's decision to give him a mere divisional command. He explained that Suchet needed rest after an arduous campaign. It was a snub and Suchet recognized it. He wrote an abject letter to Bonaparte explaining that he was young and consumed by the pursuit of glory. Yet he could not help but take another swipe at Masséna by including the comment, "I am ignorant of how jealousy, perhaps even perfidy, can mislead certain people." Squirm as he might, he missed out in the post-Marengo scramble for recognition and rewards. He never entered Napoleon's inner circle. Not until 1811 would he receive his baton.

Claude Victor (M)

To his great disappointment, Victor was not among those named in the first promotion to marshal. Official accounts of Marengo dwelt on the heroes of the late afternoon counterattack and overshadowed the importance of Victor's lonely four-hour struggle when he faced Melas' entire army. Bonaparte gave Victor little praise although he owed him a great deal. Victor had combined courage with tactical judgment to provide Bonaparte with excellent combat leadership. He did not achieve his baton until 1807.

Louis Vogelsang (M)

After recovering from his wound at Marengo, Vogelsang served as commander of the grenadier reserve under Karl during the 1805 campaign in Italy. At the battle of Caldiero he distinguished himself and was rewarded with appointment as inhaber of the Franz Kinski Infantry Regiment. He commanded the I Corps' 1st Division in 1809. The following year, at the age of 62, Vogelsang retired from active duty to serve as governor of the fortress of Josphstadt.

Frederic Walther (H)

Following his service under Richepance, Walther recovered from his wound and rose to become commander of the Imperial Guard's cavalry at Wagram.

Anton Zach (M)

Following his service under Melas and Bellegarde, Zach next served as Erzherzog Karl's chief of staff during the 1805 Campaign. The pair opposed Masséna in Italy, where Karl managed narrowly to win the Battle of Caldiero. It was Austria's single major success of the 1805 campaign and helped alleviate Zach's memory of Marengo. During the next interlude of peace, Karl judged Zach too elderly and replaced him with a younger man.

NOTES

1. Louis de Bourrienne, *Memoirs of Napoleon Bonaparte*, II (New York, 1906), p. 16.
2. Louis Cohen, *Napoleonic Anecdotes* (London, 1925), p. 57.
3. Jeanne A Ojala, "Suchet," in David G. Chandler, *Napoleon's Marshals* (New York, 1987), p. 485.

Bibliography

Primary Sources

Barras, Paul. *Memoirs of Barras*. Vol. 4. New York, 1896.

Beauharnais, Eugène de. *Mémoirs et Correspondance Politique et Militaires du Prince Eugène*. Vol. 1. Paris, 1858.

Bonaparte, Lucien. *Memoirs of Lucien Bonaparte*. Part 1. New York, 1836.

Bonaparte, Lucien. *Memoirs of Lucien Bonaparte*. London, 1835. A curiously different translation, purportedly based upon the transmission of personal documents to the publisher.

Bonaparte, Lucien. *Révolution de Brumaire*. Paris, 1846. Possibly Lucien's most candid account of what transpired.

Bon Boulart, Jean François. *Mémoires Militaires du Général Bon Boulart*. Paris, 1892.

Bonneval, General Marquis de. *Mémoires Anecdotiques du Général Marquis de Bonneval*. Paris, 1900.

Bourrienne, Louis de. *Memoirs of Napoleon Bonaparte*. 2 vols. New York, 1906. Unreliable for specific dates and the like, but valuable for a general understanding of Bonaparte's character and the atmosphere of his court.

Bugeaud, Marshal Thomas. *Memoirs of Marshal Bugeaud*. Vol. 1. London, 1884. He commanded the 9th Light in 1814.

Bulow, Dietrich. *Histoire de la Campagne de 1800 en Allemagne et en Italie*. Paris, 1804.

Cambacères, Jean. *Lettres Inédites à Napoléon, 1802-1814*. 2 vols. Paris, 1973. The Second Consul who helped Bonaparte secure his position and then served as Arch-Chancellor of the Empire.

Campredon, Jacques. *La Défense du Var et Le Passage Des Alpes 1800*. Paris, 1889. General Campredon was chief engineer in Suchet's corps during the 1800 campaign. This is an annotated collection of his documents.

Chamans, Antoine-Marie, Compte de Lavalette. *Mémoires et Souvenirs*. Paris, 1994.

Constant, Wairy. *Memoirs of Constant*, Tr. Percy Pinkerton. Vol. 1. London, 1896.

Crossard, Jean Baptiste. *Mémoires Militaires et Historiques*. Vol. 2. Paris, 1829. Far from reliable, but full of detail about the inner workings of the Austrian army with which he served.

Decaen, Charles. *Mémoires et Journaux du Général Decaen*. Paris, 1911. Shows the influence of subordinate initiative and the fog of war at the Battle of Hohenlinden.

Dienst reglement fur die kaiserlich-königliche Cavallerie. Vienna, 1807.

Drouet, Jean-Baptiste. *Vie Militaire*. Paris, 1844.

Du Casse, André. *Mémoirs et Correspondance Politique et Militaire du Prince Eugène*. Paris, 1859.

Dupuy, Victor. *Souvenirs Militaires*. Paris, 1892.

Elliot, Gilbert. *Life and Letters of Sir Gilbert Elliot, First Earl of Minto from 1751 to 1806*. Vol. 3. London, 1874.

Exercier-Reglement fur die kaiserlich-königliche Infanterie. Vienna, 1807.

Fouché, Joseph. *The Memoirs of Joseph Fouché*. Vol. 1. London, 1846.

Foudras, C. *Marengo or the Campaign of Italy by the Army of Reserve*. Philadelphia, 1801. A translation of Bonaparte's official account for the American market.

"French Account of the Battle of Marengo." *British Military Library*, II:XXV (October, 1800) 417-423.

Gohier, Louis-Jerome. *Mémoires des Contemporains*. 2 vols. Paris, 1824. The view from one of the consuls whom Bonaparte supplanted.

Gourgaud, Gaspard. *Memoirs of the History of France During the Reign of Napoleon, Dictated by the Emperor*. Vol. 1. London, 1823. History according to how Napoleon wanted it to be remembered.

Graham, Thomas. *The History of the Campaign of 1796 in Germany and Italy*. London, 1800.

Grandin, F. *Souvenirs Historiques du Capitaine Krettly, ancien trompette-major*. Vol. 1. Paris, 1839.

Grouchy, Marquis de. *Mémoires du Maréchal de Grouchy.* Vol. 2. Paris, 1873. Nominally a biography, it mostly contains Grouchy's writings and reports.

Gurwood, Lt. Col., ed. *The Dispatches of the Field Marshal the Duke of Wellington During His Various Campaigns in India, Denmark, Portugal, Spain, the Low Countries, and France From 1799 to 1818.* London, 1837-1838.

Hardÿ de Perini, General, ed. *Correspondence Intime du Général Jean Hardÿ de 1797 à 1802.* Paris, 1901.

J., C. "Other Interesting Particulars respecting the Battle of Marengo," *British Military Library or Journal,* II. London, 1799-1801.

Junot, Laure. *Memoirs of Napoleon.* Vol. 1. New York, 1880. Entertaining, gossipy history filled with human insights and factual errors.

Larchey, Lorédan, ed. *The Narrative of Captain Coignet.* New York, 1890.

Lejeune, General. *Mémoires du Général Lejeune.* Paris, 1896. He was a newly commissioned engineer captain serving with Berthier and later a famous painter. His paintings are full of meticulous detail but Savary claims his Marengo painting places Kellermann's cavalry incorrectly.

Lejeune, Baron. *Memoirs of Baron Lejeune.* 2 vols. London, 1897.

Macdonald, Etienne. *Recollections of Marshal Macdonald.* Vol. 1. New York, 1892.

Marmont, Auguste. *Mémoires du Maréchal Marmont Duc de Raguse.* Vol. 2. Paris, 1857. Substantially, but not entirely, reliable.

MetternichWinneburg, Clemens. *Memoirs of Prince Metternich: 1773-1815.* Vol. 2. New York, 1970.

Miot, André. *Memoirs of Count Miot de Melito.* New York, 1881. Observations from a patriot but not a sycophant.

Montholon, Count de. *Memoirs of the History of France During the Reign of Napoleon Dictated by the Emperor at Saint Helena.* London, 1823.

Napoleon's Own Memoirs. London, 1823.

Correspondance de Napoléon Ier. Vol. 6. Paris, 1860.

Letters and Documents of Napoleon, ed. John Howard. Vol. 1. New York, 1961.

Ordres et Apostiles de Napoléon. Vol. 4. Paris, 1912.

Unpublished Correspondence of Napoleon I. Vol. 3. New York, 1913.

Noel, J. N. A. *Souvenirs Militaires d'un Officier du Premier Empire.* Paris, 1895.

Oudinot, Marie Charlotte. *Memoirs of Marshal Oudinot Duc de Reggio.* New York, 1897. Compiled from Madame Oudinot's writings, a not terribly accurate memoir.

Pasquier, Etienne-Denis. *Memoirs of Chancellor Pasquier.* Vol. 1. New York, 1893.

Pelet, Jean Jacques. *The French Campaign in Portugal, 1810-11.* Minneapolis, 1973. Includes observations about events and personalities from Masséna's early campaigns.

Pelleport, Pierre. *Souvenirs Militaires et Intimes du Général Vicomte de Pelleport.* Vol. 1. Paris, 1857. A colonel in the 18th Ligne who served in Egypt.

Perrin, Claude-Victor. *Extraits de Mémoires Inédits de feu.* Paris, 1846. Victor was proud of what he accomplished and provides a detailed description. The battle account also appears in *Le Spectateur Militaire*, XC (1845-46) 496-522.

Petit, Joseph. *Marengo or the Campaign of Italy, by the Army of Reserve Under the Command of the Chief Consul Bonaparte.* Philadelphia, 1801. A participant's account composed while events were still fresh and published before Bonaparte's revisions held sway. A marvelous source.

Rapp, Jean. *Memoirs of General Count Rapp.* London, 1823.

Reiset, Lt. General. *Souvenirs du Lieutenant Général Vicomte de Reiset.* Vol. 1. Paris, 1899.

Rémusat, Claire. *Memoirs of Madame de Rémusat.* New York, 1880. A delightful story. Many Napoleonic aphorisms come from this book.

Richepance, Antoine. "Bataille de Hohenlinden," *Le Spectateur Militaire*, XXII (Paris, 1836), 260-266. This is a copy of Richepance's official report.

Roguet, François. *Mémoires Militaires du Lieutenant Général Comte*

Roguet. Vol. 2. Paris, 1862.

Saint-Cyr, Laurent Gouvion. *Mémoires pour servir a l'histoire militaire sous le directoire, Le Consulat, et l'empire.* Vol. 2. Paris, 1831.

Savary, Anne. *Mémoires du Duc de Rovigo.* Vol. 1. Paris, 1901. As noted in my 1809 studies, it is very important to read the French original. The English translation, published in London in 1828, omits text and contains many misleading translations.

Seruzier, Baron. *Mémoires Militaires du Baron Seruzier.* Paris, 1823.

Sevelinges, Ch.-L., trans. "Précis de la campagne de 1800, la Souabe, la Bavière et l'Autriche," in Okouneff, U. *Considerations sur les Grandes Operations de la Campagne de 1812, en Russie.* Brussels, 1841. The campaign outline written by a Wurttemberg officer who served on the Austrian staff.

Soult, Nicolas Jean. *Mémoires du Maréchal-Général Soult.* Vols. 2, 3. Paris, 1854.

Talleyrand, Charles. *Memoirs of the Prince de Talleyrand.* Vol. 1. New York, 1891.

Thibaudeau, Antoine Claire. *Bonaparte and the Consulate.* New York, 1908.

Thibaudeau, Antoine Claire. *Mémoires de A.C. Thibaudeau, 1799-1815.* Paris, 1913. A legislator's memoirs full of Bonaparte's conversations and arguments in the Council of State. The basis for many of Napoleon's most famous utterances are in Thibaudeau's account. It is instructive to see how popular usage has twisted or even entirely missed Bonaparte's original intent.

Thiébault, Paul. M*emoirs of Baron Thiébault.* Vol. 2. New York, 1896. Thiébault's candid account of the Siege of Genoa (published as a separate document) and his refusal to toe the Bonaparte party line about the events of 1800 caused him to fall into disfavor with the Emperor.

Tour du Pin, Gouvernet Henriette Lucie Dillon Marquise de la. *Recollections of the Revolution and the Empire.* London, 1933.

Wickham, William. *Correspondence of the Right Hon. William Wickham from the year 1794.* Vol. 2. London, 1870. The view of one of the paymasters who dispensed British gold during the Second Coalition's effort to defeat France.

Secondary Sources

Adye, John. *Napoleon of the Snows*. London, 1931. Popular but insightful history based upon de Cugnac's work.

Angeli, Moriz Edlin von. *Erzherzog Carl*. 5 vols. Vienna, 1896-1897.

Arnold, James R. *Crisis on the Danube: Napoleon's Austrian Campaign of 1809*. New York, 1990.

Arnold, James R. *Napoleon Conquers Austria: The 1809 Campaign for Vienna*. Westport, CT, 1995.

Bergerot, Bernard. *Le Maréchal Suchet, duc d'Albufera*. Paris, 1986.

Bernard, Jack F. *Talleyrand; A Biography*. New York, 1973.

Bertaud, Jean-Paul. *The Army of the French Revolution*. Princeton, NJ, 1988.

Bessières, Albert. *Le Bayard de la Grande Armée*. Paris, 1952.

Bodart, Gaston. *Militär-historisches kriegs-lexicon 1618-1905*. Vienna, 1908.

Bonnal, H. *La Vie Militaire du Maréchal Ney*. Vol. 1. Paris, 1910.

Bonnal, M.E. *Histoire de Desaix*. Paris, 1881.

Boudard, Rene. "La Conscription Militaire et ses Problemes dans le Department de la Creuse," *Revue de L'Institut Napoleonic*, #145, (Paris, 1985-92) 23-57.

Brinton, Crane. *The Life of Talleyrand*. New York, 1936.

Carrion-Nisas, Marquis de. *Campagne des Français en Allemagne*. Paris, 1829. A well-researched document prepared by an officer at the Dépôt de la Guerre utilizing official archives.

Chandler, David G. *The Campaigns of Napoleon*. New York, 1966. A recognized classic.

Chandler, David G. *Dictionary of the Napoleonic Wars*. New York, 1979. A really useful source.

Chandler, David G., ed. *The Military Maxims of Napoleon*. New York, 1988.

Chandler, David G. *Napoleon's Marshals*. New York, 1987. The best modern account. David's assignment to write about Victor led me to investigate the significance of Victor's performance at Marengo.

Chandler, David G. *On the Napoleonic Wars: Collected Essays.* London, 1994.

Cohen, Louis. *Napoleonic Anecdotes.* London, 1925.

Cole, Hubert. Fouché: *The Unprincipled Patriot.* New York, 1971.

Colin, J. *La Tactique et la Discipline dans les Armées de la Révolution.* Paris, 1902.

Connelly, Owen, ed. *Historical Dictionary of Napoleonic France, 1799-1815.* Westport, CT, 1985.

Cooper, Duff. *Talleyrand.* Stanford, CA, 1967.

Craig, Gordon A. *War, Politics, and Diplomacy.* New York, 1966. The essays on Austrian command problems and the frictions of coalition warfare are of interest to Napoleonic students.

Cugnac, Gaspar Jean Marie Rene de. *Campagne de l'Armée de Réserve en 1800.* 2 vols. Paris, 1901.

The Campaign of the Reserve Army in 1800 According to Documents Collected by Captain de Cugnac. United States Army Command and General Staff School Library, Fort Leavenworth, KS, 1922.

Dard, Emile. *Napoleon and Talleyrand.* New York, 1937.

Detaille, Edouard. *L'Armée Française.* New York, 1992.

Duffy, Christopher. *The Army of Maria Theresa.* New York, 1977.

Dumas, Mathieu. *Précis des evenemens militaires ou essais historiques sur les campagnes de 1799 à 1814.* Vol. 3. Paris, 1816.

Dupuy, Raoul. *Historique de 12e Regiment de Chasseurs de 1788 à 1891.* Paris, 1891.

Esposito, General Vincent J. and Colonel John Elting. *Military History and Atlas of the Napoleonic Wars.* New York, 1964. Wonderful maps with an opinionated but succint text.

Fiebeger, Colonel G. J. *The Campaigns of Napoleon Bonaparte of 1796-97.* West Point, NY, 1911.

Fisher, H. A. L. "Brumaire," in *The Cambridge Modern History,* VIII (New York, 1908), 665-688. A clear account of the coup.

Gachot, Édouard. *La Deuxième Campagne d'Italie.* Paris, 1899. Full of excerpts from original documents.

Gachot, Édouard. *Le Siège de Gênes.* Paris, 1908.

Griffith, Paddy. *The Art of War of Revolutionary France 1789-1802*. London, 1998.

Guerrini, Maurice. *Napoleon and Paris*. New York, 1970.

Guilland, Anton. "The Pacification of Europe, 1799-1802," in *The Cambridge Modern History*, IX (New York, 1909), 55-80.

Hayman, Sir Peter. Soult: *Napoleon's Maligned Marshal*. London, 1990.

Haythornthwaite, Philip J. *Die Hard! Dramatic Actions from the Napoleonic Wars*. London, 1996.

Headley, J.T. *The Imperial Guard of Napoleon*. New York, 1852.

Herold, J. Christopher, ed. *The Mind of Napoleon: A Selection from His Written and Spoken Words*. New York, 1955. A splendid compilation.

Howarth, David. *Trafalgar: The Nelson Touch*. New York, 1969. Enjoyable popular history.

Lachouque, Henry. *Anatomy of Glory*. Providence, RI, 1961.

Langsam, Walter. *The Napoleonic Wars and German Nationalism in Austria*. New York, 1930. A fine, scholarly work.

Lefebvre, Georges. *Napoleon From 18 Brumaire to Tilsit*. New York, 1969.

Lynn, John A. *The Bayonets of the Republic: Motivation and tactics in the Army of Revolutionary France, 1791-95*. Chicago, 1984.

Mackesy, Piers. *British Victory in Egypt, 1801*. London, 1995. A very readable and well-informed account.

Mackesy, Piers. *The Strategy of Overthrow 1798-1799*. London, 1974. Anti-French bias aside (seemingly part of all British historians' baggage) this, along with its companion volume, provides a really fine account of British strategy during the War of the Second Coalition. This volume includes a detailed account of the Netherlands campaign.

Mackesy, Piers. *War Without Victory: The Downfall of Pitt, 1799-1802*. Oxford, 1984.

Meynier, Albert. "Levées et Pertes D'Hommes sous le Consulat et l'Empire," *Revue des Etudes*, XXX (Paris, 1930).

Mitchell, Harvey. *The Underground War Against Revolutionary France*. London, 1965.

Montgomery, Frances. "General Moreau and the Conspiracy Against Napoleon in 1804: The Verdict of the Court and of History," *The Consortium on Revolutionary Europe Proceedings* (1988) 165-187.

Morton, J.B. *Brumaire: The Rise of Napoleon.* London, 1948. Well-written popular history.

Mras, Karl. "Gefchichte Des Feldzuges 1800 in Italien," *Öestereichische Militärische Zeitschrift,* VII-XII (Vienna, 1822); V-IX (1823). In lieu of an official report, which was never published, Mras offers a "semi-official" account.

Muller, Paul. *L'Espionnage Militaire sous Napoléon I.* Paris, 1896.

Nosworthy, Brent. *With Musket, Cannon and Sword: Battle Tactics of Napoleon and His Enemies.* New York, 1996.

Pariset, Georges. "The Consulate, 1799-1804," in *The Cambridge Modern History,* IX (New York, 1909) 1-33.

Perin, Rene. *Vie Militaire du Duc de Montebello.* Paris, n.d.

Phipps, Ramsay W. *The Armies of the First French Republic.* 5 vols. London, 1926-1939.

Picard, Ernest. *Hohenlinden.* Paris, 1909. The best French account written during 'the golden age of staff studies.'

Picard, Ernest, ed. *Preceptes et Jugements de Napoléon.* Paris, 1913.

Rath, R. John. *The Viennese Revolution of 1848.* Austin, TX, 1957. Describes Johann's role in the overthrow of Metternich and the events of 1848.

Rodger, Alexander B. *The War of the Second Coalition.* Oxford, 1964. The British view. Strong on political and diplomatic perspectives.

Rose, John Holland. *The Life of Napoleon I.* Vol. 1. London, 1907. While incorrect in various details, strong in analysis and useful for citations to British Official Records.

Ross, Steven T. *From Flintlock to Rifle.* Rutherford, NJ, 1979. A study of tactical evolution.

Rothenberg, Gunther E. *The Art of Warfare in the Age of Napoleon.* London, 1977.

Rothenberg, Gunther E. *Napoleon's Great Adversaries.* Bloomington, IN, 1982.

Sargent, Herbert H. *The Campaign of Marengo.* Chicago, 1901.

Savant, Jean. *Les Espions de Napoleon.* Paris, 1957.

Schom, Alan. *Napoleon Bonaparte.* New York, 1997. Highly opinionated, highly entertaining.

Sherwig, John M. *Guineas and Gunpowder: British Foreign Aid in the Wars with France.* Cambridge, MA, 1969. Another scholarly work.

Six, Georges. *Dictionnaire Biographique des Généraux & Amiraux Français de la Révolution et de l'Empire.* 2 vols. Paris, 1934. A fountain of biographical facts.

Souham, Gerard. *Le Général Souham sur tous les champs de bataille de la Révolution et de l'Empire.* Paris, 1990.

Thiers, Adolphe. *History of the Consulate and the Empire.* Vol. 1. London, 1845.

Thoumas, Charles A. *Le Maréchal Lannes.* Paris, 1891.

Tulard, Jean and Louis Garros. *Itineraire de Napoléon au jour le jour.* Paris, 1992. What did he do and when did he do it? This wonderful compilation provides the answers.

United States Army Service Schools. *Source Book of the Marengo Campaign in 1800.* The General Service Schools Press, Fort Leavenworth, KS, 1922.

Victoires, Conquêtes, Désastres, Revers et Guerres Civiles des Français. Vols. 12, 13. Paris, 1819-20. Entertaining propoganda.

Voykowitsch, Bernhard. *Castiglione 1796.* Maria Enzersdorf, Austria, 1998.

Walker, T.A. and H.W. Wilson. "The Armed Neutrality, 1780-1801," in *The Cambridge Modern History*, IX (New York, 1909) 34-54.

Wilkinson, Spenser. *The French Army Before Napoleon.* Aldershot, UK, 1991. A reprint of the 1915 classic.

Wood, General Sir Evelyn. *Achievements of Cavalry.* London, 1897.

Index

Because of the limitations of space, the names of Napoleon Bonaparte, Jean Moreau, and Michael Melas and the words Marengo and Hohenlinden are not included in the Index.

L

Lannes, Jean: 9,16-17,24; through Saint Bernard 86-88;
in Aosta Valley 92-97;101,104-105, 106-107,113, 116-117, 120-121;
at Montebello 122-127;129,132,146;
at Marengo 156,160-162,164,165,168, 170,173,175;193,264,278-279,285
Lattermann, Franz: 153,156,162,171, 177,180,191
von Lauer, Baron Franz: background 205-206;208,213-214,220-221
Lebrun, Charles: 24
Lefebvre, François: 7,16-17, 28
Legrand, Claude: 219; at Hohenlinden 225,234,248-249;279,285
Liechtenstein, Johannes: at Hohenlinden 238
Loepper, Franz: at Hohenlinden 229-231;279
Loison, Louis: 42,89,97,109,128
Lunéville: 205,207,210,258
Luxembourg Palace: 14,24,29

M

Macdonald, Jacques Etienne Joseph Alexandre: 33,211,257,285
Mack, Karl: 65,286
Mainoni, Joseph: 38,149,161,190, 278-279
Manual of 1791: 39-40
Marmont, Auguste: 16-17,44-45, 89-90,96-98,121,131,156;
at Marengo 176-180; 255
Masséna, André: 10-11,25,34;
assumes command of Army of Italy 52-57; siege of Genoa 70-76;80, 82-83,106,112,151,194,207,255, 257,283,286-287
Metternich, Clemens: 58
Milan: 82,91,106-109,111-112, 114-116,121,143,190,193-194,202
Moncey, Bon: 38,101,111,128
Monnier, Jean-Charles: 128,132,165, 168-170,173,175,182,264,279,285-286
Montebello, battle of, June 9, 1800: 38,40, 59,63,

see especially 122-127;129,156
Mortier, Edouard: 10
Morzin, Peter: 149
Moulin, Jean-Francois-Auguste: 17-18
Mouton, Georges: 71
Murat, Joachim: 9,16-17, 20,96,105, 107-109,116-117,132;
at Marengo 176,180-181;258,279,285

N

Naples: 3,4,7
Ney, Michel: 10, 28,128,217-220;
at Hohenlinden 225,234,243-244, 247-249;254-255,279,282-283,286
Novi, battle of: 9-10,60

O

O'Reilly, Andreas: 60-61,115, 117,120,122;
at Montebello 124-126;
on eve of Marengo 131,144-146;
at Marengo 149-150,160-161,163,171, 182-183
Ott, Peter: 60,65;
at siege of Genoa 72-75;100, 115,120;
at Montebello 121-126;127, 129,144,146;
at Marengo 160-162,165,173,181, 183;189
Oudinot, Nicolas: 38,74

P

Pichegru, Jean: 31,33,265
Piedmontese forces: 64,114,116,194
Pilati (Pellati), Giovanni: at Marengo 158-160,173,181
Pitt, William: 11, 25-26,29,260
Po River: 4,107,109,112,115-117, 120-121,146

R

Radetzky, Josef: at Hohenlinden 247
Rhine River: 6,9,31,197-198,200-201,204,